WILLIAM WORDSWORTH
HIS LIFE, WORKS, AND INFLUENCE

WILLIAM WORDSWORTH

HIS LIFE, WORKS, AND INFLUENCE

By GEORGE McLEAN HARPER

WOODROW WILSON PROFESSOR OF LITERATURE IN
PRINCETON UNIVERSITY

" A man of uncommon genius is a man of high passions
and lofty design."—WILLIAM GODWIN

VOLUME ONE

New York
RUSSELL & RUSSELL
1960

Reprinted, 1960, Russell & Russell, Inc.,
by arrangement with John Murray Ltd., London
who published the original edition in 1929

Library of Congress Catalog Card Number: 60–11020

PRINTED IN THE UNITED STATES OF AMERICA

TO

MY DEAR WIFE

WHO HAS SHARED THE JOYS AND TOIL OF
THIS WORK

PREFACE

IN preparing for the press this revised edition the author has availed himself of much new material which has been brought to light since 1916, when the work was first published, and also of numerous and helpful reviews. Among fresh sources may be mentioned especially his own little book " Wordsworth's French Daughter," 1921, Professor Emile Legouis's " William Wordsworth and Annette Vallon," 1922, and Professor Ernest de Selincourt's superb *variorum* edition of " The Prelude," 1926. There has been in these thirteen years a great revival of Wordsworthian study, to which many critics have contributed, notably Professor Arthur Beatty in his " William Wordsworth, his Doctrine and Art in their Historical Relations," 1922. The chief documentary sources used in the former editions of the present work, and acknowledged there fully, were the " Memoirs " by the poet's nephew Christopher, 1851, the letters of Dorothy Wordsworth to Mrs. Marshall (Jane Pollard), Knight's " Letters of the Wordsworth Family," Ernest Hartley Coleridge's collection of his grandfather's " Letters," Mr. E. V. Lucas's " The Works of Charles and Mary Lamb," Mrs. Sandford's " Thomas Poole and his Friends," Dorothy Wordsworth's Journals, the unpublished correspondence between her and Mrs. Clarkson, the Crabb Robinson manuscripts, Coleridge's notebooks, " Le Général Michel Beaupuy," by MM. Bussière and

Legouis, and the comments dictated by Wordsworth in 1843 to Miss Fenwick. In this edition detailed references to these sources have generally been omitted, but the author could not, without ingratitude, fail to mention once more his appreciation of the fruitful labours of Professor Legouis and the helpful counsel of Mr. Gordon Wordsworth.

CONTENTS

VOLUME ONE

ILLUSTRATIONS

VOLUME ONE

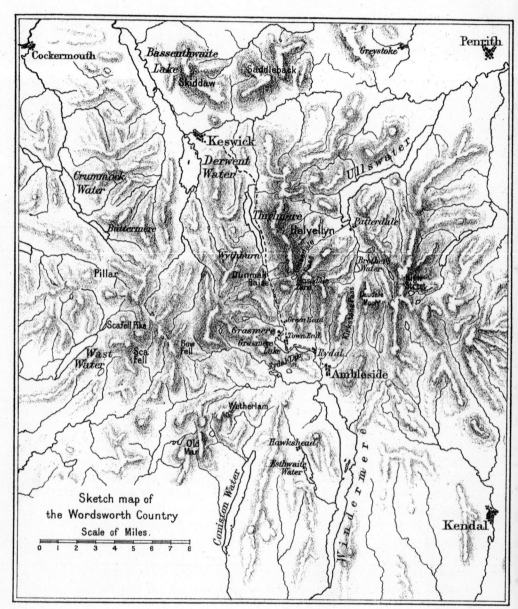

Cockermouth

Bassenthwaite
Lake

Greystoke

Penrith

Skiddaw

Saddleback

Keswick

Derwent
Water

Ullswater

Crummock
Water

Thirlmere

Patterdale

Buttermere

Helvellyn

Wythburn

Brothers
Water

Pillar

Dunmail
Raise

Grisedale
Tarn

Daudale
Moor

High
Street

Scafell Pike

Green Head

Town End

Grasmere

Grasmere
Lake

Kirkstone

Wast
Water

Sca
Fell

Bow
Fell

Rydal Lake

Rydal

Ambleside

Wetherlam

Old
Man

Hawkshead

Esthwaite
Water

Windermere

Sketch map of
the Wordsworth Country

Scale of Miles.

0 1 2 3 4 5 6 7 8

Coniston Water

Kendal

To face p. I.

WILLIAM WORDSWORTH

HIS LIFE, WORKS, AND INFLUENCE

CHAPTER I

THE PERMANENCE OF WORDSWORTH

WORDSWORTH is more widely read and more often quoted than any other English poet, except Shakespeare and Milton. He is therefore a power in the world. Countless thousands of English-speaking men and women have died and been forgotten. The influence of every one of them lives, no doubt, and will live for ever, but only a few survive by name and with some degree of fulness. Wordsworth's mind and heart, his view of life as a whole, his most delicate perceptions, his innermost feelings, are still a part of the spiritual world in which we move, and there is every likelihood that what we may call his personality will continue to exist for many generations.

I can imagine the ghosts of great discoverers, conquerors, and statesmen, complaining among the shades that they are forgotten in the upper world, while poets continue to walk in the sunshine of human gratitude and are as real a thousand years after death as when they moved on earth. " Men of action," as they called themselves, they wonder why, not to them, but to poets, should be given " the name that honoureth most and most endureth." A little reflection on the haunting love of companionship which dwells in every soul would furnish an answer. The poets give us themselves. They have the simplicity to suppose that we will care for their confidences. And they possess an art of communication which is so pleasing to our senses that, almost for its sake alone, we should be willing to listen.

The first question we must ask, then, in estimating the qualities of Wordsworth's poetry which may be expected to give it permanence, concerns his possession of artistic mastery. And it is certainly not overbold to say that in perfection and range of technical skill he is a master. Taking into account the whole of his poetry, and not merely the best or the most well-known part of it, one is impressed with the correctness, the vigour, the ingenuity, and the variety of his versification. He is rich in metrical forms. His devices for entrapping the eye and ear are endless, and are the more subtly effective as they seldom obtrude themselves upon our attention, which he always occupies with something beyond the music and the form.

His diction, too, and syntax are of vast range and singular exactness. He keeps, as regards the grammatical elements of style, strictly to the sound English tradition. To an uncommon extent his language is free from learned affectations and ephemeral fashions. He was an observant and purposeful student of our elder poets, of Chaucer and Spenser and Shakespeare, of Drayton and Daniel and Milton, of Dryden and Collins and Gray. His is pure English and undefiled. With only the very smallest allowance for exceptions, we may say that his language would have passed current at any time in the last three hundred and fifty years. This is some guarantee of its future acceptance. In the main it is not charged with a temporal alloy, is not the product of a " movement " or a " period," is neither Classical nor Romantic, is not a revival, is not local, is not exotic, is not pedantic.

In one respect, at least, the quality of Wordsworth's thought matches the breadth of his style. His mind was excessively masculine; yet through almost lifelong association with gifted women, and a peculiar dependence upon womanly sympathy, his natural asperity became tempered with feminine tenderness, and his disposition to generalize was balanced by a feminine

interest in particulars. Still, he is the most philosophical of all our great poets; he dwells in a region of
ideas, which he endeavours to correlate to the sum of
human experience. In all things, animate or inanimate,
he perceives a spiritual life. The strength of this perception and the faith with which he tries to impart it to
other minds make him a seer and prophet, though he
neither repels a simple-hearted reader by setting up a
system, nor creates distrust by claiming to enjoy a
mystical illumination. Yet he professes, with good
reason, to be a teacher.

On the other hand, except Dante, no poet capable of
sustaining such flights is more rich in concrete detail.
Things in themselves interest him, apart from their
possible connection with the mind of man or their share
in the great soul of nature. He enjoys them and finds
it worth while to describe them, for the sake of their
inherent attractiveness, quite apart from their ulterior
significance. Whether he would have subscribed to
the statement that the external world is a symbol of the
Infinite Idea, I very much doubt. There were moments
when he said so; but when he is most himself he is most
content with nature as reality and not symbol. He
never taught that nature existed as an object-lesson.
He did not, in his prime, habitually think of nature as
leading up to God; he thought of nature as having the
Life of Life abiding in her. With reverence, then, as
well as curiosity and delight, did he note her features.
Until his powers and his courage for independent vision
had begun to fail, he did not accept the view, so para-
lyzing to the pursuit and enjoyment of knowledge, that
it is impious to study nature except as we behold in her
a warning or a stage to an inconceivable life beyond.
He dealt with this goodly frame more worthily, accepting the " joy in widest commonalty spread."

But though a great poet owes his place among his peers
to qualities of style and thought that are traditionally
acceptable there may yet be room in him for peculiarities
of a local, temporary, or personal kind. Indeed, if he is
to win a life of his own in our affections he must possess

these. Otherwise, to establish his generality he would
have stripped himself of the traits which give to every
human being a something all his own. There is much in
Wordsworth's versification, language, choice of subjects, and mode of thought, that belongs to him alone;
much, also, that belongs to his age; and not a little that
is local. He experimented boldly, and was deeply
moved by sympathies which made him willing to risk
the disapproval of even very excellent judges. His
peculiarities have at different times and for various
reasons repelled readers. At first there was the complaint that his characters and diction were " low."
Then a certain class objected that his philosophy was
unorthodox, that it was materialistic, or at least pan-
theistic. Later it was discovered that it was mystical
and out of touch with an age of reason and science.
The style of his longer works has by some been deemed
too vague and ecstatic; by others, hard and uninspired.
Notwithstanding the wide scope and general applic-
ability of his works, he is still mentioned now and then
as " one of the Lake poets." He is likewise known as
a poet for children, though perhaps more commonly as
the poet best fitted to console the afflicted, restore the
erring, and comfort the aged.

After all, it is greatly to Wordsworth's advantage
that there is a certain amount of truth in every one of
these limited views. They prove that he is not to be
disposed of in a formula. They show how immensely
varied his excellence is, how wide his appeal, how he
transcends and embraces the special domains of almost
all English poets who were his contemporaries. Some
of the features of his work that were once peculiar to
him, or to him and Coleridge, have now in large measure
become elements in the method of all poets, in every
land. In any case, his idiosyncrasies enrich the sum
of his value by giving personal colour to his pages and
saving them from that featureless perfection which we
acknowledge languidly in Racine, for example, and
Lamartine and Schiller. It is an enrichment of his art
that the great interpreter of universal nature should have

known every foot of ground in one or two narrow valleys; for, the whole being the sum of all its parts, not to know intimately at least one part disables the judgment of a philosopher, and how much more the insight of a poet ! Wordsworth studied with what seemed a petty curiosity certain individuals, preferably simple souls, in an effort to divine their motives and resources. He has been foolishly blamed for taking so much interest in paupers, idiots, weak old men, and quite ordinary children. His justification blazes forth in many a hundred lines of high political wisdom. He found his way, through the least defended approaches, to the inner recesses of human character. He became like a little child or like a poor beggar, and learned what man is. With the knowledge thus acquired of human needs and passions, he was able to understand, better even than Byron or Shelley, the effect of the French Revolution upon the feelings and conduct of men in all classes of society.

Of course, even a sound and vigorous style would not suffice to win and hold for any poet a position such as Wordsworth's. There must also be an altogether un-common weight of character, intensity of emotional force, and reach of intellect. To note and estimate these is the special task of biography. In Wordsworth's case we have to take into account not only poetry, but several prose compositions, which deal with subjects so diverse as politics and the principles of æsthetics. His opinions, whenever he gives definite expression to them, are found to be rooted in some principle below the surface. They are original in that they are a part of his very self. He utters them grudgingly, as if loath to part with what has been so long cherished. Even when they concern matters of seeming indifference, or upon which, at least, no momentous consequences appear to hang, they are so personal to him, and have been so long pondered by him, that they carry some of the heat and passion of his soul. That they do not cohere in a system is due to the fact that his life, if reckoned by convictions and feelings, was broken in the middle. Up to a certain point he was guided by hope; later he was

driven by fear. The two halves of his life are in-
congruous.

The extent of the difference has never been fully
appreciated, because it is not so perceptible in his
poetry as it is in his letters and the reports of his conversation that have come down to us. A careful study,
not only of what he said and wrote, but of what others
said and wrote to him and about him, makes it quite clear
that in the second half of his life he cursed what he once
blessed, and blessed what he once cursed. The transition was fairly rapid, and it was complete. Moreover,
it affected his poetry, affected not merely the subjects
he chose and the general direction in which he turned
his thoughts and feelings, but even the choice of words
and the structure of his verse. As I believe that Wordsworth has influenced the tone of English and American
thought, for the last eighty or ninety years, more than
any other poet who lived in the nineteenth century, I
have found much dramatic interest in the play and
counter-play of two contending forces operating in him.
In either period, considered by itself, there is essential
unity; his conduct, his doctrine, and the works of his
imagination, are consistent with one another. But the
Wordsworth of 1816 is a different man from the Wordsworth of 1800. Since it is that later man whom we
find represented in a dozen portraits and innumerable
anecdotes, and not often to his advantage, the earlier
and far more attractive Wordsworth is almost entirely
obscured. There is, to be sure, less material for getting
acquainted with that fiery and adventurous youth, now
dead for more than a century, than with the famous old
man who died in 1850.

Investigation of those earlier years is all the more
thrilling because, while some of them are revealed to
us with remarkable fulness in his sister's letters and
journals and in the poet's own works and those of
Coleridge, and show him in a light as attractive as it is
clear, other periods, of many months' duration, are
shrouded in mystery. An additional touch of romance
is imparted by the presence of that sister, herself a

genius, full of originality and charm, and by the friendship of both these wayward spirits with Coleridge, a community of mind unique in human story. These " three persons and one soul " represent the fine flower of English literary culture in the eighteenth century, and the beginning of much that was most distinctive and valuable in the nineteenth. When they wandered together, heart in heart, " on sunny Quantock's airy ridge," or held high converse in the bare little cottage at Grasmere, they were moulding, in no small degree, the intellectual destiny of future generations, establishing a fresh style in poetry, and especially creating a new and vitalizing sense of the relation between poetry and life.

Poetry was to be no longer regarded as a merely decorative art. It was to spring more than ever from experience and to bear more than ever upon conduct. It was to be less academic and exclusive, and by becoming simpler in form was to appeal to a larger audience. Yet the broadening-down has been accomplished without recourse to vulgarizing methods. No one can say that Wordsworth's influence has had the effect of blunting the poetical sensibilities of our race. On the contrary, while poetry and every art associated with poetry have through his efforts become more popular, they have also attained superior delicacy. New powers of perception have been awakened, and exquisite workings of emotion have been for the first time recognized. Humanity at large has been found immensely more interesting and important than even the choicest selection from its more favoured classes. In nature herself, contemplated with a wider glance and a freer curiosity, many objects previously unregarded or even despised have been found to possess fine moral and æsthetic values. Like many another experiment in democracy, in which, after much delay, hesitation, and prophesying of evil, it has been decided to open to profane feet some ancient preserve of opportunity and enjoyment, this appeal to wider circles has been amply justified by results. Strange as it may at first seem, the fact is that in proportion as poetry has become less aristocratic it has become more refined, and that by being universalized it has become more sacred. We require from poets a stricter warrant of heaven-given authority than our forefathers in the eighteenth century insisted upon. We are less easily contented with talent and clever workmanship, or even with mere intellectual power and emotional violence. Wordsworth taught us to expect that a poet should be a dedicated spirit, obliged by a sense of his calling and enabled by his genius to conceive of nature and of human life more worthily than other men.

A further reason for believing that Wordsworth will hold a permanent place in English literature is that still, after the lapse of two generations, he remains pre-eminent among our poets, from the fourteenth century to the twentieth, for the truth of his report about nature. None of his successors has equalled him in this. In his own phrase, he wrote " with his eye on the object." From the beginning, this has not been the practice of poets nearly so much as is often supposed. If poets have, since Wordsworth's time, been striving, and with very gratifying success, to report more strictly of nature and in words unencumbered with conventional meaning, the credit is in large measure due to him. Poetry would have had small chance of holding its ground in the nineteenth century except by establishing a strong claim to respect for an exactness of its own, comparable with the exactness of science. Wordsworth's poetry, in particular, has been enjoyed by men to whom no other kind of imaginative writing appeals. They have valued it for the natural way in which it rises to the loftiest flights from a firm basis in observation. Others, having regard to the end rather than the beginning, value his poetry none the less because it is from things plainly seen and intimately known that it ascends to what is beyond sight and beyond knowledge. His initial impulse towards naturalness and simplicity was political, social, and moral, not literary. It was only when his heart had been profoundly moved, and

certain convictions, having no necessary or at least no
immediate connection with poetry, had been formed
within him, that his style and method of writing began
to change. He then immediately abandoned the standards which he had unquestioningly followed. All that
he wrote before 1792 is conventional; all that he
wrote between 1792 and 1798 is Revolutionary. In this
second period he worked out and put in practice a
theory of composition, which he thought fitting in one
who had determined to obey the command, " What God
hath cleansed, that call not thou common." The
attempt was heroic. It had something of the self-
sacrificing recklessness of a forlorn hope. It was a
gallant forward movement, but desperately lonely, and
not likely to succeed unless reinforced. Coleridge
brought up the needed support. Falling in with
Wordsworth's advance, he strengthened it at a time
when, through its own *élan*, it was in danger of wasting
away. He added those elements which have been
termed romantic, and interested Wordsworth, who till
then was a severe realist, in legends of the wonderful.
If Wordsworth could ever be termed a Romanticist, it
was during the last three years of the eighteenth century. Originally and characteristically he was nothing
of the sort. When he was most himself, he found
sufficient inspiration in the natural world. Romanticism looked to the past, to the supernatural, to the
extraordinary. Wordsworth, the true Wordsworth,
dwelt in the present, felt that nature was herself divine,
and strove, with the zeal of a controversialist, and at
considerable risk, to show that the ordinary is as wonderful and instructive as the exceptional.

It is in this sense that he was peculiarly the prophet
of an age of science. What biologists and chemists
have done to reveal the wonders of the physical world,
he did, in a measure, for the relations between man's
mind and the objects upon which the mind plays. This
vast domain of perceptions and feelings he treated with
something like the self-restraint, respect, and fidelity
with which men of science investigate the material uni-

verse. Nothing, he thought, was unworthy of regard.
All things were so interesting, so justified in their existence and special working, that distinctions of high and
low lost much of their meaning, just as mountains must
appear of no peculiar significance to a man accustomed
to use a powerful microscope. This state of mind in
Wordsworth was a result of his conversion to the equalitarian creed of the French Revolution. Some sort of
faith in human equality was the religion of that movement. Say what they will, neither the Carlyles nor the
Taines can obscure this fact. And the doctrine being
once accepted, it affected the very words he used.

But, after all, the first steps in his new spiritual life
merely placed him, as a literary artist, on a plane with
many older English poets, who wrote in a natural
manner without having gone through a religious or
political experience such as his. There have always
been in English poetry two manners or methods. The
one is natural, simple, free, and full of variety, the other
artificial and much restricted. The latter prevailed,
on the whole, from the time of Milton until near the close
of the eighteenth century. It may be called the academic manner. Until Wordsworth and Coleridge were
lifted on the ground-swell of the Revolution, they were
satisfied with the fashion that prevailed in their youth.
Their revolt was at first not literary, but political.
Wordsworth, for example, continued to write in the
academic manner when composing even those passages
of " Descriptive Sketches," in 1792, which proclaimed
his republican principles so vehemently that he afterwards felt constrained to suppress and alter them.
However, since he respected his own genius, he was not
long in changing his style to match his opinions.

Too much emphasis can hardly be laid upon the
statement that Wordsworth at his best, in his great
years, when he was most truly himself, when he was
animated by courage and hope, was a fervent Revolutionist. His words were acts. His decisions, even in
so quiet an affair as the choice of subjects and words for
pastoral poems, were based on principles of the widest

scope, and were in truth momentous, as he supposed. He breathed, with joy and awe, the spirit of a glorious time. And the time found in him its most faithful and inspired interpreter. He alone, of all who have experienced or contemplated the Revolution, has left an adequate artistic record of its effect upon the spiritual life of those who welcomed it and those who opposed it.

The circumstances of his birth and early life had prepared him to embrace the Revolutionary doctrines and to fill worthily the office to which this acceptance committed him. It is probable that even the most reactionary man now living would be shocked, if he were to awake some morning in the last decade of the eighteenth century in England, by the oppressiveness of the social atmosphere. Wordsworth's boyhood was passed in a pleasant nook of English ground, where the contrast between the privileged classes and the body of the oppressed was not so violent as elsewhere. When he left it he was struck by the unhappy condition of his country. After his first visit to France he found England half choked, as he thought, with noxious fumes. He had breathed the exhilarating air of a country that had roused itself from even deadlier slumber. He came home with a new consciousness, a new outlook, and new aspirations. The contrast between what was and what he believed might be was presently deepened by the poverty and unrest occasioned by prolonged war. He himself, in the vicissitudes of his own life, was affected by both extremes of social difference. His family name and university education brought him into contact with persons of wealth and power, but the background of his memory was already filled with homely figures of poor, uneducated people, and his associations in the years before he became well known covered an unusually wide range in the social scale. He had to endure a certain share of prejudice, social as well as literary, and a certain amount of legal injustice, and he lived for some years on the verge of poverty. The sympathy which he felt for those whose lot was different from his own was not purely imaginative, but was based on much real experience. A sense of social responsibility lay heavy upon him. He was never contented with a make-believe world or a world of books.

His excellence as an artist, the special work he performed in renovating the spirit and the style of English poetry, and his pre-eminent position as interpreter of the Revolution, assure for Wordsworth an enduring place among the greatest of our poets. He acknowledged Milton as his master. That he equalled or perhaps surpassed Milton in the quality and variety of his best achievements may be the opinion of Wordsworthians, though it is hardly the judgment of mankind. But more and more the conviction is growing that he is the greatest of our poets since Milton. There is still another ground on which he is venerated. This is the belief that, more than any other eminent poet, in any language, he reveals a mystical relation between nature and the mind of man. It is quite possible that some of his admirers exaggerate the value of this revelation; but there can be no doubt that he endeavoured, with courage and originality, and from deep conviction, to establish as a religious principle what to all genuine poets is at least a sacred instinct.

CHAPTER II

HOME, SCHOOL, COLLEGE

THE poet was born at Cockermouth, in the county of Cumberland, the second son of John Wordsworth, an attorney and law-agent to Sir James Lowther, afterwards Earl of Lonsdale. His mother was Anne, only daughter of William Cookson, mercer, of Penrith, and of Dorothy, born Crackanthorp. Cockermouth and Penrith are small market towns situated twenty-five miles apart, on the northern border of the mountainous region known as the Lake District. Five children were born to John and Anne Wordsworth: Richard, on August 19, 1768; William, on April 7, 1770; Dorothy, on December 25, 1771; John, on December 4, 1772; and Christopher, on June 9, 1774. William passed his infancy and early boyhood partly at Cockermouth and partly with his mother's parents at Penrith. He remembered that his mother once said of him that he was the only one of her five children about whose future life she was anxious, and that he would be remarkable either for good or for evil, being of a stiff, moody, and violent temper. He carried the same toughness of resolution through life, bearing himself high in all affairs and seldom taking counsel of other men.

The Wordsworth house was a spacious brick mansion, with its face to the main street and its back towards the river Derwent and the ruins of Cockermouth Castle. The children were left much to themselves and roamed freely in a little world abounding in natural pleasures and fair humanities. He tells us in the first book of " The Prelude " that the bright blue river was a tempting playmate, and exclaims:

> Oh, many a time have I, a five years' child,
> In a small mill-race severed from his stream,
> Made one long bathing of a summer's day,
> Basked in the sun, and plunged and basked again
> Alternate, all a summer's day.

In the fifth book of " The Prelude " he contrasts the freedom of his early years with the close guidance enjoined by Rousseau, and illustrated in Thomas Day's " Sandford and Merton," expressing his gratitude for his mother's wisdom in permitting his instincts to unfold themselves without irreverent and fretful meddling. In the large quiet of her simple nature he enjoyed the immunities of childhood, its indifference to the future, its absorption in the present, its long spaces of happy solitude. The passage is of great biographical interest, in view of the high importance of childhood instincts in Wordsworth's philosophy.

Even in these earliest days William's favourite companion was his sister Dorothy, near to him in age and similar in her tastes. Late in life, speaking of her extreme sensibility, he recalled the fact that when she first heard the voice of the sea and beheld the waves breaking against the quays and piers of Whitehaven, she burst out weeping.

In 1801, when he and his sister had settled at Town-end, Grasmere, he wrote the following poem in the orchard there:

> Behold, within the leafy shade,
> Those bright blue eggs together laid !
> On me the chance-discovered sight
> Gleamed like a vision of delight.
> I started, seeming to espy
> The home and sheltered bed,
> The sparrow's dwelling, which, hard by
> My Father's house, in wet or dry
> My sister Emmeline and I
>   Together visited.
>
> She looked at it and seemed to fear it;
> Dreading, tho' wishing, to be near it:
> Such heart was in her, being then
> A little Prattler among men.
> The Blessing of my later years
> Was with me when a boy;
> She gave me eyes, she gave me ears;
> And humble cares, and delicate fears;
> A heart, the fountain of sweet tears;
> And love, and thought, and joy.

The manuscript sent originally to the printer had the name " Dorothy " for " Emmeline." In a note to this poem, dictated to Miss Fenwick, in 1843, the poet said:

" At the end of the garden of my father's house at Cockermouth was a high terrace that commanded a fine view of the river Derwent and Cockermouth Castle. This was our favourite playground. The terrace wall, a low one, was covered with closely-clipt privet and roses, which gave an almost impervious shelter to birds who built their nests there. The latter of these stanzas alludes to one of those nests."

Once again, in the peace of those first months with his sister at Grasmere, he wrote a poem reminiscent of their early childhood, the lines " To a Butterfly ":

> Stay near me—do not take thy flight !
> A little longer stay in sight !
> Much converse do I find in thee,
> Historian of my infancy !
> Float near me; do not yet depart !
> Dead times revive in thee:
> Thou bring'st, gay creature as thou art !
> A solemn image to my heart,
> My father's family !
>
> Oh ! pleasant, pleasant were the days,
> The time, when in our childish plays,
> My sister Emmeline and I
> Together chased the butterfly !
> A very hunter did I rush
> Upon the prey;—with leaps and springs
> I followed on from brake to bush;
> But she, God love her ! feared to brush
> The dust from off its wings.

The superiority of Wordsworth was inborn. A congenital gift of intelligence and susceptibility was shared between him and his sister, while his brother John possessed a rare appreciation of poetry, and his brother Christopher, who became Master of Trinity College, Cambridge, was endowed with eminent strength of mind. A spirit of light must therefore have dwelt in the rather severe brick house at Cockermouth, where this extraordinary brood came into existence. Both

parents happily rejected the temptation to warp the
well-born natures, of whose fine quality they must have
been aware.   Long visits to their mother's old home
at Penrith and occasional trips to the seashore appear
to have been the only variations in the placid lives of
the children.

Mrs. Wordsworth died in March, 1778, and was buried
at Penrith.   Then began the dispersal, to which Dorothy
in her letters ruefully refers, using more than once the
expression, " How we are squandered abroad !"   She
was sent to live with her grandmother Cookson at
Penrith, and Richard and William were sent to school
at Hawkshead.   For Dorothy this was the beginning of
a long period of lonely suffering and spiritual homeless-
ness.   For William it was an auspicious turning-point,
from which we may date one of the happiest and most
receptive portions of his life.   From his ninth to his
eighteenth year Hawkshead was virtually his home.
His younger brothers, John and Christopher, joined
him there in due season; and although there must have
been many reunions at Cockermouth, few traces of them
remain.   His father died December 30, 1783.   The
family estate consisted chiefly of claims, amounting to
about £4,700, on the Earl of Lonsdale, who had withheld money due to his agent, and even forced from
him considerable loans.   He held himself superior to
the law, and when subsequently the case came up for
trial, he retained all the best counsel, and succeeded in
thwarting justice during the rest of his life.   Meanwhile,
for nineteen years, the Wordsworth children lived on
prospects, which would not have carried them far had
not their relatives come to their assistance.   The children were put in charge of their father's brother Richard
and their mother's uncle Christopher Crackanthorpe
Cookson.   Upon the earl's death, in 1802, their property
was paid to them with interest by his successor.

The village of Hawkshead is little changed from what
it was in 1778.   It lies in the shallow vale of Esthwaite,
near the head of Esthwaite Water, a lake about two
miles long, between and almost equally distant from the

larger lakes of Windermere and Coniston. The valley
is sprinkled with small farms, and its higher grounds
are wooded with beech and oak and fir. The little town
is of great antiquity, and has long held the distinction of
being a market for the wool grown in the surrounding
country. It is situated near the extreme northern
angle of Lancashire, which is wedged between Cumberland on the west and Westmorland on the east. Its
houses, of grey stone, with thick slabbed roofs, stand
in a charmingly haphazard way around several open
spaces of irregular shape, called squares. There are no
mansions here, and no hovels. The dwellings bear
witness to that equality and that general diffusion of
humble comfort which were formerly even more characteristic of the Lake country than they are now. A
mountain brook flows through a buried conduit under
one of the streets. It once was only half hidden by
flagstones, and was an object of interest to children.
On a hill that rises abruptly from one side of the village
stands a noble Gothic church, of unknown age and origin.
Its long grey mass can scarcely be distinguished at a
distance from the rock on which it rests, so naturally,
as regards colour and form, does it harmonize with its
surroundings. The turf of the churchyard creeps up to
the very doors, and the black foliage of immemorial yew-
trees masks the gravestones of many generations, removed only a few paces from the scene of their activity.
Inside, the nave spreads wide, and the aisles, with their
dignified perpendicular tracery, lift their arches high,
so that the light streams free in every part, and the outer
world seems to mingle unquestioned with the sacred
enclosure.

The free grammar-school to which the Wordsworth
boys were sent was founded in 1585 by Edwin Sandys,
Archbishop of York, a native of the region. The building, which stands at the edge of the village and contains
no dormitory for pupils, is a substantial and simple
structure.. A large square schoolroom, with an ample
fireplace, occupies most of the ground-floor, and above
are apartments for the master and the usher. The old

" forms," or long desks, still stand about the walls, and in one of them can be seen the name " William Wordsworth " deep carved in schoolboy fashion. Pure country air, blowing unchecked from field and lake, enters through the wide door and big windows. Not even the Gothic luxuriance of Winchester or Eton gives so full a sense of appropriate surroundings for the education of boys. The provision for their minds may not have been as complex as that to be found in the more famous Southern seminaries, but it was well selected, and quite generous enough when to it were added the outside influences that co-operated with books and teachers. Latin, mathematics, and the elements of Greek, were the staple subjects taught. The morning session began between six and half-past in summer, and at seven in winter, and lasted till eleven. The afternoon session was from one to five in summer, and from one to four in winter. At all other times the boys were free, since the preparation of lessons was made in school.

William Taylor, who was master from 1782 to 1786, when he died in the midst of his scholars, is the person to whom the poet refers in the lines beginning, " I come, ye little noisy Crew," and in the succeeding elegies. He also furnished some of the traits for the old man in " The Two April Mornings " and " The Fountain," and perhaps for one of the characters in " Expostulation and Reply " and " The Tables Turned." Years after Taylor's death, the poet, standing opposite the tablet in the schoolroom on which the teacher's name and the record of his service were inscribed, composed his " Matthew," in which he gives a glimpse of the happy schoolmaster:

> Poor Matthew, all his frolics o'er,
> Is silent as a standing pool;
> Far from the chimney's merry roar,
> And murmur of the village school.

> The sighs which Matthew heaved were sighs
> Of one tired out with fun and madness;
> The tears which came to Matthew's eyes
> Were tears of light, the dew of gladness.

WILLIAM WORDSWORTH

From the drawing by W. Shuter, April, 1798

THE HOUSE IN WHICH WORDSWORTH WAS BORN

From a photograph by Walmsley

DAME TYSON'S COTTAGE, HAWKSHEAD

From a photograph by Walmsley

WORDSWORTH'S LETTER FROM ORLEANS, DECEMBER, 1792

Facsimile of page 1

WILLIAM WORDSWORTH

From a drawing by Hancock about 1796

THE HOUSE IN GOSLAR WHERE THE WORDSWORTHS
LIVED IN 1798

DOVE COTTAGE FROM THE FRONT

From a photograph by Walmsley

FACSIMILE OF TWO PAGES OF DOROTHY WORDSWORTH'S JOURNAL
FOR SEPTEMBER 1, 2, AND 3, 1800

The gay old man, something between a schoolmaster and a retired labourer, whose image shapes itself in one's mind on reading these poems, can have been only suggested by Taylor, who was but thirty-two when he died; yet the fact that the poet could think thus of a teacher many years his senior shows that the latter must have been a singularly gentle and humorous person, and the boy beyond his age advanced in sympathy with mature minds. Taylor died in office, bidding farewell to the boys from his death-bed.

Wordsworth's schoolmates were drawn from a wide range of society; sons of country clergymen and the professional and business men of north-country towns, sons of villagers and small farmers. The most fortunate class of all Englishmen who laboured with their hands, in the eighteenth and nineteenth centuries, were the small farmers or " statesmen " in the vales of Westmorland, Cumberland and northern Lancashire. Their ancestors came into possession of the soil before the Reformation, when the monks of Furness Abbey and other great land-owning ecclesiastical establishments encouraged independent settlement in place of feudal tenure or mere tenantship, in the hope of providing a larger and more stubborn population for defence against the Scottish raiders. They had thus, in Wordsworth's time, been for several centuries raised above the position of tenant farmers. They tilled their own soil, to which they clung with deep attachment, sentimental considerations blending with economic. They were equally disposed to guard with jealous defiance their rights of pasturage on the fells or mountain-tops. The boldness of character which they inherited from their Scandinavian forefathers was re-enforced by the sense of possession. Like the corresponding class in Scotland, they were alive to the superiority of mental attainments, and ready to make sacrifices to educate their children.

The boys lived frugally and on a plane of equality, lodging and boarding with Hawkshead families, of whose home-life they made a part. Some of the boys the poet mentions by name, and not a few of their exploits he

records in " The Prelude " and in scattered notes. The
kind dame with whom he lived was Anne Tyson, whom
he always held in grateful memory for her motherly
care. Her cottage was, and is, a grey stone dwelling,
two stories high, in a side-street. An ash-tree stood
before it, and through its garden sang the imprisoned
brook. A sweet harmony bound together the hours in
school with the unmeasured time of play and repose in
Hawkshead homes, and of adventure in the open country; and the sunny seat " round the stone table under
the dark pine," before Dame Tyson's cottage, was
friendly alike " to studious or to festive hours." The
happiness of the boys was due no less to natural advantages than to the wise liberality with which they were
governed. In two minutes every boy could run from
his dame's doorstep to the open fields, and at no great
distance lay tracts of wood and moor. They ranged
the open heights, trapping birds after dark, and hunting
their eggs by day, " shouldering the naked crag." They
crept forth before dawn on mysterious errands, and
played late into the " soft starry nights," around the
stone where an old woman, in the largest square, sold
cakes and apples.

> Duly were our games
> Prolonged in summer till the daylight failed:
> No chair remained before the doors; the bench
> And threshold steps were empty; fast asleep
> The labourer, and the old man who had sate
> A later lingerer; yet the revelry
> Continued and the loud uproar: at last,
> When all the ground was dark, and twinkling stars
> Edged the black clouds, home and to bed we went,
> Feverish with weary joints and beating minds.*

In autumn they explored the hazel copses for nuts,
and all the green summer they fished " by rocks and
pools shut out from every star." From hill-top and
meadow they flew their kites. In winter,

> when the sun
> Was set, and visible for many a mile
> The cottage windows blazed through twilight gloom,†

---

* " Prelude," II. 9.   † " Prelude," I. 425.

they skated through the darkness below the solitary cliffs till,

with the din
Smitten, the precipices rang aloud;
The leafless trees and every icy crag
Tinkled like iron; while far-distant hills
Into the tumult sent an alien sound
Of melancholy not unnoticed, while the stars
Eastward were sparkling clear, and in the west
The orange sky of evening died away.

Thus, the poet tells us, his sympathies were enlarged, and the daily range of visible things grew dear to him. He beheld familiar scenes change with the revolving year till they were not what they had been, and yet were mysteriously the same. He watched the expression of nature run on in endless variety while the majestic presence remained for ever. The pathos, the charm, and the power of nature showed themselves in this contrast. Monotony was as necessary as alteration to reveal the fulness of the eternal being and impress with awe the beholder's mind. The events that fill earth and sky with dramatic action forced themselves upon him in unsolicited invasion. His soul lay passive at first; then it awoke to observe actively, and at last to contemplate and respond. From the danger of being prematurely lured away from the commonplace he was saved by the lusty sports of his fellows; yet he was always so much unlike ordinary boys as to remind one of Rousseau's remark, " Thoughtless boys make commonplace men."

His acquaintance extended from high to low throughout the neighbourhood. In his comment upon the lines beginning " Nay, Traveller, rest," which were composed in part at school in Hawkshead, he tells us that his delight in a rocky peninsula on Windermere was so great that he led thither a youngster about his own age, an Irish boy, who was servant to an itinerant conjurer. His purpose was to witness the lad's pleasure in the prospect, and he was not disappointed. It was probably in the roads about Hawkshead that he observed

the old Cumberland beggar, whose helpless existence
was an appeal to the charity of farmers' wives and passing horsemen riding in the pride of life. The Two
Thieves, one a doting old man of more than ninety
years, the other equally innocent, his grandson, aged
three, were familiar figures in the village, where they
performed an unconscious ministry of tender-hearted-
ness. No one could behold them sinlessly committing
their daily crimes, without reflecting on the nature of
moral responsibility and making allowance for im-
maturity and decay. The original of the Pedlar, in the
poem which at first went by that name and was later
called " The Excursion," was a packman who occasionally lived at Hawkshead, with whom the boy Wordsworth " had frequent conversations upon what had
befallen him, and what he had observed, during his
wandering life." And, as he told a friend in after-years,
they took much to one another, " as was natural." It
is to this Pedlar that the following lines in " The Excursion " refer. They are but the beginning of a long
and very attractive description, one of the most complete portraits in Wordsworth's gallery of worthies :

> We were tried Friends: amid a pleasant vale,
> In the antique market-village where was passed
> My school-time, an apartment he had owned,
> To which at intervals the Wanderer drew,
> And found a kind of home or harbour there.
> He loved me; from a swarm of rosy boys
> Singled out me, as he in sport would say,
> For my grave looks, too thoughtful for my years.
> As I grew up, it was my best delight
> To be his chosen comrade. Many a time,
> On holidays, we rambled through the woods:
> We sate—we walked; he pleased me with report
> Of things which he had seen; and often touched
> Abstrusest matter, reasonings of the mind
> Turned inwards; or at my request would sing
> Old songs, the product of his native hills.*

Another of his grown-up friends, living near Hawkshead, was the man to whom he attached himself one day

* I. 52.

when the common delusion of anglers caused him to believe that the farther from home the better the fishing. They worked their way to the sources of the Duddon, high in the mountains, and with small success. When the rain began to fall in torrents, the little fisherman, hungry and tired and wet, had to be carried home on his friend's back. The Jacobite and the Hanoverian, who figure in the same poem, were drawn from " two individuals who, by their several fortunes, were at different times driven to take refuge at the small and obscure town of Hawkshead on the skirt of these mountains. Their stories I had from the dear old dame with whom, as a schoolboy and afterwards, I lodged for the space of nearly ten years."*

In wilder flight, the boys rowed races on Windermere, played on the bowling-green, and ate strawberries and cream upon its farther shore, and, as their utmost extravagance, visited on horseback ancient landmarks far away, such as Furness Abbey. These were exceptional treats, exhausting their little weekly stipend, so that three-quarters of the year they " lived in penniless poverty." Plain and simple was the ordinary fare, and quiet were the usual pursuits. They had their " home amusements by the warm peat-fire," at evening, when a well-worn pack of cards did faithful service, while abroad

> Incessant rain was falling, or the frost
> Raged bitterly, with keen and silent tooth.

There are two ways of keeping a schoolboy busy, which is the first condition of his welfare. One is by rigorous discipline. The other and safer way is by alluring him to occupy himself in the pursuit of such happiness as is proper to his age and conducive to his development. These truisms were less commonly accepted in the eighteenth century than they are now, and there can be no doubt that Wordsworth's experience at Hawkshead was exceptional. The liberty he enjoyed

* Note to " The Excursion," dictated by Wordsworth to Miss Fenwick, about 1843.

could hardly be accorded even now in a large town. It
was his good-fortune to be brought up in the country,
under generous rules and among plain people. He
learned at Hawkshead to value at their just worth the
intelligence and morality of the poor. His judgment
of people in humble life was unmarred either by sentimental exaggeration or unfeeling ignorance. He had
lived among them, eating at their tables and playing
with their children.

The consciousness of nature as a source of love and as
a monitor came to him in moments when his being was
invaded by a higher power than himself, taking tranquil
possession of his senses, and unexpectedly of his affections too. A frequently recurring joy, if it be pure and
bring no painful consequences, creates love for the
source whence it is bestowed. So his heart became
engaged more deeply with every sweeping return of
these dear delights. The occasions of noticeable growth
to which he directs our attention in the first book of " The
Prelude " were moments when natural duty and childish
fear met in his heart. In the following passage he relates
how his moral consciousness was bound for ever, though
by what might be called a mere illusion, to the ineluctable
presences of nature:

> Ere I had told
> Ten birth-days, when among the mountain slopes
> Frost, and the breath of frosty wind, had snapped
> The last autumnal crocus, 'twas my joy
> With store of springes o'er my shoulder hung
> To range the open heights where woodcocks run
> Along the smooth green turf.   Through half the night,
> Scudding away from snare to snare, I plied
> That anxious visitation;—moon and stars
> Were shining o'er my head.   I was alone,
> And seemed to be a trouble to the peace
> That dwelt among them.   Sometimes it befell,
> In these night-wanderings, that a strong desire
> O'erpowered my better reason, and the bird
> Which was the captive of another's toil
> Became my prey; and when the deed was done
> I heard among the solitary hills
> Low breathings coming after me, and sounds

> Of undistinguishable motion, steps
> Almost as silent as the turf they trod.*

This passage no doubt had a significance to Wordsworth beyond the grasp of those who would limit the origin of moral admonition to some historic " authority," or even to " the inner voice " of conscience.　He believed, and probably for this reason treasured up this incident and gave it prominence, that the soul of the universe, uttering its august precepts through the clean air and the unsullied earth, speaks an intelligible language to the heart of man; because law and duty are the same for man and star and flower.　Many instincts that we deem superstition are probably based on a vague apprehension of this truth.　Many observances among primitive people bear witness to it.　A much larger part of our impulses and restraints than we are commonly disposed to admit are due to an unconscious imitation of nature in her qualities analogous to human virtues such as rectitude and prudence.　" Thanks," the poet wrote,

> Thanks to the means which Nature deigned to employ;
> Whether her fearless visitings, or those
> That came with soft alarm, like hurtless light
> Opening the peaceful clouds; or she would use
> Severer interventions, ministry
> More palpable, as best might suit her aim.†

Innumerable passages in his poetry developed this thought, now subtly and speculatively, as in " Peter Bell," now with eloquent assurance, as in the " Ode to Duty."

Another instance, almost crudely definite, may be cited to illustrate Wordsworth's belief, by no means vague, that nature exercised a moralizing influence over him in his boyhood.　One summer evening, " led by her," he unloosed a boat and rowed away in the starlight:

> Lustily
> I dipped my oars into the silent lake,
> And, as I rose upon the stroke, my boat
> Went heaving through the water like a swan;

---

† " Prelude," I. 306.　　‡ *Ibid.*, I. 351.

When, from behind that craggy steep till then
The horizon's bound, a huge peak, black and huge
As if with voluntary power instinct,
Upreared its head.   I struck and struck again,
And growing still in stature the grim shape
Towered up between me and the stars, and still,
For so it seemed, with purpose of its own
And measured motion like a living thing,
Strode after me.   With trembling oars I turned,
And through the silent water stole my way
Back to the covert of the willow tree;
There in her mooring-place I left my bark,—
And through the meadows homeward went, in grave
And serious mood; but after I had seen
That spectacle, for many days, my brain
Worked with a dim and undetermined sense
Of unknown modes of being; o'er my thoughts
There hung a darkness, call it solitude
Or blank desertion.   No familiar shapes
Remained, no pleasant images of trees,
Of sea or sky, no colours of green fields;
But huge and mighty forms, that do not live
Like living men, moved slowly through the mind
By day, and were a trouble to my dreams.*

Call it ecstasy or the unconscious exercise of reason,
the state of mind when such influxes of experience are
possible is the requisite condition of growth in childhood.   The soul is startled into self-consciousness,
and then awed by becoming aware of the deep community that binds it to the life even of insensate things.

In " The Prelude " the poet preserves the distinction
between the process by which intellectual life is kindled
in the child and that by which " the Youth, who daily
farther from the east must travel," and who is less
splendidly ministered to, must win his way to a wise
independence.   The examples of the former which he
gives in the first two books are of great significance, not
merely because they are gleams of elusive truth in a
twilight region of human experience.   Wordsworth is
almost, though not quite, unique in the reality of his
recollections of these high places of childhood.   Other
poets have made their revelations, too.   But he is unique

* " Prelude," I. 356.

in the degree of assurance with which he insists that these shadowy recollections

> Are yet the fountain light of all our day,
> Are yet a master light of all our seeing.

Not only to the psychology of childhood does he contribute these visions of the soul in lonely places, but his final word for the moral guidance of maturity is to search out the secrets of innocence and follow the voice of nature. The boys were thrown upon their own resources for entertainment as well as for intellectual advancement, " for, exclude," he writes,

> A little weekly stipend, and we lived
> Through three divisions of the quartered year
> In penniless poverty.

In this vacancy, nature deigned to work; and her operation was described in terms to which we are bound to attach a meaning none the less real because we cannot understand the process ourselves:

> Ye Presences of Nature in the sky
> And on the earth !   Ye Visions of the hills !
> And Souls of lonely places ! can I think
> A vulgar hope was yours when ye employed
> Such ministry, when ye through many a year
> Haunting me thus among my boyish sports,
> On caves and trees, upon the woods and hills,
> Impressed, upon all forms, the characters
> Of danger or desire; and thus did make
> The surface of the universal earth,
> With triumph and delight, with hope and fear,
> Work like a sea ?*

These were tribute brought by nature to her child from earth and sky; but a finer harvest of delights was his also, when his mind, turning inward, became aware of a divine relationship not expressed through objects of sense. And when once this consciousness was awake in him, he faced about to the external world with a new power of apprehension, a feeling of oneness, so that

* " Prelude," I. 463.

> [He] held unconscious intercourse with beauty
> Old as creation, drinking in a pure
> Organic pleasure.*

And this he could do because he had felt an intellectual charm in the hallowed and pure motions of sense, a calm delight, he says, which surely must belong

> To those first-born affinities that fit
> Our new existence to existing things,
> And, in our dawn of being, constitute
> A bond of union between life and joy.†

Through pure and natural pleasures, whether half physical or altogether of the intelligence, " the common round of visible things " grew dear to him; his sympathies were enlarged; at last his soul could stand alone, unassisted by the " incidental charms " which first attached his heart to rural objects, and

> Nature, intervenient till this time
> And secondary, now at length was sought
> For her own sake.

Alone or with a friend he often walked, before school hours, the full round of Esthwaite Water, " five miles of pleasant wandering," exulting in fellowship with nature's beauty, finding kindred moods in nature's morning face, and storing up " an obscure sense of possible sublimity," whereto he might aspire, as to an unattainable goal of his growing faculties. His liberty extended to choice of books. Such liberty Coleridge, too, enjoyed, and to this Wordsworth refers, when he rejoices for them both, that they have escaped the interference of system-mongers, with their surveillance, their examinations, their artificial standards. Among his treasures was a volume of " The Arabian Nights," and when he discovered that this was but one of four, he and another boy hoarded their joint savings to buy them; but after several months their resolution failed. His taste was for romances, legends, fictions of love, and tales of warlike adventure. They corresponded to dumb yearnings,

* "Prelude," I. 562.   † *Ibid.*, I. 555.

hidden appetites, and from this instinctive reaching out after the wonderful he draws the inference that

> Our simple childhood sits upon a throne
> That hath more power than all the elements.*

Something divine is indicated by this faculty, which enables a child to sweep away the objects of sense and create out of its own mind a world not altogether unreal. The poet cannot guess

> what this tells of Being past,
> Nor what it augurs of the life to come;

he can only infer that the mind which can build without regard to space or matter may itself be independent of time, eternal in self-activity.

The gift of verse is not granted to all poetic souls. Yet through some undiscovered law there is doubtless a connection between the power to think synthetically and a tendency to rhythmic expression. Thoughts that cohere with nature's order flow of their own motion in musical numbers. A poet bred in a civilized community can hardly help observing the advantages of verse as an appropriate mould for his deepest and most natural thoughts. The examples he finds in books are to him discoveries of the utmost importance. And thus we see Wordsworth at the age of ten rejoicing in the possession of a new faculty, or rather, a new facility:

> Twice five years
> Or less I might have seen, when first my mind
> With conscious pleasure opened to the charm
> Of words in tuneful order, found them sweet
> For their own *sakes*, a passion and a power.†

This was his introduction to the world of art, and he was quick to recognize its identity with the one already familiar to his dauntless tread. He who has been intimate, he declared, with living nature, receives from verse

> Knowledge and increase of enduring joy
> From the great Nature that exists in works
> Of mighty Poets. Visionary power
> Attends the motions of the viewless winds,
> Embodied in the mystery of words ‡

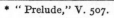

---

* " Prelude," V. 507.   † *Ibid.*, V. 552.   ‡ *Ibid.*, V. 593.

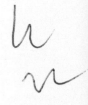

Before leaving Hawkshead Wordsworth composed a poem of many hundred lines, from which, as he told a friend in his old age, most of the thoughts and images were to be found dispersed through his other writings. Its conclusion, which suggested itself to him as he and his companions were resting in a boat on Coniston Water under a row of magnificent sycamores, has been preserved, with some alterations, in the following verses:

> Dear native regions, I foretell,
> From what I feel at this farewell,
> That, wheresoe'er my steps may tend,
> And whensoe'er my course shall end,
> If in that hour a single tie
> Survive of local sympathy,
> My soul will cast the backward view,
> The longing look alone on you.
>
> Thus, while the Sun sinks down to rest
> Far in the regions of the west,
> Though to the vale no parting beam
> Be given, not one memorial gleam,
> A lingering light he fondly throws
> On the dear hills where first he rose.

In October, 1787, Wordsworth was sent to St. John's College, Cambridge, of which his uncle, the Reverend Mr. Cookson, had been a fellow. Having a year's start of the other freshmen in mathematics, he neglected that branch of learning, but read classic authors according to his fancy, and Italian poetry. A few of the letters written by him and his sister between 1787 and 1791 exist, and are of great interest, but the chief source of knowledge concerning him for these three years and four months is "The Prelude." In spite of certain expressions of discontent, or rather want of sympathy, with Cambridge, it is evident that he really enjoyed his life at the university and benefited by it, though it is no doubt true, as he says, that the discipline was not severe enough to make him put forth his utmost energy in scholastic pursuits, while, on the other hand, he missed the opportunities for solitary wanderings and quiet observation which he had enjoyed at Hawkshead. There was considerable intellectual ferment at Cambridge shortly before and during his time of residence. Eddies from the great world-current of rationalism, the so-called Enlightenment, stirred the university from time to time, as is evident from the number of heresy trials that took place there. Such indications of independent thinking, accompanied by the hazarding of livelihood and reputation, show that the place was not altogether stagnant. If Wordsworth had been inclined to purely scholastic pursuits, particularly in theology or mathematics, he need not have complained that the atmosphere of Cambridge was uncongenial. His brother Christopher, who followed him from Hawkshead in October, 1791, certainly did not find it so. The latter was a member of Trinity College. His diary, beginning October 9, 1793, is full of attendance at lectures, conferences with tutors, conversations and debates on intellectual subjects with fellow-students, among whom was Coleridge, exercise taken with a view to mental hygiene, wide reading, and computation of the number of hours devoted to study. The following are the records of two typical days:*

" *Thurs.*, 17 [*Oct.*, 1793].—Rose to chapel.   Read till one.   Trigonometry (plane).   In the afternoon lounged in the library.   Walked with Reynolds.   Drank tea at home.   Read Tweddell's Panegyric on Locke.   Proceeded in my syllabus of Trigonometry.   Read part of Æschylus' Seven against Thebes.   Bilsborrow saw the Letter in which Johnson offers Dr. Darwin £1,000 for his Ζωονομια, without having ever seen it.   Dr. D. confesses it in his Botanic Garden, etc.; he propounds many opinions which he does not himself believe.   Hayley, Bilsborrow says, is employed upon a life of Milton."

" *Wednesday*, 23.—Chapel.   A Latin declamation brought to me.   All morning spent in choosing a subject, finding my opponent, going to the Dean, procuring books, etc."

He was attending Wollaston's lectures and reading Euclid, plane and spherical trigonometry, mechanics,

* Christopher Wordsworth: " Social Life at the English Universities in the Eighteenth Century."

astronomy, Locke, Æschylus, Sophocles, and Euripides, not to mention Boswell's " Johnson," *The Spectator*, and the early poetical ventures of his brother and of Coleridge.

Christopher Wordsworth manifested even in his youth the qualities that made him ultimately a successful Churchman and a great academic figure. He was naturally fond of reading, and not averse from hard study for its own sake or for the sake of distinction. He was docile and orthodox, and his social inclinations were strong. The ambitions which appear to have been the mainspring of his life were decidedly practical. It is hardly necessary to say that young men of this type are the round pegs for whom the round holes of prefer- ment are intended. If his brother had been like him, or, on the other hand, had been content to enjoy the easy tasks required and the harmless pleasures tolerated by the college and university authorities, we should have heard no complaint. But he asked of Cambridge what it is to be feared no university ever gave continu- ously and as a matter of course—namely, a great stimu- lus to the emotions, coinciding with a steady advance in knowledge and intellectual strength.

A still more instructive inference from these glimpses of Cambridge life is that the poet may have been imbued during his residence at the university with the radical opinions in religion and politics for which it has been commonly supposed that his sojourn in France was re- sponsible. He could hardly have escaped the influence which was to be, within a year or two, very effective with Coleridge, who, without going to France, became as much a radical as Wordsworth. It was in part, no doubt, Wordsworth's sympathy with this element of Cambridge life, an element discountenanced by the authorities and practically ineffective, that kept him from feeling at home. A reflexion of his state of mind may be seen in a suppressed passage of " The Prelude," dating from 1804 or earlier, which has been printed on p. 91 of Professor de Selincourt's *variorum* edition. The poet, addressing the university, exclaims:

Wear not the vizard of the ancient time
Upon a modern face, fling to the ground
Thy monkish Caul; and run no more abroad,
A greybeard Masquerader, dizen'd out
In Superstition's cast-off garb.

All that is certain, however, is that he held himself quietly aloof. He had grown up to be his own judge and master. Since his father's death he had been restrained by no authority save the mild rules of Hawkshead. He had lived much alone and out of doors, subject to a grander discipline, and seeking nobler rewards than those of any school. His heart, which had expanded generously, as we have seen, in the society of other boys and of simple rustics, closed upon its tender secrets in the unaccustomed air of a larger place. An uneasy wonder, not real admiration, took the place of those deep satisfactions, those unquestioning acceptances, that filled his mind among his native mountains. He half regretted, half cherished, the consciousness of being different from the young men about him, and of being out of sympathy with the spirit of the university. It was not merely disdain that taught him to feel he " was not for that place."

Wordsworth's great autobiographical poem, which towards the close of the second book becomes deeper and slower in its movement, bursts at the opening of the third into a rapid narrative, and streams along with lively interest. He records with Chaucerian simplicity his arrival on the coach, the aspect of the many-towered town, his fresh sensations, his important visits to tutor and tailor, and the welcome given him by old Hawkshead boys, " now hung round with honour and importance ":

I was the Dreamer, they the Dream; I roamed
Delighted through the motley spectacle;
Gowns grave, or gaudy, doctors, students, streets,
Courts, cloisters, flocks of churches, gateways, towers:
Migration strange for a stripling of the hills,
A northern villager.*

---

* " Prelude," III. 29.

He occupied rooms, since demolished, in the beautiful
First Court, which were over the kitchens, and looked
out upon the chapel of Trinity.   From his bedroom
window he

> could behold
> The antechapel, where the statue stood
> Of Newton with his prism and silent face,
> The marble index of a mind for ever
> Voyaging through strange seas of Thought, alone.*

The routine of lectures and examinations failed from
the very first to awaken his interest.   He was untouched
by the excessive hopes, small jealousies, and triumphs,
of student life.   Yet he was disturbed at times by
prudent thoughts about his future worldly maintenance,
which depressed him amid the crowd of eager aspirants.
And then he did for himself what he has since done
for thousands—he strengthened his heart by commun-
ing with nature.   It is a hackneyed phrase, but to him
it represented a most real and important experience.
As he paced along the level fields of Cambridgeshire,
far from the grander scenes that had inspired his
boyhood, he felt even there an uplifting of his mind and
a sense that all was well—felt what independent solaces
were his

> To mitigate the injurious sway of place
> Or circumstance.

He looked for universal things, called on them to be his
teachers, gave a moral life even to the loose stones that
covered the highway, " saw them feel, or linked them
to some feeling."   " The great mass," he says,

> Lay bedded in a quickening soul, and all
> That I beheld respired with inward meaning.

He flung himself upon nature, fearing that she might not
be the same in these less lovely regions, and found her
ready as ever to soothe and exalt.   He could then return
and look unabashed at the memorials of intellectual
greatness that admonished him from their honourable

* " Prelude," III. 59.

niches in college gateways or their gilded frames in college halls.   What wonder if he held himself somewhat apart from his companions !   It was not easy for him to come down to their level, and evidently in his first year he acted strangely.   They thought him mad, and so, he says, he was indeed,

> If prophecy be madness; if things viewed
> By poets in old time, or higher up
> By the first men, earth's first inhabitants,
> May in these tutored days no more be seen
> With undisordered sight.*

But as proof that his vision of Oneness was no blear illusion, he asserts that at this time his analytic powers were keen and active.   He perceived not only similitudes, but differences.   He might have said, with William Blake, " every Minute Particular is holy." He is anxious to avert the charge that he was too attentive to generalities, and therefore incapable of that direct sense of the actual and individual which is common to men.   He is concerned to show that in so far, at least, he was not unaffected by the logical severity which was supposed to dominate Cambridge thought.

Gradually he adapted himself more to the ideals of the place, and began to take part in its enjoyments.   His heart, he tells us, was social, and if a throng was near, that way he inclined.   He welcomed new acquaintances, made friends, sauntered, talked, drifted about the streets and walks, read lazily in trivial books, rode horseback, and sailed boisterously on the river.   With no one did he share his deeper thoughts.   He scarcely gave them definite form in his own mind, and made no attempt to express them in writing.   Now and then he forced himself to work at the appointed tasks, and felt a faint hope of success.   We must not suppose that he was really as neglectful of classical studies as " The Prelude " might lead us to think.   In later life he showed evidence of fairly wide and accurate reading in classical authors, and prepared his son for college.   And yet, for him, as

* " Prelude," III. 150.

indeed for many minds, there could be no complete
absorption in work unless imagination led the way.
And imagination, he says, slept, though not utterly.
Had he been more mature in scholarship, or more experienced, he might have been moved, as Goethe was
moved, by the contrast between active life and the
systems of speculative idealism which were echoing on
their way from Berkeley to Kant. Or he might have
been thus early aroused, as Lessing and Voltaire were
aroused, to shoulder his responsibility in the warfare
between rationalism and mysticism. It is to sceptical
impulses, perhaps, that he refers when he mentions
with annoyance

> a treasonable growth
> Of indecisive judgments, that impaired
> And shook the mind's simplicity.*

The English universities in his day were not, in a
broad sense, national institutions. They were organs of
the Church of England. Much of their mediæval character as groups of religious houses still survived. The
clergy were conspicuous in almost all high academic
posts, and a steady circulation between fellowships and
church livings in the gift of colleges was maintained.
In academic groups religious and political doubt were
treated with the disgust due to filial ingratitude. Wordsworth, if he doubted, was too simple-hearted to resent
this feeling and to realize its impertinence.

After all, the most memorable pages of the third book
of " The Prelude " are those which recall the deep floods
of reverence that flowed into the young poet's soul when
he remembered his illustrious predecessors, Newton,
Chaucer, Spenser, Milton. In those precincts he could
not move and sleep and wake untouched by their
ennobling influence. " I could not lightly pass," he
says,

> Through the same gateways, sleep where they had slept,
> Wake where they waked, range that inclosure old,
> That garden of great intellects, undisturbed.†

---

* " Prelude," III. 211.   † *Ibid.*, III. 261.

In the neighbouring village of Trumpington he " laughed
with Chaucer in the hawthorn shade." In lines that
exquisitely imitate the music of his great Brother,
Englishman, and Friend, he records how he hailed

> Sweet Spenser, moving through his clouded heaven
> With the moon's beauty and the moon's soft pace.

Milton, " soul awful," he says, " I seemed to see "

> Familiarly, and in his scholar's dress
> Bounding before me, yet a stripling youth—
> A boy, no better, with his rosy cheeks
> Angelical, keen eye, courageous look,
> And conscious step of purity and pride.

One of his acquaintances occupied Milton's rooms in
Christ's College, and there, on a dark winter evening,
betrayed by enthusiasm, he poured out libations to his
memory,

> till pride
> And gratitude grew dizzy in a brain
> Never excited by the fumes of wine
> Before that hour, or since,*

and in fear of being too late for evening prayers he ran
ostrich-like through the streets, with flowing gown, and,
shouldering up his surplice with careless ostentation, hurried through the antechapel of St. John's.

Those mighty dead roused his enthusiasm, but through
his own fault, as he admits, failed to stir in him

> A fervent love of rigorous discipline.

What he missed was some compelling force which should
break the light composure of his easy spirits and bend
him to a task demanding all his efforts. He did not
slight his books, but he knew full well that he possessed
powers that might have been exerted to great purpose
had the passion for study been awakened in him. Other
passions already filled his mind, passions engendered by
crystalline rivers and solemn heights, lovely forms that
left less space for learning's soberer visions.

* " Prelude," III. 275-321.

Out of these regrets he framed, later, an ideal of a place of learning " whose studious aspect " should have bent him down " to instantaneous service," a place where the gregarious instincts should be turned to the highest account in a generous co-operation, where knowledge should be prized for its own sake, where youth, under the impulse of a truly religious zeal, should stand abashed

> Before antiquity and steadfast truth
> And strong book-mindedness; and over all
> A healthy sound simplicity should reign,
> A seemly plainness, name it what you will,
> Republican or pious.*

He fancied that the universities possessed such a character in the Renaissance,

> When all who dwelt within these famous walls
> Led in abstemiousness a studious life,†

when princes froze at matins and peasants' sons begged their way from remote villages, journeying to these centres of learning "with ponderous folios in their hands," and illustrious scholars,

> Lovers of truth, by penury constrained,
> Bucer, Erasmus, or Melanchthon, read
> Before the doors or windows of their cells
> By moonshine through mere lack of taper light.

The glorious dream is by no means vain. It may yet be realized, and Wordsworth was right in thinking that poverty, compulsory or voluntary, with the plainness that poverty entails, is one of the first conditions of its fulfilment. The religion of such a place, upon which it will depend wholly for dignity, grace, integrity, and inspiration, must, however, be a faith in those things which are recognized by the best spirits of the times as the supremely good things. A mediæval or a seventeenth-century type of religion will not vivify a modern university. Nowhere is there a more disastrous effect on morality than in a college or school whose real religion

* " Prelude," III. 394.   † *Ibid.*, III. 446-478.

does not heartily support its ceremonial of worship.   In a vein of fervent satire Wordsworth comments on the practice of compulsory chapel services, which the younger members of his college attended unwillingly and the older members very irregularly or not at all. " Be wise," he says,

> Ye Presidents and Deans, and, till the spirit
> Of ancient times revive, and youth be trained
> At home in pious service, to your bells
> Give seasonable rest, for 'tis a sound
> Hollow as ever vexed the tranquil air;
> And your officious doings bring disgrace
> On the plain steeples of our English Church,
> Whose worship, 'mid remotest village trees,
> Suffers for this.*

All authority, he held, was weakened by the irreverence produced by this forced attendance, and even Science was " smitten thence with an unnatural taint."

He was impatient, too, of the narrow range of scholastic studies. Modern subjects attracted him, and he spent much time reading in branches not recognized as part of the official course. He learned Italian. His private tutor, Agostino Isola, a native of Milan, whence he had fled for political reasons, had taught Gray in his time. Isola's granddaughter, Emma, was adopted, or at least brought up in part, by Charles and Mary Lamb. Wordsworth was never a discursive reader. More intense study would have suited him better, and he does indeed mention, with minute and curious detail, the way in which geometry strengthened and elevated his mind. From the same source he says he drew

> A pleasure quiet and profound, a sense
> Of permanent and universal sway,

and thus a recognition of God, which comforted him with transcendent peace. He craved discipline and insight, not experience, and so, in the large part of " The Prelude " devoted to his education, few books—the doors to experience—are mentioned, even in the canto

* " Prelude," III. 409.

entitled " Books." It is significant, too, that almost the
only books he mentions in connection with this time—
and with great delight—are " The Arabian Nights "
and " Don Quixote," which pleased him, evidently, by
their extravagance and fancifulness, more than for any
outlook on reality they offered. His very considerable
acquaintance with books of travel was gained later,
perhaps as a relief from too much concentration, and
because he had, as he said, a passion for wandering.

After the manner of undergraduates, he derived much
amusement from the oddities of his seniors. " Rich
pastime," he found it, to observe " the grave Elders,
men unscoured, grotesque in character," with so little
to do that they fell into random and strange practices.
The employment of what is termed " academic leisure "
creates bewilderment in the young. This is especially
the case when apparent idleness is not disconnected
with academic distinction. Wordsworth was perhaps
more tender than his fellow-students in his criticism of
the old dons, for he remembered the aged shepherds of
the hills, and found that, though different in expression,
the eccentricities of age were essentially the same in
Cambridge as in Hawkshead. But he scourges the
system which encouraged a rapid decline into useless-
ness; and thinking of the " old humorists " who sat at
the college high tables in his youth, he bursts into an
indignant passage.

At the end of his first college year he had no home to
go to, and turned eagerly towards Hawkshead. His old
dame welcomed him with almost a mother's pride. He
re-entered her cottage with the assurance of a son.
Language failed him in which to express the complex
feelings that filled his heart on this occasion, as he
recognized a hundred once familiar objects, beholding
everything in duplicate, its present aspect mingling
strangely with its remembered form. The richest part
of this experience is seeing one's old self peeping unexpectedly at its new playfellow. No one can communicate to anyone else more than the barest outline of what
the first home-coming after a long absence means to an

imaginative person, and although the fourth book of
" The Prelude " is probably the most successful attempt
to do so ever made, the poet asks as in despair :

> Why should I speak of what a thousand hearts.
> Have felt, and every man alive can guess ?

He greeted the rooms, the court, the garden of Dame
Tyson's dwelling, and the unruly brook boxed up in its
paved channel, which was an emblem of his own mountain origin and recent restraint. He hailed old friends
at their work, or on the roads, or across fields. He felt
embarrassed among his old schoolmates because of his
fashionable dress. He took his place with delight at
the domestic table, and, after a day of many sensations,
laid him down in the lowly accustomed bed whence he
" had heard the wind roar and the rain beat hard," and
oft

> Had lain awake on summer nights to watch
> The moon in splendour couched among the leaves
> Of a tall ash, that near our cottage stood ;
> Had watched her with fixed eyes while to and fro
> In the dark summit of the waving tree
> She rocked with every impulse of the breeze.*

After this first riot of boyish spirits the ferment of
poetry revived in him, and, accompanied by an old
favourite, a rough hill terrier, he wandered in the
country, " harassed with the toil of verse," rushing
forward boyishly to pat the dog when some lovely
image rose full-formed in the song, and putting on the
air of a mere saunterer if the animal gave warning of
approaching passengers. By contrast with the fens of
Cambridgeshire, the lakes and hills seemed more beautiful than ever. That he had felt their beauty a year
before, when as yet he had never lived outside the circle
of their power, is proof of his inborn distinction of spirit,
for not every son of the mountains is aware of the
majesty that surrounds him. Now to this original
realization was added the result of comparison. He
recognized the peculiar appeal of these old haunts which

* " Prelude," IV. 87.

had once seemed a whole world to him. He felt, with pensive sympathy, that even this beauty must be transient.

With clearer knowledge than of old, he was now able to read, also, the characters of his former companions, the dalesmen and their children. He found a freshness in human life. He observed with increased respect the daily occupations which he really loved. They had gained dignity in the eyes of one who had been puzzling vainly over the mystery of endowed leisure. The peaceful scene,

> Changed like a garden in the heat of spring
> After an eight days' absence,

filled him with surprise. Many things which before had seemed natural now began to take their places in the order of conventional society. He saw with his own unclouded eye of childhood, and at the same time with the eye of the world. In this first long vacation many a day was

> Spent in a round of strenuous idleness.

He flung himself into the innocent gaieties of country life, " feast, and dance, and public revelry." This course he afterwards, taking himself strictly to task, regretted. Like Rousseau, Wordsworth believed that the development of the child should be held back until adolescence, and that then, in a few crowded years or even months, the reasoning powers should be subjected to rigorous discipline, the imagination enriched, and purposes ennobled. He therefore looked back with some disapproval on the waste of many golden hours at that important time. For, he declared, except some casual knowledge of character or life, he gained no real experience;

> Far better had it been to exalt the mind
> By solitary study, to uphold
> Intense desire through meditative peace.*

Yet one hour of profound insight set the balance straight. It was the hour of his baptism with the fire of poesy,

* " Prelude," IV. 304.

an hour memorable in his life and in the history of
literature.   It was the supreme religious moment of his
life, the point when solitude closed in on all sides of him,
and his being stood cut off for the first time from every
other human soul, distinct in conscious self-hood; the
point, too, when by this very isolation his soul lay bare
to divine influence and he communed with God, sub-—
missive to the heavenly voice.   He then accepted—he
could not help accepting—the call of a power beyond
his control.   And from that time his faculties were
released.   The incident does not admit of paraphrase,
and must be read in his own words, the momentous
conclusion being:

> bond unknown to me
> Was given, that I should be, else sinning greatly,
> A dedicated Spirit.*

Penrith is nearly thirty miles northeast of Hawkshead.   The shortest route between them lies over
Kirkstone Pass and along Brother's Water and Ullswater.   At the halfway point the most beautiful little
beck in the whole Lake Country comes tumbling out
of Dovedale, from " the springs of Dove," and then
winds quietly past " one green field " until it finds rest
in Brother's Water.   An ancient manor-house or superior
farmhouse, Hartsop Hall, seated beside the brook, com-
mands a prospect of the upper part of the vale.   It
seems likely that this is the scene and that the summer
of 1788 was the time of the experience which is exquisitely
idealized in the Lucy poems, written in Germany more
than ten years later.   I am convinced that these five
poems, and less obviously four or five others, record, in
the delicate distillation of memory, a real experience of
youthful love and bewildering grief.   The maiden whom
Wordsworth loved was a child.   He loved her with the
ennobling passion of a high-minded boy.   She died, but
her image survived in his heart.
    There is nothing in " The Prelude " or in any published
letters of the Wordsworth family to indicate that the

* " Prelude," IV, 309-338.

young collegian spent any considerable part of this first long vacation with his sister, or elsewhere than at Hawkshead. But it is, of course, extremely probable that he visited her at Penrith, to which his good long legs would easily carry him in a day. He had been with her before going to Cambridge, in October, 1787. She had bravely helped to get him ready for the journey, and then fallen back in mute despair into a lonely life. She was made to feel her dependence upon her grandparents and her uncle Christopher. Her duties in the mercer shop were uncongenial, and were not lightened by much sympathy. Her grandmother's eye was on her there, and she could not indulge her love of reading. The grandfather was ill and cross. There was not in all England a spirit naturally more gladsome than Dorothy Wordsworth's, nor a constitution that called so eagerly as hers did for space and exercise and change. Two passions possessed her wholly—love of nature and love of her brothers; and at sixteen she was cut off from both nature and her brothers. Her mobile apprehension had to accommodate its pace to the torpid current of events in a small market-town. Her tameless enthusiasm was checked by the disapproval of a commonplace family. There exist two letters which she wrote from Penrith to a girl friend, Jane Pollard, of Halifax, before William went to Cambridge. They are remarkable productions for a child of fifteen. The handwriting is that of a person accustomed to rapid composition. It is neither unformed nor " commercial." The style is singularly correct, and flexible enough to express a wide range of anger, affection, and playfulness. The words flow as from a pent-up fountain. Never was there a heart more eager to love. It is worth remarking as a distinguishing trait and a noble one, that, while craving a chance to bestow her love, she expresses little anxiety about being loved. Possibly some abatement from what she writes about her gloom and its causes should be made on the ground that she takes an artistic pleasure in describing them. In the first letter, which is dated merely " Sunday evening," but apparently was written at Penrith in the summer of 1787, excusing herself for negligence, she says:

" On Thursday night I began writing, but my brother William was sitting by me, and I could not help talking with him till it was too late to finish. . . . I might perhaps have employed an hour or two in writing to you, but I have so few, so very few, to pass with my brothers that I could not leave them. You know how happy I am in their company. I do not now want a friend who will share with me my distresses. I do not now pass half my time alone. I can bear the ill-nature of all my relations, for the affection of my brothers consoles me in all my griefs; but how soon, alas ! shall I be deprived of this consolation, and how soon shall I then become melancholy, even more melancholy than before ! They are just the boys I could wish them, they are so affectionate and so kind to me as makes me love them more and more every day. William and Christopher are very clever boys, at least so they appear in the partial eyes of a sister. No doubt I am partial and see virtues in them that by everybody else will pass unnoticed. John, who is to be the sailor, has a most excellent heart. He is not so bright as either William or Christopher, but he has very good common sense, and is well calculated for the profession he has chosen. Richard, the eldest, I have seen. He is equally affectionate and good, but is far from being as clever as William, but I have no doubt of his succeeding in his business, for he is very diligent and far from being dull. He only spent a night with us. Many a time have William, John, Christopher and myself shed tears together, tears of the bitterest sorrow. We all of us each day feel more sensibly the loss we sustained when we were deprived of our parents, and each day do we receive fresh insults. . . . Our fortunes will, I fear, be very small, as Lord Lonsdale will most likely only pay a very small part of his debt, which is £4,700. My uncle Kit (who is our guardian) having said many disrespectful things of him, and having always espoused the cause of the Duke of Norfolk, has incensed him so much that I fear we shall feel through life the effects of his imprudence. We shall, however, have sufficient to educate my brothers. John, poor fellow ! says that he shall have occasion for very little, £200 will be sufficient to fit him out, and he should wish William to have the rest for his education, as he has a wish to be a lawyer if his health will permit, and it will be very expensive. We shall have, I believe, about £600 apiece, if Lord Lonsdale does not pay. It is but very little, but it will be quite enough for my brothers' education, and after they are once put forward in the world there is little doubt of their succeeding, and for me while they live I shall never want a friend. Oh, Jane! when they have left me I shall be quite unhappy. I shall long more ardently than ever for you, my dearest, dearest friend. We have been told thousands of times that we were liars, but we treat such behaviour with the contempt it deserves. We always finish our conversations, which generally take a melancholy train, with wishing we had a father and a home. Oh, Jane! I hope it may be long ere you experience the loss of your parents, but till you feel that loss you will never know how dear to you your sisters are."

The uncle mentioned in this letter, Christopher Crackanthorpe Cookson, was a brother of the poet's mother. On his own mother's death, in 1792, he took the surname of Crackanthorpe instead of Cookson, and became Christopher Crackanthorpe Crackanthorpe.

The second letter bears the Penrith stamp, and was evidently written late in the summer or early in the autumn of 1787. It is dated merely "Monday evening, 10 o'clock."

"Yesterday morning I parted from the kindest and most affectionate of brothers. I cannot paint to you my distress at their departure. For a few hours I was absolutely miserable. A thousand tormenting fears rushed upon me—the approaching winter, the ill-nature of my grandfather and uncle Christopher, the little probability there is of my soon again seeing my youngest brother, and still less likelihood of my revisiting my Halifax friends, in quick succession filled my mind. . . . [She tells how she has to look for chances to write, avoiding her grandmother's watchful eye. There is something merely romantic, but also perhaps something morbid and overstrained, in all this.] A gentleman of my father's intimate acquaintance, who is not worth less than two or three thousand pounds a year, and who always professed himself to be the real friend of my father, refused to pay a bill of £700 to his children without considerable reductions. . . . I am sure as long as my brothers have a farthing in their pockets I shall never want. My brother William goes to Cambridge in October, but he will be at Penrith before his departure. He wishes very much to be a lawyer, if his health will permit, but he is troubled with violent headaches and a pain in his side, but I hope they will leave him in a little while. You must not be surprised if you see him at Halifax in a short time. I think he will not be able to call there on his way to Cambridge, as my uncle William [the Rev. William Cookson] and a young gentleman who is going to the same college will accompany him. When I wrote to you last I had some faint hopes that he might have been permitted to stay with me till October. You may guess how much I was mortified and vexed at his being obliged to go away. I absolutely dislike my uncle Kit. He never speaks a pleasant word to one, and behaves to my brother William in a particularly ungenerous manner. . . . I have a very pretty collection of books from my brothers, which they have given me. I will give you a catalogue. I have the Iliad and Odyssey, Pope's Works, Fielding's Works, Hayley's poems, Gil Blas, Dr. Gregory's letters to his daughters; and my brother Richard intends sending me Shakespeare's plays and the Spectator. I have also Milton's works, Dr. Goldsmith's poems, etc. . . . I am determined to do a great deal now both in French and English. My grandmother sits in the shop in the afternoons, and by working particularly hard for one hour I think I may read the next without being discovered. I rise pretty early in the morning, so I hope in time to have perused them all. I am at present reading the Iliad, and like it very much. My brother William read part of it."

After these formidable projects it is pleasant to read a feminine description of her looks: " I am so little, and wish to appear as girlish as possible; I wear my hair curled about my face in light curls frizzed at the bottom and turned at the ends."

In another letter, written late in the autumn, occurs a more particular description:

" My grandmother is now gone to bed, and I am quite alone. Imagine me sitting in my bed-gown, my hair out of curl and hanging about my face, with a small candle beside me, and my whole person the picture of poverty (as it always is in a bed-gown), and you will then see your friend Dorothy. It is after 11 o'clock. I begin to find myself very sleepy, and I have my hair to curl, so I must bid my very dear friend a Good-night."

One perceives that, after all, " poverty," a dragon grandmother, and the dreadful necessity of writing letters at eleven o'clock at night, were not without a certain romantic delightfulness to this young lady.

A few weeks later, as the autumn evenings lengthened, she wrote to her friend with bitterer feeling:

" I often wish for you. I think how happy we could be together notwithstanding the cold insensibility of my grandmother and the ill-nature of my grandfather. . . . . I often go to the Cowpers and like Miss D. C. better than ever. I wish my uncle and she would marry. [She means her favourite uncle, the Rev. William Cookson, who did marry Miss Cowper, on October 17, 1788.] . . . I am now writing beside that uncle I so much love. He is a friend to whom next to my aunt I owe the greatest obligations. Every day gives me new proofs of his affection, and every day I like him better than I did before. I am now with him two hours every morning, from nine till eleven. I then read and write French, and learn arithmetic. When I am a good arithmetician I am to learn geography. I sit in his room when we have a fire. . . . I had my brother William with me for three weeks. I was very busy during his stay, preparing him for Cambridge, so that I had very little leisure, and what I had you may be sure I wished to spend with him. I have heard from my brother William since his arrival at Cambridge. He spent three or four days at York upon the road."

In her next letter to Miss Pollard, dated Friday, December 17, she refers to a copy of the Kilmarnock edition of Burns's poems, published the year before. William " had read it, and admired many of the pieces very much, and promised to get it for me at the book-club, which he did." She found the Address to a Louse " very comical," and the one to a Mountain Daisy " very pretty." But she longs for liberty.

" Oh, Jane, Jane," she cries, " that I could but see
you ! how happy, how very happy, we should be ! I
really think that for an hour after our meeting there
would nothing pass betwixt us but tears of joy, fits of
laughter, and unconnected exclamations, such as ' Oh
Jane !' ' Oh Dolly !' It is now seven months since we
parted. What a long time ! We have never been
separated so long for these nine years. I shall soon
have been here a year, and in two years more I am
determined I will come to Halifax if I cannot sooner,
but I hope my uncle William is now on the road to preferment. If I do not flatter myself without having any
right, he will soon be married. I must certainly in a
little time go to see him, and then I shall visit Halifax. . .
I daresay *you* look forward with pleasure to the approaching season; I am sorry to say I cannot. Believe me, my
dear Jane, I wish you many merry evenings and agreeable dances. I shall often think of you, and flatter
myself that on Christmas Day, which you know is my
birthday, you will cast a melancholy thought upon your
friend Dorothy. . . . The assemblies are indeed begun,
but they are no amusement for me. There was one on
Wednesday evening, where there were a number of
ladies, but alas ! only six gentlemen, so two ladies were
obliged to dance together."

In a letter to Miss Pollard, written apparently in
January, 1788, she mentions the recent sudden death of
her grandfather. More than once, writing of her
brothers—Richard in London, William at Cambridge,
Christopher at Hawkshead, and John, sailing now to the
West Indies, now to the East—she exclaims, " How we
are squandered abroad !" Her ardent nature yearned
for affection and intimacy. At last her uncle William
married Miss Cowper, and was appointed rector of
Forncett, near Long Stretton, in Norfolk. Thither
they went in December, 1788, taking the happy girl
with them. Writing to Jane from Norwich, where they
stayed a few days, in December, 1788, before settling at
Forncett, she says: " I have now nothing left to wish
for on my own account. Every day gives me fresh
proofs of my uncle and aunt's goodness. . . . My
happiness was very unexpected. When my uncle told
me, I was almost mad with joy. I cried and laughed

alternately. It was in a walk with him that it was communicated to me."

On the way they had stopped for a few hours at Cambridge, where she greatly admired the buildings, and walked with delight in the college courts and groves. She thought it odd to see the " smart powdered heads " of the students, " with black caps like helmets, only that they had a square piece of wood at the top, and gowns something like those that clergymen wear," but she considered the costume " exceedingly becoming." She saw her brother there.

For about four years Forncett rectory was to be her home, until what she called " the day of my felicity, the day on which I am to find a home under the same roof as my brother." She was so happy with her uncle and aunt, and so busy gardening, raising poultry, teaching the country children, visiting the sick, and reading, that only one desire was left unsatisfied—the desire to be with William. This longing, however, grew until it drove every other thought from her mind. She wrote about him and to him with the warmth and abandonment of a lover. Her occasional journeys to the North, to Halifax, Sockburn, and Penrith, only revived his memory. Her visits to Windsor, where her uncle was occasionally on duty as a canon of the Chapel Royal, and where she saw many grand people and was introduced to the royal family, only increased her admiration and solicitude for the plain and no doubt rustic collegian.

He who has not lingered in the Lake country till far into the autumn cannot realize the meaning of Wordsworth's lines at the opening of the sixth book of " The Prelude," in which he relates that he turned his face

    from the coves and heights
Clothed in the sunshine of the withering fern;
Quitted, not loth, the mild magnificence
Of calmer lakes and louder streams.

The golden bracken and the voice of full-fed streams are nature's signals to depart. They remind the visitor that summer is gone and winter is at hand. Wordsworth, as one not yet fitted to dwell uninterruptedly in this retreat, went back willingly enough to Cambridge. But though refreshed and cheerful, he withdrew now for the first time in his life into something like solitude. He read copiously, but without a settled plan. He troubled himself very little about the prescribed studies, except from a sense of duty to his friends and kindred. He knew he was a poet, and was calmly happy in the present sense of joy and the certain anticipation of future power. In those days he first dared to hope that he might leave behind him some monument " which pure hearts should reverence." The analogy with Milton is evident, and perhaps Milton's example gave him courage. He declares that

> the dread awe
> Of mighty names was softened down and seemed
> Approachable, admitting fellowship
> Of modest sympathy.

Such boldness did the *alma mater* of Spenser, Marlowe, Fletcher, Ben Jonson, Milton, Crashaw, Herrick, Herbert, Cowley, and Gray, instil into her nursling. All winter long it was his habit to walk in the groves of his college in the evening till the nine o'clock bell summoned him to go indoors. The human beauty of Cambridge, her peculiar blending of quiet, unobtrusive, and half-rural simplicity with some of the noblest monuments of Gothic architecture to be found in the world, charmed him in spite of himself. His three sonnets, " Inside of King's College Chapel, Cambridge," are sufficient evidence that he was neither unappreciative nor ungrateful. And no doubt his mind, " in hours of fear or grovelling thought," sought refuge in the memory of that " glorious work of fine intelligence."

Yet we have only two poems, originally one, but printed as two, of which it is known with certainty that he composed them at Cambridge. These are the " Lines written while sailing in a Boat at Evening " and the three additional stanzas entitled " Remembrance

* " Prelude," VI. 59.

of Collins," in which he has arbitrarily changed the
scene to the Thames.

His second summer vacation, that of 1789, was spent
in the north again. He explored Dovedale in Derby-
shire, and some of the valleys in western Yorkshire
and hidden tracts of his own native region. Between
these wanderings he was blessed, he tells us, with a
joy "that seemed another morn risen on mid-noon,"
the presence of his sister, from whom he had been so
long separated that "she seemed a gift then first
bestowed." At their age time had wrought many
changes in both of them, all tending to make them more
interesting in each other's eyes. She had returned
from Forncett to Penrith or to Penrith and Halifax
for the summer. She was now old enough to take
some of the freedom from household restraints which
she had longed for, and under her brother's charge she
visited the many romantic scenes within easy reach of
Penrith. Side by side they strolled along the banks of
Emont, and climbed among the ruins of Brougham
Castle, thinking of Sidney, who, as tradition said, penned
there snatches of his "Arcadia," which was written
for his sister, the Countess of Pembroke. Here they
clambered up broken stairs and out into the sunlight
on ridges of fractured walls, to lie on an old turret,

> Catching from tufts of grass and hare-bell flowers
> Their faintest whisper to the passing breeze,
> Given out while mid-day heat oppressed the plains.*

The long companionship, the deep and unbroken
communion of spirits, really began in this happy season.
It was then, too, that he first felt the stirrings of affection
for Mary Hutchinson, his sister's friend, to him at that
time

> By her exulting outside look of youth
> And placid under-countenance, first endeared.†

Their haunts were the high hill beyond Penrith called
the Beacon, on which the signal fires used to blaze in
times of Border warfare, and the crags and pools on the

* "Prelude," VI. 221.   † Ibid., VI. 226.

bare fell, and the shady woods and lanes of eglantine, whence he gathered thoughts of love—

> The spirit of pleasure, and youth's golden gleam.

In their wanderings they passed the spot where, as a child, he had once been struck with sombre fear by its loneliness and the remembered story of an execution. Now, " in the blessed hours of early love," and with the loved one by his side, the same melancholy place gave him only joy, for

> The mind is lord and master—outward sense
> The obedient servant of her will.

It is difficult to believe that this awakening of interest in Mary Hutchinson, in the summer of 1789, deepened at once into the passion of love. Many years, filled with other associations, were to intervene between this idyll and their marriage in 1802. Wordsworth's ardour and self-will were so intense that, had he at this time really loved, he would have been unlikely to suppress his feelings. It is to be supposed, also, that in such case more frequent mention of Miss Hutchinson would have been made in Dorothy Wordsworth's letters to Miss Pollard.

In one of these, written at Forncett, January 25, 1790, she says:

" My brother John, I imagine, sailed for India on Saturday or Sunday in the ' Earl of Abergavenny.' He wrote to me the other day in excellent spirits. William is at Cambridge, Richard in London, Kit at Hawkshead. How we are squandered abroad !" She tells about her little voluntary school of nine pupils, and adds this interesting paragraph: " Mr. Wilberforce has been with us rather better than a month. Tell your father I hope he will give him his vote at the next general election. I believe him to be one of the best of men. He allows me ten guineas a year to distribute in what manner I think best to the poor."

Defending herself from Miss Pollard's insinuation that Mr. W. (Wilberforce ?) may have come as a suitor, she says, in a letter of March 30, 1790, " Your way of accounting for my absence of mind diverted me exceedingly. I will set forward with assuring you that my heart is perfectly disengaged, and then endeavour to show you how very improbable it is that Mr. W. would think of me. As to the first point, I can only say that no man I have seen has appeared to regard me with any degree of partiality, nor has anyone gained my affections." She says she is reading Pope's works, and a little treatise on Regeneration, which, with Mrs. Trimmer's " Œconomy of Charity," Mr. Wilberforce had given her. She is going to read the New Testament with Doddridge's exposition. In this letter we find her first mention of her brother's future wife: " The seal you showed so much sagacity in your conjectures about was given me by a Penrith friend, Mary Hutchinson." Of her brother she writes: " I long to have an opportunity of introducing you to my dear William. I am very anxious about him just now, as he will shortly have to provide for himself. Next year he takes his degree. When he will go into orders I do not know, nor how he will employ himself. He must, when he is three-and-twenty, either go into orders or take pupils. He will be twenty in April."

It must not be inferred from the expression " provide for himself " that her brother was being educated at the expense of her uncles. His own share of his parents' estates would be sufficient to pay for his education, though, until the money came in, his uncles were probably obliged to advance part of the sum required. But at best, if Lord Lonsdale should pay his debt and all other business matters should be satisfactorily settled, very little would remain for William and Christopher after deducting their college expenses. We find Dorothy writing as follows on December 7, 1791 :*

" Our grandmother has shown us great kindness, and has promised to give us five hundred pounds (£100 apiece), the first time she receives her rents. . . . Our several resources are these: £500 which my grandmother is to

---

* Erroneously printed " 1790 " in Professor Knight's " Letters of the Wordsworth Family." From the original manuscript.

give us, £500 which is due on account of my mother's fortune, about £200 which my uncle Kit owes us, and £1,000 at present in the hands of our guardians, and about £150 which we are to receive out of the Newbiggin estate, with what may be adjudged as due to us from Lord Lonsdale. My brother Richard has about £100 per annum, and William has received his education, for which a reduction will be made; so that I hope, unless we are treated in the most unjust manner possible, my three younger brothers and I will have £1,000 apiece, deducting in William's share the expense of his education."

If the young collegian could have made up his mind to be a clergyman, his connection with his uncle Cookson would probably have helped him to a church " living." But doubtless the taint communicated to the profession by its dependence on worldly favour and the patronage of the rich rendered it unattractive to his pure and generous mind. It was possible for a young graduate, with little more theological reading than that required for the general degree of Bachelor of Arts, to be placed almost at once in a curacy. Of course, standing in the university affected a candidate's chances of securing what is known as a " good " living— that is, one with a large salary.

CHAPTER III

ADRIFT

THE academic year, or at least that part of it in which residence was required, being only about half the calendar year, students who expected to distinguish themselves in the examinations were accustomed to spend their final long vacation in hard study, either at Cambridge or in some quieter place. Wordsworth's relatives, therefore, were disappointed when he decided to make use of the summer and early autumn of 1790 in a way which apparently would not lead to academic honours nor to a profession nor to pecuniary profit. It was most natural, however, that Wordsworth, in his unsettled state of mind, should yield to his love of landscape and his fondness for walking, and hasten as soon as possible from the indoor restraints and the bookishness of the university. And the events then occurring with such good augury in France would arouse the hopeful curiosity of an open-minded and democratic youth. Undergraduate society at Cambridge was on the whole liberal as compared with the tone of thought in most of the homes from which the students came, and Wordsworth was predisposed by his Hawkshead life to practise, if not to profess, a belief in human equality. Nature had taught him that her laws, her faithfulness, and her beauty, could be observed as well in small as in great objects. Experience in divers ranks of society had shown him how ill-based were the conventional distinctions. It is not to be thought that the system of ideas known as Revolutionary had penetrated Cambridge without arousing his sympathetic interest. Yet it is likely, too, that, with the indifference to politics which characterizes Anglo-Saxon youth, he failed to realize at this time the importance or even the dramatic values of the great world-movement of

56

which he was soon to catch a glimpse. He cared far
more for landscape. Indeed, the enjoyment of natural
beauty was apparently his one absorbing passion. In
planning a journey on foot from Calais to the Alps, he
was willing to pass within a day's march of Amiens and
Rheims without breaking his bird-like flight to see
their cathedrals, and within fifty miles of Paris without
being drawn into what was then, more than ever, the
heart of the world's political circulation. The only
object for which he turned aside was the Grande
Chartreuse, where great natural beauty combined with
religious interest to produce a peculiar romantic charm.
A similar attraction led him once and only once again
to interrupt his enjoyment of landscape for the sake of
a monument of human design, the convent of Einsiedeln.

His companion was a fellow-collegian, Robert Jones,
of Plas-yn-llan, in Wales, who remained his friend
through life. They arrived in Calais on July 13, 1790,
and set out next day on a " march of military speed,"
that carried them in precisely two weeks to Châlons on
the Saône, a distance of over three hundred and fifty
miles. They descended the Saône by boat to Lyons
and sailed down the Rhone to St. Vallier, whence they
walked to the Lake of Geneva. Climbing over the
Simplon Pass, they visited Lakes Maggiore and Como,
turned north again, and made a comprehensive survey
of Switzerland, ending at Basel about September 21,
where they bought a boat, in which they floated down
the Rhine to Cologne in one week. It took them about
a fortnight more to reach Calais, and the whole trip
lasted exactly three months, with hardly a day of rest.
Writing to Jane Pollard from Forncett on October 6,
1790, Dorothy quotes admiringly from a long letter she
has received from her brother, in which he expresses
great enthusiasm for the grand and beautiful scenes he
has beheld and the tenderest affection for his sister.
The following passages are the most interesting:

" We had perpetual occasion to observe that cheerfulness and sprightliness for which the French have always
been remarkable. But I must remind you that we

crossed at the time when the whole nation was mad with
joy in consequence of the revolution. It was a most
interesting period to be in France; and we had many
delightful scenes, where the interest of the picture was
owing solely to this cause. I was also much pleased with
what I saw of the Italians during the short time we were
among them. We had several times occasion to observe
a softness and elegance which contrasted strongly
with the severe austereness of their neighbours on the
other side of the Alps. . . . We have both enjoyed most
excellent health; and we have been so inured to walking
that we are both become almost insensible to fatigue.
We have several times performed a journey of thirteen
leagues over the most mountainous parts of Switzerland
without any more weariness than if we had been walking
an hour in the groves of Cambridge. Our appearance
is singular; and we have often observed that, in passing
through a village, we have excited a general smile.
Our coats, which we had made light on purpose for the
journey, are of the same piece; and our manner of carrying our bundles, which is upon our heads, with each an
oak stick in our hands, contributes not a little to that
general curiosity which we seem to excite. . . . I flatter
myself still with the hope of seeing you for a fortnight
or three weeks, if it be agreeable to my uncle, as there
will be no necessity for me to be in Cambridge before
the 10th of November. I shall be better able to judge
whether I am likely to enjoy this pleasure in about
three weeks. I shall probably write to you again before
I quit France; if not, most certainly immediately on my
landing in England. You will remember me affectionately to my uncle and aunt; as he was acquainted with
my giving up all thoughts of a fellowship, he may,
perhaps, not be so displeased at this journey. I should
be sorry if I have offended him by it."

Three years after their delightful journey, Wordsworth dedicated to his fellow-traveller, by that time
the Rev. Robert Jones, fellow of St. John's College,
Cambridge, a little volume entitled "Descriptive
Sketches. In Verse. Taken during a Pedestrian Tour
in the Italian, Grison, Swiss, and Savoyard Alps. By
W. Wordsworth, B.A., of St. John's, Cambridge."
"In inscribing this little book to you," he says, "I
consult my heart. You know well how great is the

difference between two companions lolling in a post-
chaise, and two travellers plodding slowly along the
road, side by side, each with his little knapsack of
necessaries upon his shoulders. How much more of
heart between the two latter !"

The original text of " Descriptive Sketches " was
materially altered by Wordsworth in the edition of
1815, and much amended in the editions of 1820, 1827,
1832, 1836, ·1845, and 1849. It was considerably
longer than in the form which it finally attained. Many
of the alterations were made in the interest of clear-
ness and artistic finish, but some were attempts to
moderate, discreetly if not prudishly, one or two passages
of glowing description, and to take the very heart out
of pages pulsing with ardent enthusiasm for liberty.
This is not the place to discuss the literary value of the
poem, but we may well expect that some of its eight
hundred lines, as originally printed, will bear witness
to its author's character and opinions in 1790, even
though it was written for the most part in 1791 and 1792.

It took all the sunshine and beauty of the first few
days' march to remove the sadness with which he set
forth:

> Me, lured by hope her sorrows to remove,
> A heart, that could not much itself approve,
> O'er Gallia's wastes of corn dejected led.

If my conjectures about his love for " Lucy," her
death, and his premature and unsuccessful endeavour
to console himself with Mary Hutchinson are well
founded, these lines have a pathetic meaning. He
altered them in subsequent editions, leaving out the
reference to his sorrows and their wasting effect, and
making them read as follows:

> A hope that prudence could not then approve,
> That clung to Nature with a truant's love,
> O'er Gallia's wastes of corn my footsteps led.

In the edition of 1793 there are touches that the caution
of his later years caused him to erase or blur—mention
of " fair dark-eyed maids," who smiled from their

arboured gardens at the swift-striding English boys.
In a strain which in maturer years he never permitted
himself to employ, he describes the languorous afternoons
and thrilled starlit evenings of an Italian summer:

> Slow glides the sail along th' illumined shore,
> And steals into the shade the lazy oar.
> Soft bosoms breathe around contagious sighs,
> And amorous music on the water dies.
> Heedless how Pliny, musing here, survey'd
> Old Roman boats and figures through the shade,
> Pale Passion, overpower'd, retires and woos
> The thicket, where th' unlisten'd stock-dove coos.

And again, in a passage only partly reproduced in
later editions, we feel the same warmth:

> Farewell! those forms that, in the noon-tide shade,
> Rest, near their little plots of wheaten glade;
> Those steadfast eyes, that beating breasts inspire
> To throw the " sultry ray " of young Desire;
> Those lips, whose tides of fragrance come, and go,
> Accordant to the cheek's unquiet glow;
> Those shadowy breasts in love's soft light array'd,
> And rising, by the moon of passion sway'd.
> Thy fragrant gales and lute-resounding streams,
> Breathe o'er the failing soul voluptuous dreams.

He describes the life of poor and humble people without
a trace of condescension. This attitude was as yet so
rare in English authors as to be almost novel. He
paints with that kind of sympathy which really shares
the feeling of its objects. He even puts himself in the
place of the superstitious pilgrims to the wonder-work-
ing image at Einsiedeln, and in a tone of dejection
cries:

> Without one hope her written griefs to blot,
> Save in the land where all things are forgot,
> My heart, alive to transports long unknown,
> Half wishes your delusion were its own.

The sight of half-starved peasants in the Vale of
Chamonix leads to the strain with which the poem
ends, the thought that poverty and disease are the
children of tyranny. He burned to free Savoy from

her oppressors. Happiness, he declares, is found only where freedom smiles encouragement.

> In the wide range of many a weary round,
> Still have my pilgrim feet unfailing found,
> As despot courts their blaze of gems display,
> E'en by the secret cottage far away
> The lily of domestic joy decay;
> While Freedom's farthest hamlets blessings share,
> Found still beneath her smile and only there.

This may not be good poetry, but it sounds like heart-felt conviction. Then follows an apostrophe to France, which echoes his thoughts of 1791 and 1792, rather than those of 1790:

> And thou ! fair favoured region ! which my soul
> Shall love, till Life has broke her golden bowl,
> Till Death's cold touch her cistern-wheel assail,
> And vain regret and vain desire shall fail.
>
> *   *   *   *   *
>
> Yet, hast thou found that Freedom spreads her pow'r
> Beyond the cottage hearth, the cottage door:
> All nature smiles; and owns beneath her eyes
> Her fields peculiar, and peculiar skies.

Under these laboured and unsuccessful phrases may be discerned a strength of belief and a fervour of zeal which were just as real as if they had received lucid and compressed expression. France, he meant, was happy because she was free, visibly and demonstrably happier than other lands. Her mill-wheels clacked more merrily, her rivers rippled with brighter blue and cleaner white, her farmyard cocks sent forth a louder challenge:

> The measured echo of the distant flail
> Winded in sweeter cadence down the vale;
> A more majestic tide the water roll'd,
> And glowed the sun-gilt groves in richer gold.

He hails exultantly the prospect of her war with " Conquest, Avarice, and Pride," and prays God to grant that " every sceptred child of clay," who attempts in his presumption to stem the tide of Freedom, shall

> With all his creature sink—to rise no more.

These terms were much moderated and qualified and generally pulled about in the course of that censorship which the Wordsworth of later years exercised over his early poems. Read in its original form, " Descriptive Sketches " confirms his statement to his sister that he was a perfect enthusiast in his admiration of nature in all her original shapes. He was correct in thinking that perhaps scarcely a day of his life would pass in which he should not derive some happiness from the images gathered on his journey. The lovely forms and flashing eyes of which he caught a glimpse at the Lake of Como were accountable for a " thousand dreams of happiness which might be enjoyed upon its banks, if heightened by conversation and the exercise of the social affections." The poem shows with what sympathy of heart and acquiescence of the mind he shared the emotions of the French " at the time when the whole nation was mad with joy in consequence of the revolution." Several of the " many delightful scenes, where the interest of the picture was owing solely to this cause," he described twelve years later in " The Prelude," with a mastery he did not command at the time he wrote " Descriptive Sketches." The style is immeasurably heightened, and the record is no longer one of mere sensations chiefly, but of imagination brooding over incidents of life and forms of outward beauty, and making them a part of the poet's soul. The well-known opening of this famous portion of " The Prelude " explains more eloquently, if not more clearly, his two reasons for making the journey:

> When the third summer freed us from restraint,
> A youthful friend, he too a mountaineer,
> Not slow to share my wishes, took his staff,
> And sallying forth, we journeyed side by side,
> Bound to the distant Alps.   A hardy slight
> Did this unprecedented course imply
> Of college studies and their set rewards;
> Nor had, in truth, the scheme been formed by me
> Without uneasy forethought of the pain,
> The censures, and ill-omening of those

To whom my worldly interests were dear.
But Nature then was sovereign in my mind,
And mighty forms, seizing a youthful fancy,
Had given a charter to irregular hopes.
In any age of uneventful calm
Among the nations, surely would my heart
Have been possessed by similar desire;
But Europe at that time was thrilled with joy,
France standing on the top of golden hours,
And human nature seeming born again.*

In " The Prelude " the journey is hastily narrated except for five broad descriptive passages. The first of these† depicts the release of " benevolence and blessedness," the triumphal arches, the garlands, the dances of liberty, the overflowing fraternity, which they witnessed in the northern French provinces, then rejoicing in the first anniversary of the fall of the Bastille. The second relates how the young wayfarers, sailing down the Rhone from Lyons to St. Vallier, were welcomed into the society of

a merry crowd
Of those emancipated, a blithe host
Of travellers, chiefly delegates, returning
From the great spousals, newly solemnized
At their chief city, in the sight of Heaven.‡

These were probably some of the representatives of Marseilles and their friends going home after the Festival of the Federation, on July 14, when the King and Lafayette, as commander of the National Guard, in the presence of the Queen, the Dauphin, and one hundred thousand delegates, had sworn fidelity to the Constitution before the Altar of the Country on the Champ de Mars. Englishmen, as children of a free nation, were in high favour in France. Wordsworth and his companion were received with open arms by these excited southerners :

Guests welcome almost as the angels were
To Abraham of old.

---

* " Prelude,'' VI. 3 22.   † *Ibid.*, 342-374.   ‡ *Ibid.*, 384-414.

Together they landed, probably at Coudrieu, to take their evening meal. Every tongue was loosed. There were brave speeches of amity and glee. There was dancing hand in hand around the table. At early dawn the voyage was renewed and the enthusiasm commenced again, lasting till the young men quitted the glad throng at St. Vallier to pursue their way on foot. The third passage* repeats, with maturer reflections, his thoughts on seeing the Grande Chartreuse on a day when its sanctity was rudely profaned by a band of reformers. The fourth† is an inadequate attempt to catch the spirit of the Alps and the Swiss people. What he saw of the mountaineers confirmed his rapidly forming political opinions, and he cries:

> With such a book
> Before our eyes, we could not choose but read
> Lessons of genuine brotherhood, the plain
> And universal lesson of mankind.

In the fifth‡ he elaborates an episode, not specially significant, of their walk above Lake Como.

In the midst of these he introduces a sublime account§ of a spiritual event, a happening within his own soul. The travellers suddenly learned, from the downward dropping of a stream, that they had crossed the Alps. When attention has been fixed for many hours upon the face of nature in a wild and difficult region, a discovery of this sort may possess a startling significance. But what struck Wordsworth was the fact that in this moment, when nature seemed very real, his own mind seemed equally real, and distinct from nature. At first, he says, he was lost, " halted without an effort to break through " the mystery of this abrupt estrangement from nature, who had been his intimate comrade and apparently of the same stuff with him. The first moment of bewilderment over, his soul rose triumphant in self-consciousness. He recognized her glory. She was not then, after all, dependent on

* " Prelude," VI. 414-488.   † Ibid., 499-540.
‡ Ibid., 691-726.   § Ibid., 557-640.

sense and subject to time and space; and assured of
this he sang:

> Our destiny, our being's heart and home,
> Is with infinitude, and only there;
> With hope it is, hope that can never die,
> Effort, and expectation, and desire,
> And something evermore about to be.

The road, having reached the summit of the Alpine
pass, cannot go higher. The stream must flow into
Italy. North must remain North, and South be ever
South; but no limit is decreed to human souls. With
this thought of the transcendence of mind, there flashed
upon him a new conception of the meaning of visible
things. The grand and terrible features of the gorge
through which he descended

> Were all like workings of one mind, the features
> Of the same face, blossoms upon one tree;
> Characters of the great Apocalypse,
> The types and symbols of Eternity,
> Of first, and last, and midst, and without end.

The day was an epoch in his life, and the passage in
which he recorded this experience is one of the most
significant in all his works.

Lastly, in a tone quite at variance with the strain
that ends " Descriptive Sketches," he attributes his
interest in the new stir that animated France, not so
much to Revolutionary principles as to " the independent spirit of pure youth," called forth by the widening
prospects of fresh glories in the universe:

> A glorious time,
> A happy time that was; triumphant looks
> Were then the common language of all eyes;
> As if awaked from sleep, the Nations hailed
> Their great expectancy: the fife of war
> Was then a spirit-stirring sound indeed,
> A blackbird's whistle in a budding grove.
> We left the Swiss exulting in the fate
> Of their near neighbours; and when shortening fast
> Our pilgrimage, nor distant far from home,
> We crossed the Brabant armies on the fret
> For battle in the cause of Liberty.

A stripling, scarcely of the household then
Of social life, I looked upon these things
As from a distance; heard, and saw, and felt,
Was touched, but with no intimate concern.*

Wordsworth visited his sister at Forncett in the Christmas holidays. He was graduated Bachelor of Arts on January 21, 1791. His sister believed he might have obtained a fellowship had he tried, and doubtless if she thought so, her uncles thought so too. In a letter to Miss Pollard, from Forncett, dated Sunday morning, June 26, 1791, she says:

" William, you may have heard, lost the chance (indeed the certainty) of a fellowship, by not combating his inclinations. He gave way to his natural dislike to studies so dry as many parts of mathematics, consequently could not succeed at Cambridge. He reads Italian, Spanish, French, Greek, Latin, and English, but never opens a mathematical book. We promise ourselves much pleasure from reading Italian together at some time. He wishes that I was acquainted with the Italian poets, but how much I have to learn which plain English will teach me! William has a great attachment for poetry; so indeed has Kit, but William particularly, which is not the most likely thing to produce his advancement in the world. His pleasures are chiefly of the imagination. He is never so happy as when in a beautiful country. Do not think in what I have said that he reads not at all, for he does read a great deal; and not only poetry, and other languages he is acquainted with, but history, etc., etc."

What delightful chatter! What touching anxiety for her brother's reputation! Dorothy will not have Miss Pollard think him less than perfect, even though he has an aversion from mathematics and had not won college honours. From a statement she made in a previous letter to Miss Pollard, written at Forncett on May 23, it appears that this notable scholar had not spent even his last Christmas holidays at work in Cambridge, but had preferred her society to that of the mathematicians. Her romantic heart doubtless excused him to itself.

* " Prelude," VI. 754.

In February, 1791, the poet, not yet twenty-one years
old, went to London, probably with no definite plan.
The following summary, at the opening of the ninth
book of " The Prelude," gives but a very loose account
of the time he spent there:

> Free as a colt at pasture on the hill,
> I ranged at large, through London's wide domain,
> Month after month. Obscurely did I live,
> Not seeking frequent intercourse with men,
> By literature, or elegance, or rank,
> Distinguished. Scarcely was a year thus spent
> Ere I forsook the crowded solitude,
> With less regret for its luxurious pomp,
> And all the nicely-guarded shows of art,
> Than for the humble book-stalls in the streets,
> Exposed to eye and hand where'er I turned.

As a matter of fact, he lived much less than a year
in London. The sources of our knowledge of this period
are few, and some of them are misleading. The seventh
and eighth books of the great autobiographical poem
contain many passages reflecting, after an interval of
thirteen years, some of the impressions made upon
him by the sights of the city, but all carefully chosen
to illustrate " the growth of a poet's mind," and particularly to show how the love of nature, by which he
means, in this connection, country scenes and sounds,
remained supreme. The incidents are not important
in themselves, nor do they furnish much information
as to his reasons for being in London and his main
occupation there. Apart from their effect on his poetic
faculties, which can scarcely, after all, have been comparable in importance to the influence of Hawkshead
and Cambridge, they were purely external and fleeting,
the things every fairly observant country-bred youth
would notice in the streets and public haunts of town.
His effort to set them forth as contributions to his
poetic development seems a little forced. His use of
them is too systematic and reveals too clearly his under-
lying design, in a way that suggests pedantry. The
want of spontaneity in these passages affects the language, which is occasionally obscure, the sentences being

long and complex. He invites us again and again
to observe the precise degree in which this or that
quality of soul, now Fancy, now Imagination, now
Love of Man, now Sense of Majesty and Power, was
affected by some happening, which one hesitates to
call trivial only because it caught the eye of Wordsworth. And the phrases are huddled back upon themselves, in these passages, as if for an onward rush, which
does not come. On the other hand, no poet before him
had ever described with the same combination of simplicity, exactness, zest, and elevation, the every-day
incidents of street-life. Where they are not spoiled by
too much moralizing reference to his own inward growth,
these descriptions are delightful, and mark a decisive
step in English poetry.

Except for two or three short visits from Cambridge,
it would appear that Wordsworth had never seen London
until this time. The wealth of sensations which could
be tasted there might well have seemed to justify
him in spending a few months in the metropolis as
a finishing touch to his scholastic education. At
least, he offers no other excuse, but says that after
quitting every comfort of that privileged ground, the
university, he was

> Well pleased to pitch a vagrant tent among
> The unfenced regions of society.

His want of occupation did not trouble him. With all
the imprudence of boyhood and with a poet's valua-
tion of whatsoever might feed his mind, regardless
of bodily sustenance, he deliberately took one more
vacation:

> undetermined to what course of life
> I should adhere, and seeming to possess
> A little space of intermediate time
> At full command, to London first I turned,
> In no disturbance of excessive hope,
> By personal ambition unenslaved,
> Frugal as there was need, and, though self-willed,
> From dangerous passions free.*

" Prelude," VII. 58.

It was an unpremeditated, natural piece of self-indul-
gence, or a yielding, rather, to the impulses which always
ruled him. His whole life was independent, but sudden
outbreaks of extreme and wayward impatience of
restraint frequently gave sharper accent to its general
tenor. At such times he was stubborn, bold, adventurous, improvident. He had no home and no parents,
and his elder brother was too young to exercise any
authority over him.

Among the public celebrities whom he saw or heard
he mentions Mrs. Siddons " in the fulness of her power "
and Burke. It is to be remembered that the tribute to
Burke in the seventh book of " The Prelude " was
added in a late version of the poem, and does not reflect
the poet's feelings in 1791. The great statesman had
published, only a few months before Wordsworth's
arrival in London, his " Reflections on the Revolution
in France." The immediate occasion of this work was
a sermon by the Rev. Richard Price, a Nonconformist
minister, before the Revolution Society, a club originally
formed to celebrate the " glorious Revolution " of 1688.
This society had not only listened to a discourse from
Dr. Price in praise of the French Revolution, but had
forwarded to the National Assembly an address which
Burke declared to have sprung from the principles of
that sermon. The nobleness of the political philosophy
embodied in Burke's famous pamphlet contrasts shiningly
with his sarcastic attack on Dr. Price, which is mean
and illiberal. And to anyone who had even a faint
idea of how just, and, indeed, how necessary, was the
French uprising, and how extravagant and unfeeling
was the Queen over whose fate Burke became eloquent,
his rhetoric must have seemed sadly out of place. The
deplorable effect of his " Reflections " in precipitating
war between England and France, and thus helping to
engender the Terror, might have been foreseen. This
book, more than anything else, turned the current of
English opinion, which had not yet been decidedly uns
favourable to the Revolution. It put majestic precept-
and august principles into the mouths of stupid people,

who used them as a covering for prejudice and ignorance and panic. As John Morley has said:

" Before the Reflections was published the predominant sentiment in England had been one of mixed astonishment and sympathy. Pitt had expressed this common mood both in the House of Commons and in private."

Those who seized most greedily upon his denunciation of the popular excesses in France, and his prophecies that the Revolution would fail, were precisely the persons least able to comprehend the great principles upon which his argument was based. As Morley again says: " It is when we come to the rank and file of reaction that we find it hard to forgive the man of genius who made himself the organ of their selfishness, their timidity, and their blindness." By the time that Wordsworth heard him in Parliament, Burke, who had once been an object of derision and fear to the Tory party, had, through vindicating the all too natural English view of French affairs, become the oracle of privilege and " patriotism." He spoke, as Wordsworth accurately records, in defence of immemorial dependencies and vested rights, for they were what was meant by " social ties endeared by Custom." The poet does not say that he was persuaded at the time that Burke was right, or that he approved the orator's keen ridicule of all systems built on abstract rights. We know that for six or eight years to come he disapproved of the national policy which Burke did so much to promote. We know that it was perhaps the deepest sorrow of his life that his country should have adopted such a policy. And " The Prelude " was written just when a reaction against his youthful ideals was most powerful within him.

He heard the popular preachers, and was not untouched by the admonitions of some, though he satirizes the affected manner, the fine dressing, and the sentimental oratory, of others. He glanced at the examples of folly, vice, and extravagance, which made London

their domain, but lingered over sights of courage and
of tenderness, rendered more touching by contrast. He
felt the sensation of kinship with passing unknown
persons, coupled with the unhappy realization that each
of us is like a ship sailing its own course upon the waters.
Interest in man, but not yet love of man, at least not
love comparable to his love of nature, grew within him.
It is evident that the town took far less hold upon his
affection, stirred shallower depths of imagination, and
was in itself less sufficient, than his native hills. This
is amply shown in the contrast between the description
of St. Bartholomew's Fair, near the end of the seventh
book, and the description of a Westmorland market in
one of the vales below Helvellyn, with which the eighth
book opens. The former appears scant in loving detail,
and rather perfunctory, while the latter breathes at
once the spirit of Wordsworth and of rural life. He
gave deep and eloquent expression to his sense of the
futility of city life as a source of spiritual strength, and
it was the memory of more permanent powers that
sustained him " in London's vast domain." This inner
calm and perception, which it occurs to few men to
strive for, were the highest good for which Wordsworth
lived. All other powers were in his estimation secondary.
But such as they were, London fed some of them. He
was taught by the memorials piled up in the ancient
city to feel his country's greatness. The place, he says,
" was thronged with impregnations." It feelingly set
forth the unity of men. It smote the soul with the
sublime idea that there is among men

> One sense for moral judgments, as one eye
> For the sun's light.

There is no trace in " The Prelude " by which we
can be sure of more than one or two things in regard to
his ordinary external life at this time. He was independent of the people with whom he lodged, could come
and go as he pleased, and had much time to spend in free
roving. The first streak of clear light in the way of
positive fact comes, unfortunately, after he had left

London.   It is in a letter from his sister to Miss Pollard, from Forncett, May 23, 1791.   She writes:

" I hope my brother William will call at Halifax on his way into Cumberland.   He is now in Wales, where he intends making a pedestrian tour, along with his old friend and companion Jones, at whose house he is at present staying. . . .   My aunt would tell you that she saw my brothers Richard and William in town."

The sojourn in London had lasted less than four months.   How long the young man remained in Wales is not known.   He visited his fellow-collegian and former companion in foreign travel, Robert Jones, at the latter's home, Plas-yn-llan, near Ruthin, in Denbighshire, and was with him, apparently, from the middle of May till about the middle of September, and certainly till August 13.   Together they made another pedestrian tour, and saw " the sea-sunsets which give such splendour to the Vale of Clwyd, Snowdon, the Chair of Idris, the quiet village of Bethgelert, Menai and her Druids, the Alpine steeps of the Conway, and the still more interesting windings of the wizard stream of the Dee."*
Wordsworth's most intimate friend at this time appears to have been another fellow-student just graduated from Cambridge, William Mathews, elder son of a London bookseller and Methodist local preacher, and brother of Charles Mathews, the comic actor.   The latter, in his " Memoirs," gives the following description of him:

" William, my brother, was my senior by seven years, and, being intended for the church, of course looked to a college education. . . .   My dear and excellent brother had great natural talents, and was indefatigable in his search after knowledge.   He was essentially a gentleman in all his feelings; and his earliest associates were high, if not in rank, certainly in talent.   The pursuits that engaged him were not those of other youths—he was devoted to profound and abstruse studies, mathematics, and had an absolute thirst for languages, six of which

* From the Dedicatory Letter to the Rev. Robert Jones, Fellow of St. John's College, Cambridge, prefixed to " Descriptive Sketches."

he could speak or read before he was twenty years of
age. To gain perfection in these, his time was occupied
day after day, night after night. The school exercises,
of course, were only Latin, Greek, and Hebrew; French
was supplied by my father's means; but at the time I
was young enough to sleep in the same room with him,
he rose at four or five o'clock in the morning to study
Italian and Spanish; of which pursuits he was so un-
ostentatious that he threatened me with the penalty of
his displeasure if I revealed to anyone the hours he stole
from sleep. Thus qualified at a very early age, he
entered Pembroke College, Cambridge, already an accomplished gentleman.''

It was a sore point with Charles Mathews that their
father tried to create '' a mortifying distinction between
the rank in society of his two sons—the eldest a gentleman, the youngest a tradesman.'' They both attended
Merchant Taylors' School, where they took part in a
rebellion against the masters, which led to the abolition
of flogging. Their home was in London. Their father
was a '' serious '' bookseller, a rigid Calvinist, the main
pillar in one of Lady Huntingdon's chapels, and the victim
of a horde of fanatical preachers, yet mild and liberal
withal in disposition. Their mother was '' strict in her
adherence to the tenets of the Church of England.''
The happiness of parents and children alike was often
troubled by the intrusion of this or that canting ex-
horter, and the boys grew up detesting what they termed
'' superstition.'' It is related of Charles Mathews that
he was in the habit of impersonating Coleridge.

Wordsworth's letters to William Mathews are the only
ones in which we see the poet indulge a vein of youthful
levity. Beginning in this tone of irresponsible banter,
they soon become more serious, though not less outspoken. Mathews entertained republican principles.
He was apparently unsettled in life and desirous of
becoming a journalist. In his correspondence with
him, Wordsworth expresses himself more plainly on
public questions and on the subject of his own course of
life than anywhere else. As was natural between young
men of the same age who had been at the university

together, there was no concealment of opinion. Their interchange of letters continued till 1796, at least, covering the most obscure period of Wordsworth's life, a period that was probably, to the few persons who knew him well, the most interesting. Time, and very likely a desire on his part and that of his family to cover his actions and sufferings in these years with oblivion, have left us only a few of his letters to Mathews, but they are very significant. The young poet's temper was impetuous. His self-will was strong. He felt the impulse of vagrant passions. His principles were of the kind that English society stamped with disapproval, as dangerous and subversive. And in 1791 he had as yet gone through or witnessed no experiences to damp his ardour and arouse misgivings. Mathews went to the West Indies to practise law, probably in 1800 or 1801, and died in the latter year, of yellow fever, in Tobago. In a letter to this friend, from Plas-yn-llan, written June 17, 1791, Wordsworth expends many words in boyish excuses for not writing sooner. He then says:

" You will see by the date of this letter that I am in Wales, and, whether you remember the place of Jones's residence or no, will immediately conclude that I am with him. I quitted London about three weeks ago, where my time passed in a strange manner; sometimes whirled about by the vortex of its *strenua inertia*, and sometimes thrown by the eddy into a corner of the stream, where I lay in almost motionless indolence. Think not, however, that I had not many very pleasant hours; a man must be unfortunate indeed who resides four months in Town without some of his time being disposed of in such a manner as he would forget with reluctance."

After the awkward gambols of William's epistolary pen, it is delightful to read one of his sister's letters, so easy are they and cordial, so open-hearted and affectionate, so full of keen remarks. She writes to Jane Pollard from Forncett, June 26, 1791:

" I often hear from my brother William, who is now in Wales, where I think he seems so happy that it is probable he will remain there all the summer, or a great part of it. Who would not be happy enjoying the company of three young ladies in the Vale of Clewyd, and without a rival ? His friend Jones is a charming young man, and has five sisters, three of whom are at home at present. Then there are mountains, rivers, woods, and rocks, whose charms without any other inducement would be sufficient to tempt William to continue amongst them as long as possible. So that most likely he will have the pleasure of seeing you when he visits Halifax, which I hope he will do in his road to the North. He thinks with great pleasure of paying that place a visit where I have so many friends. I confess you are right in supposing me partial to William. I hope when you see him you will think my regard not misplaced. Probably, when I next see Kit, I shall love him as well; the difference between our ages at the time I was with him was much more perceptible than it will be at our next meeting. His disposition is of the same cast as William's, and his inclinations have taken the same turn, but he is much more likely to make his fortune. He is not so warm as William, but has a most affectionate heart. His abilities, though not so great perhaps as his brother's, may be of more use to him, as he has not fixed his mind upon any particular species of reading or conceived an aversion to any. He is not fond of mathematics, but has resolution sufficient to study them, because it will be impossible for him to obtain a fellowship without them."

William's second letter to Mathews from Plas-yn-llan, August 13, of the same summer, is in the same frivolous and mock-bombastic vein as the first.

" You desire me to communicate to you copiously my observations on modern literature, and transmit to you a cup replete with the waters of that fountain. You might as well have solicited me to send you an account of the tribes inhabiting the central regions of the African Continent. God knows my incursions into the fields of modern literature—excepting in our own language three volumes of Tristram Shandy, and two or three papers of the Spectator, half subdued—are absolutely nothing. Were I furnished with a dictionary and a grammar, and other requisites, I might perhaps make an attempt upon Italy, an attack valiant; but probably my expedition, like a redoubted one of Caligula's of old, though of another kind, might terminate in gathering shells out of Petrarch, or seaweed from Marino. The truth of the matter is that when in Town I did *little*, and since I came here I have done nothing. A miserable account! However, I have not in addition to all this to complain of bad spirits. That would be the devil indeed. I rather think that this gaiety increases with my ignorance, as a spendthrift grows more extravagant the nearer he approximates to a final dissipation of his property. I was obliged to leave all my books but one or two behind me. I regret much not having brought my Spanish grammar along with me. By peeping into it occasionally I might perhaps have contrived to keep the little Spanish or some part of it, that I was master of. I am prodigiously incensed at those rascal creditors of yours. What do they not deserve? Pains, stripes, imprisonments, etc., etc. . . . Adieu, hoping to hear from you soon, and that your letter will bring gladder tidings of yourself. I remain most affectionately yours. Chear up is the word."

Mathews was discontented with his work, and made some wild proposal to Wordsworth, to which the latter composed a very sensible reply, dated Cambridge, September 23.

They were dallying with the idea of throwing themselves upon the world as vagrants, wandering from place to place in the manner of Goldsmith with his flute. But Wordsworth rejected the alluring project, sagely remarking:

" I should not be able to reconcile to my ideas of right the thought of wandering about a country without a certainty of being able to maintain myself, being indebted for my existence to those charities of which the acceptance might rob people not half so able to support themselves as myself."

On October 9 Dorothy Wordsworth writes to Jane Pollard from Forncett:

" William is at Cambridge. . . . Mr. Wilberforce is at Forncett. I know not when my brother William will go into the North; probably not so soon as he intends, as he is going to begin a new course of study, which he may perhaps not be able to go on with so well in that part of the world, as I conjecture he may find it difficult to meet with books. He is going, by the advice of my uncle William, to study the Oriental languages."

No doubt his uncle wished to fix him in some settled pursuit, preferably the study of divinity, to which " the Oriental languages," presumably represented by Hebrew, would be a beginning. His friend Mathews, like himself, was either attracted or urged by circumstances to enter the ministry. Like Milton, the young poet shrank from giving up his independence, though he could not have said with Milton: " No delay, no rest, no care or thought almost of anything, holds me aside until I reach the end I am making for, and round off, as it were, some great period of my studies." Delay was what he sought. He was conscious of possessing peculiar powers, as we know from " The Prelude," although his letters to Mathews do not give that impression. They are as modest as could be. He blames himself for his hesitation, confesses he is no scholar, does not attempt to excuse himself by reason of any special ambition, but raises the objection that he is unwilling to be tied down to any pursuit. As he had no home, and could not be for ever visiting his friends, he seems to have spent about half the autumn of 1791 at Cambridge, reading Italian and Spanish, and not following a definite plan of study. The likeliest opening for a young man of literary tastes, but without fortune, was to take holy orders. To stay about the university after graduation with any other purpose was rather unusual. There was pressure from his family; on the other hand, there was the inward urging after freedom, experience, knowledge of the beauties and wonders of the world. Like many another young graduate, he thought of foreign travel as a means of combining study with the gratification of a craving for these things. From the general tone of his correspondence with Mathews, in which he frequently mentions his desire to preserve intellectual liberty, it is evident that he hesitated on moral grounds to commit himself to entering the clerical profession. He, no less than his friend, panted ardently after independence. He could not have failed, moreover, to see that the principles of established religion were seriously brought into question by some of the most acute minds in his own country and elsewhere, and that the trend of public events was making against anything like placid acceptance of even the most venerable traditions. His letters are those of an awakened and restive spirit. It is not possible to assert, from the evidence which remains, that he was at this time a believer in Christianity, nor is it possible to be certain that he was not.

CHAPTER IV

INFLUENCE OF ROUSSEAU

WE hear from Wordsworth next at Brighton, November 23, 1791, waiting for favourable winds to take him to France. He writes thence to Mathews:

" I have been prevented from replying to your letter by an uncertainty respecting the manner in which I should dispose of myself for the winter, and which I have expected to be determined every day this month past. I am now on my way to Orleans, where I purpose to pass the winter, and am detained here by adverse winds. I was very happy to hear that you had given up your travelling scheme, that your father had consented to your changing your situation, and in consequence your mind was much easier. I approve much of your resolution to stay where you are till you meet with a more eligible engagement, provided your health does not materially suffer by it. It argues a manly spirit which you will undoubtedly be careful to preserve. I am happy to find that my letter afforded you some consolation. There are few reflections more pleasing than the consciousness that one has contributed in the smallest degree to diminish the anxiety of one's friends. . . .

" I expect I assure you considerable pleasure from my sojourn on the other side of the water, and some little improvement, which God knows I stand in sufficient need of.

" I am doomed to be an idler through my whole life. I have read nothing this age, nor indeed did I ever. Yet with all this I am tolerably happy. Do you think this ought to be a matter of congratulation to me, or no? For my own part I think certainly not. My uncle, the clergyman, proposed to me a short time ago to begin a course of Oriental literature, thinking that that was the best field for a person to distinguish himself in, as a man of letters. To oblige him I consented to pursue the plan upon my return from the Continent. But what must I do amongst that immense wilderness, I who have no resolution, and who have not prepared myself for the enterprise by any sort of discipline amongst the Western languages ? who know little of Latin, and scarce anything of Greek.　A pretty confession for a young gentleman whose whole life ought to have been devoted to study.　And thus the world wags.　But away with this outrageous egotism.　Tell me what you are doing, and what you read.　What authors are your favourites, and what number of that venerable body you wish in the Red Sea ?　I shall be happy to hear from you immediately.　My address, Mons. W. Wordsworth, Les Trois Empereurs, à Orléans.　I am no Frenchman, but I believe that is the way that a letter is addressed in France.　I should have deferred this epistle till I had crossed the water, when I might have had an opportunity of giving you something new; had I not imagined you would be surprised at not hearing from me, and had I not had more time on my hands at present than I am likely to have for some time.　Adieu.　Yours most affectionately and sincerely, W. WORDSWORTH."

Why did Wordsworth make choice of France ?　No doubt the agreeable impression produced by the French whom he had met on his long foot-tour had something to do with it.　They had charmed him by their manners, their alertness, and their speech.　He knew the language fairly well by this time.　And there was no doubt a more significant reason, in his sympathy with the Revolutionary spirit, now at its height.　Love of adventure, a desire to be near the scene of great events, a feeling that the air of France would be good for him at that particular time when he was hesitating and France was rushing confidently forward—all these elements were doubtless present in his mind as motives.　The study of the Oriental languages was becoming a faint and distant prospect.　We have seen that he was studying several of the Romanic languages, evidently with a view to fitting himself for teaching them.　It was doubtful whether he would settle in England on his return.　His brother John was coming and going between home and the Indies, both East and West.　William's thoughts were often turned in the direction of Barbados. As he has told us, he felt a leaning towards a military career, or at least towards being a General ! In fact, he had big hopes, and thought the world was all before him where to choose. His sister, whose nature was equally ardent, but who seems to have been up to this time richer in real heart experience, was making quiet observations at Forncett. She chafed against restraint, but her only outlet was to share, in sympathy, the actions of her roving brothers, John and William, and the scholastic triumphs of Christopher. She was as anxious as a mother that William and Christopher and John should have every advantage. One of her great concerns was to see them educated and started in life before the modest fortune of the family was quite exhausted. And so it was with great relief that she wrote to her friend on December 7, 1791 :

" Poor Richard is quite harassed with our vexatious business with that tyrannical Lord Lonsdale; he has all the plague of it. William is, I hope, by this time arrived in Orleans, where he means to pass the winter for the purpose of learning the French language, which will qualify him for the office of travelling companion to some young gentleman, if he can get recommended; it will at any rate be very useful to him, and as he can live at as little expense in France as in England, or nearly so, the scheme is not an ineligible one. He is at the same time engaged in the study of the Spanish language, and if he settles in England on his return (I mean if he has not the opportunity of becoming a travelling tutor) he will begin the study of the Oriental languages."

Wordsworth's life was by no means uneventful. If contact with supremely important public affairs and intimacy with great spirits make a life eventful, we may say, indeed, that no other English poet, since the years when Milton sat at the council table with Cromwell, has undergone experiences so heart-stirring as those which came in a few years to the quiet young poet from the North Country. What would not any student of history give to have walked across France in the inspiring summer of 1790 ? In the calendar of great days, what lover of literature would not mark as memorable above all others one on which he had met Coleridge and won his heart for ever ? How many occurrences in any man's life could have been reckoned so notable as making friends with Charles Lamb and Walter Scott ? And we have now come to an epoch in Wordsworth's personal history which had all the charm of adventure and romance, together with a spice of danger, and in which he touched, as with his bare hand, the vast coils that were generating heat and light for a world that was to move faster than ever before and through clearer spaces. His poetry yields sustenance to old and young, to the ignorant and the well informed, but can be really appreciated only by those who have entered into its spirit in two ways—by natural sympathy with his mode of thought, and by knowledge of his life. One of the most decisive periods of that life was the thirteen or fourteen months of his second visit to France. From the seclusion of Hawkshead, the sheltered luxury of Cambridge, the slow pace and quiet tone of English and Welsh parsonages and country-houses, he stepped in a single day into the brilliancy, the hardness, the peril, and excitement, of Revolutionary France.

The contrast between the two countries would have been stimulating at any time; in 1791 it was almost overpowering. His sojourn in France enabled him to gather into the solidity of a system those faint impulses of love for humanity which were stirring in him during his stay in London. It confirmed his doubts of the validity of the religion in which he had been brought up. It strengthened his implicit republicanism into an explicit and outspoken political creed, and shook his faith in the paramount excellence of his own country. It widened immensely the scope of his " civism," to use a word more current then than now, for the step from patriotism to a love which embraces one's own country and another is enormous.

Until recently very little information has been available about Wordsworth's life in France and, indeed, throughout the entire period between 1790 and 1795,

except the abundant revelations of his inward growth
which he made in " The Prelude." Such knowledge of
his actions as we now possess is extremely valuable for
the study of his character and his poetry and also of
human history, for even had he been no poet, but only
the clear and passionate observer that he was, his
experiences would rank among the most precious docu-
ments of the Revolution.   In later years he was unwilling
to let the world know how extreme had been his opinions
and how irregular his conduct; yet the agony of his
spirit for a long time after his return from France
showed that he had identified himself more completely
with the Revolutionary cause and with French life than
he was willing to admit in plain terms.

Before endeavouring to penetrate this mystery, and
even before piecing together the most significant of his
own poetical statements concerning the effect of his
experiences in France, we must consider an influence to
which he was probably exposed before he left England,
and which unquestionably continued and deepened on
the other side of the Channel.   This was the influence
of Rousseau.

Wordsworth was never a browsing reader.   In the
course of his long life, so uncommonly exempt from
petty cares and interruptions, he read much, to be sure,
but seldom with avidity.   He went to books as to a
serious task.   His sister's Grasmere Journal, if we had
not the evidence of his own diction, would show that
he studied Chaucer and the Elizabethan and Jacobean
poets with extreme care.   He found pleasure especially
in books of travel and description.   He was familiar
with much classical and Italian literature.   Books to
him were " a substantial world," very real, as real
almost as living persons, and therefore not to be lightly
treated.   Amid their pressure, as amid the unremitting
urgency of friends, he still preserved his independence
and, on the whole, few other great poets are so little
indebted to books.   As we have seen, he reproached
himself for his indifference during his months of leisure
after leaving college.

One author, however, he almost certainly read before the close of 1791, and, curiously enough, this was a writer who himself had been indifferent to books. Rousseau it is, far more than any other man of letters, either of antiquity or of modern times, whose works have left their trace in Wordsworth's poetry. This poor, half-educated dreamer, just because he was poor, half educated, and a dreamer, found his way to the centre of his age, the centre of its intellectual and emotional life. And here all original and simple souls met him. They were drawn thither by the same force that drew him, by a desire to return to nature. Exaggeration apart, and thinking not so much of his systematic working out of his views, which was generally too abstract and speciously consistent, as of their origin, purpose, and spirit, one must acknowledge their truth. They are as obviously true now as they were startlingly true when first uttered. They could not have seemed novel to Wordsworth, who was prepared for them by having lived with lowly people, of stalwart intelligence and worthy morals, at Hawkshead. Originality often consists in having remained unconscious of perverse departures from simple and natural ways of thought. A person who has been brought up to know and speak plain truth appears original in perverse and artificial society. We can imagine Wordsworth becoming, without the aid of Rousseau, very nearly what he did become. Nevertheless, the points of agreement are too numerous to be the result of mere coincidence.

What, in fine, are the distinctive elements in Rousseau? In the first place, we recognize in him the prevalence of reverie as a mode of thought. Reverie is an inactive, unsystematic kind of meditation, distinguished from logical processes of discourse by the absence of consciously perceived steps. External events and objects are not primary essentials of this state, though they may induce or stimulate it. This is truly the poetic process, and Rousseau, in all his most original, vital, and characteristic passages, is a poet. We are reminded when we read them of

Wordsworth's remark, " Poetry is emotion recollected in tranquillity."

A second element in Rousseau is his desire to simplify : to reduce the number and complexity of experiences and ideals. The mode of reverie always tends to concentrate and unite a multitude of concepts which have come into the dreamer's mind from many and diverse sources. To one who contemplates in this way, all dispersal of energy is painful and repugnant. When applied to things outside himself, to the social problem, the domestic life, the politics, the religion of his age, Rousseau's desire to simplify gave him the master-touch. He laid his finger on the racked nerves and prescribed quiet, concentration, and simplicity. But this meant revolution. For the habits and laws of society had been made on a different principle. Rousseau's Discourses, " Whether the Restoration of the Arts and Sciences has tended to purify Manners," and " On the Sources of Inequality among Men," show by their very titles the sequence of his thought and how the idea of simplification leads to the idea of equality.

Now, inequality is a sign and a cause of unstable equilibrium. Where inequality exists there is a constant pressure to restore the balance. He, therefore, who desires that life shall be simple, and that men shall attain, as nearly as possible, a level of opportunity, loves permanence and is the true conservative. Moreover, a man who thinks by means of reverie is by this peculiarity inclined to prefer permanence to change. The ruminative process is slow. Its objects are lovingly retained and caressed. Self as an active agent seems to the dreamer to be of less consequence than self as a receptive, passive organ, inwardly transforming and assimilating what comes to it. By this persistent association of self with the objects of contemplation, the latter become infused with life from the former. They lose their difference. They become humanized. Harmony is thus established between the poet or dreamer and the world which has been so long *his* world. He endows it with his own consciousness.

He sympathizes with it, after first projecting himself into it.

The permanent is the natural; the truly permanent, I mean, which in the long-run holds out against all artifice. And the natural qualities of human beings are common to nearly all. To the many, and not to the privileged or perverted few, must he go who would understand life. This conviction, proceeding from his habit of reverie and his love of simplicity, is the third characteristic of Rousseau. Being a child of the people, knowing their soundness and vigour, he felt no surprise in connection with such a principle, and set it forth as self-evident in his books. But it surprised Europe. To him it was a matter of course that wisdom should be justified of *all* her children: *securus judicat orbis terrarum.* There was nothing new in this conviction. It has, no doubt, been held always by nine-tenths of the human race. But it was new in a man of letters. It was not the opinion of cultured people. To culture as a process of distinction, Wordsworth, too, showed repugnance at Cambridge and in his London life. He, who was to write

> Of joy in widest commonalty spread,

scarcely needed the formulas in which Rousseau stated the instinctive faith that was in them both. The social aspect of the French Revolution, its glorious recognition of equal rights and common brotherhood, seemed to him—so gracious had been the influences of his boyhood —only natural, and he consequently sings:

> If at the first great outbreak I rejoiced
> Less than might well befit my youth, the cause
> In part lay here, that unto me the events
> Seemed nothing out of nature's certain course,
> A gift that was come rather late than soon.*

A fourth quality of Rousseau is his intense individualism. Men in a state of nature, in close contact with the earth, with animals, and with other men not overpoweringly different from themselves, have to rely on

* " Prelude," IX., 244.

their own resources. A brooding, introspective person
in such circumstances is liable to form a very high, if
not an exaggerated, estimate of his own consequence
as compared with that of his fellow-mortals. He is
more likely to acknowledge the dependence of man upon
nature than the solidarity of men with one another.
The political views of Rousseau, as stated, for example,
in " The Social Contract," are extremely individualistic.
They are based on the assumption that society was
originally anarchical, a collection of independent persons or families; and the individual, not having been
a co-ordinate part of a pre-existing harmony, still
retains, as it were, the right of secession; he has merely
entered into a pact with other free and independent
beings, and his surrender of some of his liberty may be
only for a time. This conception would hardly have
been possible in a Catholic. It was ultra-Protestant.
It was Calvinistic. Wordsworth, with his Anglican
training, never went to the individualistic extreme in
his love of liberty. Even when most rebellious against
the spirit of his bringing-up and his environment, he
still felt that social ties had something of the naturalness
and permanence of the external world. He thus acted
the mediating part of a true Anglican, and even, one
might say, of a true Englishman, by trying to preserve
historic continuity without surrendering the right of
private judgment.

Rousseau reasoned more abstractly and trenchantly.
But trenchant abstract reasoning, in the complex field
of social relations, is peculiarly liable to error. The
natural, which is permanent, is also rational, and the
rude popular way of arguing from analogy and precedent
is therefore, after all, a sort of reasoning. Thus Wordsworth was not less rational than Rousseau, though in him
pure reason was steadily counterbalanced by instinct.
In Rousseau there was rarely an equilibrium between
the two; he was alternately swayed by the one or the
other; he at times surrendered himself to reverie and
earned the name of sentimentalist; and, again, he was
seduced by the speciousness of abstract reasoning, and

CHAPTER V

IN REVOLUTIONARY FRANCE

WHEN the young English poet set foot on French soil, near the end of November, 1791, the prospects for a successful issue of the Revolution were very bright. The movement was still apparently under the control of sober men, the disciples of Montesquieu, whose object was to model a State after the English pattern, with constitution, hereditary sovereignty, and legal safeguards of personal freedom. The excellent elements, also, of Rousseau's doctrines were being put into practice. The net result of the work of the Constituent Assembly was such as to win the approval of all French patriots and of nearly all progressive Englishmen, Burke being one of the few notable exceptions. What generous and emancipated spirit could fail to applaud its great achievements ? It had abolished feudal privileges, many of the nobles themselves voluntarily renouncing their immemorial advantages in local government. It had taken from the king and reserved for the representatives of the people the power to make laws, to impose taxes, and to declare war and peace. It had wiped out the *octroi* and many other restrictions on agriculture, industry, and internal trade. It had abolished titles and the law of primogeniture, and thus reduced the nobles to the rank of ordinary citizens. It had thrown open all civil and military careers to all citizens, regardless of birth and religion. It had replaced the ancient provinces with eighty-three departments nearly equal in size. It had begun a vast reform of the national finances. It had firmly established an equally great and necessary judicial reform, by replacing the four hundred local systems of custom law with a uniform procedure, and setting on foot the work of codification.

It had undertaken with equal energy, though perhaps
too drastically, to reform the abuses of ecclesiastical
power, by granting freedom of worship to Jews and
Protestants and admitting them to civil office, by
destroying the corporate status of the Church, with
respect to its right to hold property, and by thus
nationalizing its immense wealth. The clergy were
in this way made public functionaries, and the State
undertook to support them and the charities which previously were maintained by the Church. The Catholic
religion in France was to be independent of the Pope.

Some of the new laws affecting the delicate question
of religion were plainly in advance of public opinion.
They were demanded by the logic of the movement,
but did not take sufficient account of either sentiment
or facts. And it was evident, before the close of the
year, that they had created an envenomed hostility.
But an English Protestant, of radical proclivities and
already less than lukewarm in his attachment to Christianity, would not be likely to resent their application
in a country to whose past he was not attached, and
whose present condition aroused in him the most
enthusiastic hope.

On the other hand, there were graver signs of disaster,
which even a youth might have read had he not been
over-sanguine. The legislature sat in Paris, where
it was subject to the threats of a populace which had
tasted the wine of violence. Fanatical men governed
the city, and were organizing its basest elements into
an instrument of their will. The riots and bloodshed
of July 17 were a bad omen of what might happen again
at any crisis. The Constituent Assembly, before dis-
solving on September 30, had unfortunately passed a
self-denying ordinance forbidding the re-election of its
members, and on that date many of the steadiest and
most experienced men disappeared from public life.
The Legislative Assembly, which took up the dangerous
task on October 1, should have laboured to conciliate
all moderate opinions, and repel all extremists; on the
contrary, it embittered the Catholics by taking severe

measures against priests who would not swear allegiance to the constitution; and by confiscating the property of emigrant nobles it exasperated those who had given asylum to these refugees.

We taste, however, the healthy savour which pervades all the relations of republican France with foreign Powers, in the firm declaration which the Assembly, on November 29, 1791, required the King to send to the foreign princes who were assembling their forces on the frontier:

" Tell them that France sees only enemies in every place where they permit preparations to be made against her; that we will religiously keep our oath to make no conquest; that we offer to be good neighbours and to give them the enviable friendship of a free and powerful country; that we will respect their laws, their customs, their constitutions, but shall require their respect for our own.   Tell them finally that if the princes of Germany continue to favour preparations made against the French, the French will carry into their midst, not fire and sword, but liberty !   Let them calculate what result may follow the awakening of nations."

Wordsworth, just arrived in Paris, must have felt the thrill of this eloquent challenge.

It was his plan to pass on at once to the Valley of the Loire, at Orleans, a region celebrated then as now for good cheer, friendly inhabitants, a soft climate, smiling landscapes, and fine old royal castles. The broad and shallow river flows with a lively current, through a fertile plain rich in orchards and wheat-fields, or under low cliffs of soft white limestone festooned with vines. In its blue mirror shakes the image of many a battlemented tower, which stood firm before the battering-ram and cannon, at Blois, Amboise, Luynes, Langeais, Angers. It mocks the ever-during walls of great cathedrals, at Orleans and Tours, with its perpetual flash and ceaseless change. Whether in the Orleannais or in Touraine, a stranger will think himself in the heart of France. Here are the grim ruins of mediæval castles, at Loches and Chinon, and the richly broidered residences of Francis I. and Henry II.—the châteaux of Chambord and Chenonceaux.

For an Englishman another attraction of this pleasant country would be the purity of the French spoken by its people. We have no means of knowing how long Wordsworth expected to remain in France, or whether he had plans more definite and far-reaching than those given for him by his sister. He intended at least to spend the winter at Orleans.

All that Wordsworth says in his autobiographical memoranda about his sojourn in France is as follows:

" In the autumn of 1791 I went to Paris, where I stayed some little time, and then went to Orleans, with a view of being out of the way of my own countrymen, that I might learn to speak the language fluently. At Orleans, and Blois, and Paris, on my return, I passed fifteen or sixteen months. It was a stirring time. The King was dethroned when I was at Blois, and the massacres of September took place when I was at Orleans, but for these matters see also the Poem. I came home before the execution of the King."

The poem is, of course, " The Prelude," of which the ninth, tenth, and eleventh books are occupied with his experiences in that period and their effect upon his mind. Events, places, and times are purposely blurred, and while the poet's feelings, or some of them, are doubtless portrayed with extraordinary fidelity, we cannot depend upon " The Prelude " for an accurate record of external facts during this long and exciting period of his life.

When he came to France, in November, 1791, Wordsworth proceeded at once to Paris. Here he visited, as he relates in the ninth book of " The Prelude,"

> In haste each spot of old or recent fame,
> The latter chiefly.

He sat in the open sun where only a few months before the sunless dungeons of the Bastille had been, and pocketed a stone as a relic, yet without much enthusiasm, and affecting more emotion than he felt. He was too young, too little versed in history, to care as much for these signs of the times as for the placid works

of art, among which he made a rather poor choice of
the Magdalen of Le Brun.* The fact of the Revolution
must have been brought home to him sharply enough,
however, when he visited the Hall of the Assembly,
the Jacobin Club, and the Palais Royal:

> In both her clamorous Halls,
> The National Synod and the Jacobins,
> I saw the Revolutionary Power
> Toss like a ship at anchor, rocked by storms.

He stayed only four days in Paris before going south
to Orleans. Here he spent part of the winter, and then
removed to Blois, a smaller town, forty miles farther
down the Loire. He was, according to his autobiographical memoranda, at Orleans again when the
prisoners were massacred in September, 1792. From
his own statement in " Descriptive Sketches " (lines
760-763, original edition), he was still there in October.
He spent some time in Paris once more, was represented
by proxy at the baptism and acknowledgment of his
child at Orleans on December 15, and had returned to
England certainly before the end of January, 1793.
He does not distinguish in " The Prelude " between
Orleans and Blois ! The first trace of his doings is
found in the following letter:

I am deeply indebted to the poet's grandson, Mr.
Gordon Wordsworth, for permission to use a hitherto unpublished letter, and part of another, which throw more
light at last upon this obscure period of Wordsworth's life:

[*William to Richard Wordsworth*, 1791.]

" ORLEANS. *Decbr.* 19*th*. My address:
" à MONSᴿ WORDSWORTH,
" chez MONSᴿ GELLET DU VIVIER,
" RUE ROYALE,
" à ORLEANS.

" DEAR BROTHER,
     " I have not been able to write to you as soon as
I wished in consequence of the time that my journey
took me, and of a wish to defer my letter till I could

---

* This picture enjoyed peculiar notoriety, because it was supposed to
be a portrait of Madame de la Vallière. Joseph Jekyll, a few years before,
made a great point of seeing it.

give you some account of my arrangements. I was detained at Brighthelmstone from Tuesday till Saturday evening, which time must have passed in a manner extremely disagreeable if I had not bethought me of introducing myself to Mrs. Charlotte Smith; she received me in the politest manner, and showed me every possible civility. This with my best affection you will be so good as to mention to Captn and Mrs. Wordsworth. On Sunday morning I got to Dieppe, and the same night to Rouen, where I was detained two days for the diligence, and on the Wednesday night I reached Paris, where I remained till the Monday following, and on the Tuesday arrived here just a fortnight after quitting London.

" I will now give you a criterion by which you may judge of my expenses here. I had in Paris six hundred and forty-three livres for £20—I give for my lodging, which is a very handsome apartment on the first floor, 30 livres per month if I stay only three months, 27 if I stay six, and 24 and ten sous, viz. halfpence, if I stay 8 months—my board, which is in the same house, with two or three officers of the Cavalry and a young gentleman of Paris, costs me fifty livres per month, breakfast excluded. There are other little expenses which it would not be easy to sum up, but this, as you will perceive, is the bulk, and I think extremely reasonable considering the comfortable manner in which I live. Mrs. Smith, who was so good as to give me letters for Paris, furnished me with one for Miss Williams, an English lady, who resided here lately, but was gone before I arrived. This circumstance was a considerable disappointment to me; however, I have in some respects remedied it by introducing myself to a Mr. Foxlow, an Englishman who has set up a cotton manufactory here—I called upon him yesterday, and he received me very politely. He and Mrs. Foxlow are going into the country for a few days, but when they return I shall, I flatter myself, by their means be introduced to the best society this place affords.

" I have as yet no acquaintance but in the house, the young Parisian, and the rest of the tables, and one family which I find very agreeable, and with which I became acquainted by the circumstance of going to look at their lodgings, which I should have liked extremely to have taken, but I found them too dear for me.

                                        I have
of my evenings there . . . . you
have heard of the news which is
in France before this letter
you; that the King has been
National Assembly and that
are going to make the emigran   [*MS. torn away*]
We are all perfectly quiet here
likely to continue so; I find
all the people of any opulen
aristocrates and all the oth
democrates—I had imagined th
there were some people of wealth and circumstance
favourers of the revolution, but here there is not one
to be found . . .

" I have every prospect of likeing this place extremely
well; the country tho' flat is pleasant, and abounds in
agreeable walks, especially by the side of the Loire,
which is a very magnificent river. I am not yet able
to speak French with decent accuracy, but must of
course improve very rapidly; I do not intend to take a
master—I think I can do nearly as well without one,
and it would be a very considerable augmentation of
my expenses.

" You will give my best love to John, and repeat to
Mrs. and Cap^n Wordsworth any parts of this letter
you may think will interest them, with my kind remem-
berances. Compts. to the Gilpins. If you see Raincock
and Fisher say I am sufficiently pleased with my situation, and tell the former he shall hear from me soon.

" I have said nothing of Paris and its splendours; it
is too copious a theme; besides, I shall return that way
and examine it much more minutely. I was at the
National Assembly, introduced by a member of whose
acquaintance I shall profit on my return to Paris.

" Adieu, Adieu."

                                        [Unsigned.]

[Post mark illegible—date possibly Dec. 27.]
Addressed to Mr. Wordsworth,
        A. Parkins, Esq.,
        Gen. Post Off.,
        London,
        Angleterre.

    Endorsed by   19*th Decr.* 1791
        Richard Wordsworth.   Wm W.⎫ Letter
                                  to   ⎬ from
                               R. W. ⎭ Orleans.

Brighthelmstone was Brighton. Mrs. Charlotte Smith was a well-known poetess. Miss Williams was undoubtedly Helen Maria Williams, the authoress. She was a celebrity at this time both in Britain and in France, well known in the former country as a poet and novelist, and in the latter as a member of a group of English residents who sympathized with the Revolution. She had gone to France in 1788 to live with her sister Cecilia, who had married a French Protestant minister, and had become acquainted with many prominent members of the Girondist party, a privilege she was to expiate during the Terror, when she was imprisoned by Robespierre. She wrote several descriptive and anecdotal books on France and Switzerland, all of them inspired by an intense and enthusiastic interest in the Revolutionary cause. Though she travelled extensively and was a close observer, the authority of her works has been contemptuously denied, partly because of their bias, but even more, I think, through the partisan prejudice of her critics. She was accused of being the mistress of John Hurford Stone, or of being secretly married to him. Stone, a native of Taunton in Somersetshire, was another English Revolutionist, associated with Price and Priestley in his own country, and with Paine in France. He was chairman at the famous banquet at White's Hotel in Paris, November 18, 1792, organized by certain Englishmen to celebrate the victories won by French arms, when Sir Robert Smith and Lord Edward Fitzgerald are said to have renounced their titles, and toasts were drunk to the speedy abolition of all hereditary titles and feudal distinctions.

Orleans harboured many aristocrats and was the scene of much unrest. Monsieur Gellet-Duvivier, with whom Wordsworth lodged and boarded, was later implicated in a local royalist uprising, and the young poet's first French companions were bitter in their hatred of the republic. From the passage in the ninth book of " The Prelude " (lines 81-389) in which he describes some of them, it is hard to tell when he is referring to Orleans

and when to Blois, a confusion intentionally made.
In Orleans lived a notary's clerk, about thirty years old,
named Paul Vallon, originally from Blois, and visiting
him at this time was his sister Marie Anne, known
familiarly as Annette. They probably were " the one
family " which Wordsworth found " very agreeable."
Annette was born at Blois on June 22, 1766, and was
therefore about four years older than the young stranger.
Her home was still at Blois, where two elder brothers,
following their dead father's profession, were practising
surgery, and two sisters older than herself were residing.
Her mother had married again. The Vallons were
royalists, but political differences melted before the fire
of sudden and passionate love which sprang up between
Annette and Wordsworth. She, like him, was unprotected by parental care; neither of them had sufficient
pecuniary means to marry; the laws of marriage were
in a state of confusion and uncertainty owing to the
struggle between the Government and the Church; and
furthermore the social ferment of the times made people
reckless. It may be that the objection to an immediate
marriage between a royalist and Catholic young woman
of little or no fortune and a foreign lad who was a
republican, a free-thinker, poor, and without a profession, trade, or business, came as much from the side
of her relatives as of his. The nobility of his character,
and his subsequent behaviour towards Annette, as well
as her continued affection for him, make it impossible
to suppose that he abandoned her voluntarily. Dorothy
Wordsworth was cognizant of the facts; yet while the
knowledge saddened and perturbed her it never weakened
her love for her brother; which alone would be sufficient
proof that he did what he could to make amends for his
false step.

When Annette went home to Blois Wordsworth
accompanied or followed her. In the spring she found
herself with child.

The letter from Blois, to which reference has been
made, shows that in May, 1792, he purposed to return
to England before the next spring, and to take orders,

though he would have wished to defer this step. His
intention, however, was to engage, together with
Mathews, in some literary undertaking. He writes as
follows:

" BLOIS,

" <i>May</i> 17, [1792].

" DEAR MATHEWS,
    " When I look back on the length of time elapsed
since my receipt of your last letter, I am overwhelmed
by a sense of shame which would deprive me of the
courage requisite to finish this sheet, did I not build
upon that indulgence which always accompanies warm
and sincere friendship. Your last reached me just at
the moment when I was busy in preparing to quit
Orleans, or certainly the sentiments which it breathes
had forced from me an immediate answer. Since my
arrival day after day and week after week have stolen
insensibly over my head with inconceivable rapidity.
I am much distressed that you have been so egregiously
deceived by Mrs. D., and still more so that those infamous calumnies prevent you from taking upon you an
office you are so well qualified to discharge. It gives
me still more heartfelt concern to find that this slander
has sunk so deep upon your spirits. Even supposing,
which is not at all probable, that it should exclude you
from the clerical office entirely, you certainly are furnished with talents and acquirements which, if properly
made use of, will enable you to get your bread, un-
shackled by the necessity of professing a particular
system of opinions.
    " You have still the hope that we may be connected
in some method of obtaining an independence. I assure
you I wish it as much as yourself. Nothing but resolution is necessary. The field of Letters is very extensive,
and it is astonishing if we cannot find some little corner,
which with a little tillage will produce us enough for the
necessities—nay, even the comforts—of life. Your residence in London gives you, if you look abroad, an excellent opportunity of starting something or other.
Pray be particular in your answer upon this subject.
It is at present my intention to take orders, in the approaching winter or spring. My uncle the clergyman
will furnish me with a title. Had it been in my power,
I certainly should have wished to defer the moment.
But though I may not be resident in London, I need
not therefore be prevented from engaging in any literary

plan, which may have the appearance of producing a decent harvest. I assure you again and again that nothing but confidence and resolution is necessary. Fluency in writing will tread fast upon the heels of practice, and elegance and strength will not be far behind. I hope you will have the goodness to write to me soon, when you will enlarge upon this head. You say you have many schemes. Submit at least a few of them to my examination. Would it not be possible for you to form an acquaintance with some of the publishing booksellers of London, from whom you might get some hints of what sort of works would be the most likely to answer?

"Till within a few days I nourished the pleasing expectation of seeing Jones upon the banks of Loire. But he informs me that at the earnest request of the Bishop of Bangor he has till Michaelmas taken upon [him] the office of usher in a school which the Bishop has just built. You know well that the Welsh Bishops are the sole patrons. This circumstance will connect him with D. Warren, and I hope prepare the way for a snug little Welsh living, of which our friend is certainly well deserving. Terrot some time ago addressed a letter to me at Orleans, promising me that it should soon be followed by another, in which he represented himself as stickling for preferment, not in the Church or the Army, but in the Custom-house. 'Tis all well. I wish heartily he may succeed. Let me entreat you most earnestly to guard against that melancholy, which appears to be making daily inroads upon your happiness. Educated as you have been, you ought to be above despair. You have the happiness of being born in a free country, where every road is open, and where talents and industry are more liberally rewarded than amongst any other nation of the Universe.

"You will naturally expect that, writing from a country agitated by the storms of a Revolution, my letter should not be confined merely to us and our friends. But the truth is that in London you have perhaps a better opportunity of being informed of the general concerns of France, than in a petty provincial town in the heart of the kingdom itself. The annals of the department are all with which I have a better opportunity of being acquainted than you, provided you feel sufficient interest in informing yourself. The horrors excited by the relation of the events consequent

upon the commencement of hostilities is general. Not
but that there are men who felt a gloomy satisfaction
from a measure which seemed to put the patriot army
out of a possibility of success. An ignominious flight,
the massacre of their general, a dance performed with
savage joy round his burning body, the murder of six
prisoners, are events which would have arrested the
attention of the reader of the annals of Morocco, or of
the most barbarous of savages. The approaching summer will undoubtedly decide the fate of France. It is
almost evident that the patriot army, however numerous, will be unable [to] withstand the superior discipline
of their enemies. But suppose that the German army
is at the gates of Paris, what will be the consequence?
It will be impossible to make any material alteration
in the Constitution, impossible to reinstate the clergy
in their antient guilty splendour, impossible to give an
existence to the *noblesse* similar to that it before enjoyed,
impossible to add much to the authority of the King.
Yet there are in France some [millions?]—I speak
without exaggeration—who expect that this will take
place.

" I shall expect your letter with impatience, though,
from my general remissness, I little deserve this attention on your part. I shall return to England in the
autumn or the beginning of winter. I am not without
the expectation of meeting you, a circumstance which,
be assured, would give me the greatest pleasure, as
we might then more advantageously than by letter
consult upon some literary scheme, a project which
I have much at heart. Adieu. I remain, my dear
Mathews,
                    " Your most affectionate friend,
                              " W. WORDSWORTH."

The only other letter known to have been written
by Wordsworth in 1792 is dated Blois, September 3,
and will be quoted later. The poem entitled " Vaudracour and Julia " is a disguised and curiously in-
verted account of his love-affair. At one time the
substance of it, in manuscript, formed part of the
ninth book of " The Prelude." The exaltation of
a happy lover sounds triumphantly in the following
lines:

> Earth breathed in one great presence of the spring;
> Life turned the meanest of her implements,
> Before his eyes, to price above all gold;
> The house she dwelt in was a sainted shrine;
> Her chamber-window did surpass in glory
> The portals of the dawn; all Paradise
> Could, by the simple opening of a door,
> Let itself in upon him:—pathways, walks,
> Swarmed with enchantment, till his spirit sank,
> Surcharged, within him, overblest to move
> Beneath a sun that wakes a weary world
> To its dull round of ordinary cares;
> A man too happy for mortality !

And the following passage, like Clärchen's song in Goethe's " Egmont," utters the anxious joy of love:

> Through all her courts
> The vacant city slept; the busy winds,
> That keep no certain intervals of rest,
> Moved not; meanwhile the galaxy displayed
> Her fires, that like mysterious pulses beat
> Aloft; momentous but uneasy bliss !
> To their full hearts the universe seemed hung
> On that brief meeting's slender filament.

When Wordsworth came to Blois his political opinions were not definitely settled, and he lacked the historical knowledge and the training in social philosophy requisite to defend them. He describes his condition in " The Prelude," Book IX., lines 93-110:

> I was unprepared
> With needful knowledge, had abruptly passed
> Into a theatre, whose stage was filled
> And busy with an action far advanced.
> Like others, I had skimmed, and sometimes read
> With care, the master-pamphlets of the day;*
> Nor wanted such half-insight as grew wild
> Upon that meagre soil, helped out by talk
> And public news; but having never seen
> A chronicle that might suffice to show
> Whence the main organs of the public power

---

* In Wordsworth's library, as catalogued after his death, was a bundle of " French Pamphlets and Ephemera "; also Rousseau's " Émile," edition of 1762, and " Confessions," edition of 1782.

Had sprung, their transmigrations, when and how
Accomplished, giving thus unto events
A form and body; all things were to me
Loose and disjointed, and the affections left
Without a vital interest. At that time,
Moreover, the first storm was overblown,
And the strong hand of outward violence
Locked up in quiet.

There were at that time in Orleans and Blois several
of those literary and philosophical societies which were
so numerous in the large French towns in the eighteenth
century. Some of them were under suspicion as sources
of royalist propaganda. With a kindness towards
strangers which is traditional in the Orléannais and in
Touraine, one or more of these academies admitted the
tall, rather impressive-looking youth to their reunions.
Travellers were rare, and Englishmen in high favour.
By a very quick transition in the poem, Wordsworth
gives the impression, although he says he " gradually
withdrew " from these circles, that he turned against
them suddenly, and that the conversion took place at
Orleans, whereas it was in reality operated at Blois,
and by slow degrees:

Night by night
Did I frequent the formal haunts of men,
Whom, in the city, privilege of birth
Sequestered from the rest, societies
Polished in arts, and in punctilio versed;
Whence, and from deeper causes, all discourse
Of good and evil of the time was shunned
With scrupulous care; but these restrictions soon
Proved tedious, and I gradually withdrew
Into a noisier world, and thus ere long
Became a patriot; and my heart was all
Given to the people, and my love was theirs.

The steps by which he reached this position are described in the rest of the ninth book. The time was the
spring and summer of 1792.

Three features of public life in Blois would necessarily interest an intelligent observer in 1792. One
was the attitude taken by the garrison, which had been
partly " purged " the year before, and was now serving

as a centre of Revolutionary propaganda. Another
and even more dramatic feature was the conduct of
Grégoire, the republican Bishop of Blois, who was one
of the most eminent members of the National Convention. He was by far the most striking personality in
the little city. A third feature was the political club
known as the Friends of the Constitution. Two Revolutionary clubs were formed at Blois early in the preceding year, the one just mentioned and another called
the Popular Society. They were presently merged
under the name of the former. The organization thus
constituted was the means by which the Jacobin Club
of Paris exercised an influence over local affairs. It
served also as a blower to the fire of Revolutionary
sentiment. It sat at first in one of the halls of the
abbey of St. Laumer, and afterwards in the church of
the Jacobin Order, as if imitating the parent society. I
have seen a manuscript roll of its members, in the
Departmental Archives at Blois. They numbered
nearly two hundred, and among them were persons of
every walk of life, clergy and laymen, rich and poor, old
men and young. Under certain restrictions the public
were admitted to its meetings, which for a long time
were held daily. So intense was the interest in funda-
mental and purely ideal questions that, even when there
was no news from Paris to discuss, crowds assembled
every evening to hear the debates in this club on the
rights of man, the relations of Church and State, new
methods of education, and the principles of government.
Special and still more open sessions were held on Sunday,
at which patriotic songs were sung, poems recited, and
the best speeches of the week repeated. I have read
the deliberations of this society, preserved in manuscript
in the Library at the Château of Blois, and found in
them a curious mixture of naïve enthusiasm, hopeful-
ness, and devotion, on the one hand, and of shrewd and
insolent interference with local government on the other.
The fanaticism of these levellers was mitigated by a
persuasion that peace and good-will were their ultimate
objects.

An intelligent young foreigner would of course hear of these meetings and desire to attend them. They were the local representation of the great drama which was being enacted all over France. Wordsworth must have been specially attracted, because he already sympathized with the general movement, and also because he wished to learn French. What better exercise for his ear could he have found than these lively debates? At the best, Blois is and was a dull town. The Revolutionary club furnished an unusual opportunity for amusement as well as instruction. There were probably very few English in Blois. Joseph Jekyll, an observant youth, had found only one Englishman there in 1775.* British subjects were regarded with favour at this moment in France because their ancestors had freed themselves from tyranny and bequeathed to them a liberal government.

At the sitting of the Friends of the Constitution on February 3, 1792, " A member asked to have the floor, and proposed two Englishmen for membership, requesting that they should be dispensed from taking the oath, as foreigners and not naturalized. The matter

* My thanks are due to Mr. Thomas Hutchinson for calling my attention to " The Correspondence of Mr. Joseph Jekyll." Jekyll, a lively young man of fortune, spent many weeks at Orleans and Blois in 1775. He found the latter place anything but dull. He mentions at least fifteen French families he knew there. His acquaintance extended to the possessors of many of the great châteaux in the neighbourhood—Herbault, Menârs, Saumery, Amboise. He describes in letters to his father the gay life he led. They echo with the laughter of girls and the rhythm of dancing feet. One is reminded of the opening chapter of " Le Vicomte de Brage-lonne." Though only seventeen years lay between Jekyll's visit and Wordsworth's, the last three of them must have made a vast difference. The careless gaiety of the earlier time became a thing long past, and even through Jekyll's recital of pleasure and " gallantry," through the tinkle of carnival music, we hear the approaching storm and perceive why it had to come. He watched a man being broken on the wheel in the great square of Orleans for burglary; he saw " three hundred wretches chained by the neck like dogs," some of them, who had undergone the torture, scarcely able to support themselves, pass through Blois in one day, and fed there on the ground in the market-place, on their way to the galleys at Brest. Even this light-hearted boy remarked of the country-people: " Ignorance approaches so near to barbarity, that I declare, when we inquired our way, the children kept aloof, for fear, as they said, that the strangers would hurt them."

being discussed, it was decided that they should not be admitted, but that nevertheless they might attend the meetings."*

It is possible, and, I think, even probable, that Wordsworth was one of these two Englishmen. If he was, the length of his stay at Blois becomes practically settled as not less than seven months.

In the meanwhile national events had happened of a nature to repel the indifferent rather than to make them converts. The first impetus of the Revolution had subsided. The membership of the Legislative Assembly was less distinguished and able than that of the Constituent. Its work for the first three months was limited almost entirely to the thorny and dolorous subject of punishing emigrant nobles and non-juring priests. It was decreed that all emigrant nobles who did not return by January 1, 1792, should lose their property and be condemned to death. The King vetoed this decree. Hostile armies were assembling on the northern and western borders, and negotiations, manifestly insincere, were going on between the King, in the name of the nation, and the foreign princes whose one desire was to give back to him the reality of power. There was actual danger from the royalist volunteers mobilizing, to the number of about 23,000, under the Prince of Condé at Worms. Coblentz was a centre of intrigue against the nation. There was a plot to capture Strassburg. The Assembly very naturally and correctly surmised that the King and Queen, together with the Emperor Leopold and the rulers of the South German States, were in correspondence on these subjects. After two months' retirement at Arras, his birthplace, Robespierre, "the incorruptible," returned to Paris on November 28, 1791, the very day after Wordsworth entered the city. Throughout the winter the Jacobin Club pursued a set policy of slander and suspicion, lest a reaction in favour of moderate laws and a limited monarchy should gain headway. They made the most

* "Registres de la Société des Amis de la Constitution," p. 115. Manuscript in the Library of the Château of Blois.

of the King's veto, destroying the remnants of his popularity and of that of his supporters. Lafayette resigned his military command and was defeated by the Jacobins when he stood for election as Mayor of Paris. The city was become openly republican. It recognized in the Jacobin Club a mirror of its own aspirations. A fatal alliance sprang up between the municipality and the club. The faubourgs armed themselves. The King also had collected a strong body-guard. Robespierre, in February, demanded the removal of the Haute Cour from Orleans to Paris. The absent were suspected. The Jacobins opposed war for fear a successful general might make terms with the monarchy. The Girondists, being less afraid of such a possible compromise, clamoured for war. On April 20, 1792, the King was forced to give his consent to a declaration of war against Austria. Envoys from the French Government, who were sent to solicit the good-will of Prussia, England, Spain, and Sardinia, were repulsed or coldly received. The opening of the campaign against the Austrian dominions in Belgium met with a lamentable check. A French division, panic-struck even before it saw the enemy, rushed back into Lille and murdered its general, Dillon, on April 29. This is the disaster of which Wordsworth writes to Mathews on May 17.

How the course of public affairs affected Frenchmen of rank, who, though loyal to the monarchy, were still in France, and indeed in the national army, but plotting reaction, is nowhere more graphically described than in " The Prelude ":

> A band of military Officers,
> Then stationed in the city, were the chief
> Of my associates; some of these wore swords
> That had been seasoned in the wars, and all
> Were men well-born; the chivalry of France.
> In age and temper differing, they had yet
> One spirit ruling in each heart; alike
> (Save only one, hereafter to be named)
> Were bent upon undoing what was done.*

---

* Book IX., line 125. The whole passage, down to line 197, should be carefully read.

Such a state of mind in the army as is here depicted goes far to explain and to justify the suspicions of Robespierre and Marat, who were unwilling to give military men, at a distance from Paris, an opportunity to distinguish themselves in war. If successful, they might rehabilitate the monarchy. Defeated, they might betray their country to the foreign foe. After the King's attempt to flee in June, 1791, officers had been obliged to swear that they would obey the National Assembly. The colonel of the Bassigny regiment, which had become the 32nd Infantry, refusing to sign the oath, had been driven out of Tours, where he was then stationed, and the fact, or one like it, is alluded to in " The Prelude," IX. 181. A detachment of four companies was transferred in August of that year from Tours to Blois. It is the officers of this detachment that Wordsworth refers to. They admitted him to their society because he was an Englishman, and tolerated his criticisms because, being an Englishman, he was *un original*.

> An Englishman,
> Born in a land whose very name appeared
> To license some unruliness of mind;
> A stranger, with youth's further privilege,
> And the indulgence that a half-learnt speech
> Wins from the courteous; I, who had been else
> Shunned and not tolerated, freely lived
> With these defenders of the Crown, and talked,
> And heard their notions; nor did they disdain
> To wish to bring me over to their cause.*

But he was invulnerable to their arguments. He had already become grounded in Revolutionary doctrine. The " master-pamphlets of the day " had convinced his reason. And a deeper source of strength, which made their talk seem crude and vain, was his natural indifference, bred in him from boyhood, to the social distinctions which meant so much to them. He was romantic, and would gladly have stopped his ears to politics and listened only to tales of ancient heroes or to the fall of waters and the madrigals of birds. Ex-

---

* " Prelude," IX, 188-197.

tremists of either side found him absent-minded when they tried to engage him. The narrow rationalism of one party and the cruel bigotry of the other, both found him smiling still at some happy thought suggested by stories or scenes of the past. Yet, when roused to controversy, he proved to be instinctively a democrat. The royalist officers sought to persuade him that their cause was just:

> But though untaught by thinking or by books
> To reason well of polity or law,
> And nice distinctions, then on every tongue,
> Of natural rights and civil; and to acts
> Of nations and their passing interests,
> (If with unworldly ends and aims compared)
> Almost indifferent, even the historian's tale
> Prizing but little otherwise than I prized
> Tales of the poets, as it made the heart
> Beat high, and filled the fancy with fair forms,
> Old heroes, and their sufferings and their deeds;
> Yet in the regal sceptre, and the pomp
> Of orders and degrees, I nothing found
> Then, or had ever, even in crudest youth,
> That dazzled me, but rather what I mourned
> And ill could brook, beholding that the best
> Ruled not, and feeling that they ought to rule.
>   For, born in a poor district, and which yet
> Retaineth more of ancient homeliness,
> Than any other nook of English ground,
> It was my fortune scarcely to have seen,
> Through the whole tenour of my schoolday time,
> The face of one, who, whether boy or man,
> Was vested with attention or respect
> Through claims of wealth or blood; nor was it least
> Of many benefits, in later years
> Derived from academic institutes
> And rules, that they held something up to view
> Of a Republic, where all stood thus far
> Upon equal ground; that we were brothers all
> In honour, as in one community,
> Scholars and gentlemen; where, furthermore,
> Distinction open lay to all that came,
> And wealth and titles were in less esteem
> Than talents, worth, and prosperous industry.
> Add unto this, subservience from the first
> To presences of God's mysterious power
> Made manifest in Nature's sovereignty,

And fellowship with venerable books,
To sanction the proud workings of the soul,
And mountain liberty.   It could not be
But that one tutored thus should look with awe
Upon the faculties of man, receive
Gladly the highest promises, and hail,
As best, the government of equal rights
And individual worth.   And hence, O Friend !
If at the first great outbreak I rejoiced
Less than might well befit my youth, the cause
In part lay here, that unto me the events
Seemed nothing out of nature's certain course,
A gift that was come rather late than soon.
No wonder, then, if advocates like these,
Inflamed by passion, blind with prejudice,
And stung with injury, at this riper day,
Were impotent to make my hopes put on
The shape of theirs, my understanding bend
In honour to their honour; zeal, which yet
Had slumbered, now in opposition burst
Forth like a Polar summer; every word
They uttered was a dart, by counterwinds
Blown back upon themselves; their reason seemed
Confusion-stricken by a higher power
Than human understanding, their discourse
Maimed, spiritless; and, in their weakness strong,
I triumphed.*

Politics apart, the human tragedy of the war affected him profoundly. He saw the roads filled with the bravest youth of France " and all the promptest of her spirits," under arms and hastening to the north. He saw the struggle in màny a family between love and patriotism. Here and there a face in the passing files of eager young men touched him with a sense of brotherhood. The martial music, the banners, quickened his blood. These moving spectacles made his heart beat high, and seemed

Arguments sent from Heaven to prove the cause
Good, pure, which no one could stand up against,
Who was not lost, abandoned, selfish, proud,
Mean, miserable, wilfully depraved,
Hater perverse of equity and truth.†

---

* " Prelude," IX. 198.   † *Ibid.*, IX. 283.

One of the oppressive laws of the old régime had been that no soldier, however brave, however accomplished, could rise above the ranks unless he were of noble blood. Among the officers stationed at Blois, there was one who viewed the patriotic rising with the same generous feelings as the young foreigner. This was a captain in the 32nd Regiment, Michel-Armand Bacharetie Beaupuy. He was thirty-six years old, and had been in the army ever since his sixteenth year. He was born at Mussidan, about fifty miles north-east of Bordeaux, July 14, 1755, of an ancient noble family. His mother was a descendant, in the sixth generation, from the great essayist Montaigne. His three elder brothers were officers in the old army, from which two of them at least retired when the Revolution began. They were all zealous partisans of liberty, and wielded great influence in their native region, being instrumental in choosing and instructing its delegates to the Constituent Assembly. His younger brother was a priest, but favoured the Revolution. At the outbreak of the troubles this young ecclesiastic gave up an easy post as Canon of Arles and became *curé* of his native parish. He joyfully swore allegiance to the constitution in 1791. Their mother had brought up these five sons on the literature and philosophy of the eighteenth century. Their home was a centre of the new culture.

Michel, the captain at Blois, had served in many parts of France, had been promoted slowly, had read and studied much, and had lately, while on furlough, been the chief figure in the politics of Mussidan. His Revolutionary principles were grounded on a thorough examination of the social philosophy which lay behind the movement. He was a democrat in heart also. He loved the poor, and lived and laboured for their sake. The annals of the Revolution present no purer spirit, none more unselfish, gallant, genial, and hopeful. Scorned by his brother officers, he rose above them by his patient dignity. He could afford to await the verdict of time, serenely confident as he was in the justice of his cause. No other man save Coleridge had so great an influence upon Wordsworth as this sweet and devoted patriot. Of him, no doubt, the poet thought, no matter of whom besides, when he wrote " The Character of the Happy Warrior." With his more systematic philosophy, tempered in the fire of persecution, Beaupuy came to Wordsworth's support. He turned the young man's vague idealism into firm principle. And at last the love of humanity, which had not yet found equal place in the poet's heart with love of nature, was raised to the double throne.   He depicts Beaupuy, in " The Prelude," with many distinct and fine touches:

> Among that band of Officers was one,
> Already hinted at, of other mould—
> A patriot, thence rejected by the rest,
> And with an oriental loathing spurned,
> As of a different caste. A meeker man
> Than this lived never, nor a more benign,
> Meek though enthusiastic.   Injuries
> Made *him* more gracious, and his nature then
> Did breathe its sweetness out most sensibly,
> As aromatic flowers on Alpine turf,
> When foot hath crushed them.   He through the events
> Of that great change wandered in perfect faith,
> As through a book, an old romance, or tale
> Of Fairy, or some dream of actions wrought
> Behind the summer clouds.   By birth he ranked
> With the most noble, but unto the poor
> Among mankind he was in service bound,
> As by some tie invisible, oaths professed
> To a religious order.   Man he loved
> As man; and, to the mean and the obscure,
> And all the homely in their homely works,
> Transferred a courtesy which had no air
> Of condescension; but did rather seem
> A passion and a gallantry, like that
> Which he, a soldier, in his idler day
> Had paid to woman: somewhat vain he was,
> Or seemed so, yet it was not vanity,
> But fondness, and a kind of radiant joy
> Diffused around him, while he was intent
> On works of love or freedom, or revolved
> Complacently the progress of a cause,
> Whereof he was a part: yet this was meek
> And placid, and took nothing from the man
> That was delightful.*

* " Prelude," IX. 288.

Beaupuy was no leveller. He did not confound distinctions. He was not blind to fact. Although he evidently was a student of Jean-Jacques, he knew from experience that some men are set apart for rule and honour by their virtues and knowledge. He loved the poor and humble, but, not being an intolerant theorist, he admitted that the ignorance of the multitude who must earn their bread by manual labour debarred them from the immediate exercise of high political power.

> Oft in solitude
> With him did I discourse about the end
> Of civil government, and its wisest forms;
> Of ancient loyalty, and chartered rights,
> Custom and habit, novelty and change;
> Of self-respect, and virtue in the few
> For patrimonial honour set apart,
> And ignorance in the labouring multitude.*

Still, at times, giving rein to pity and scorn, and employing the pompous language of the day, they indulged themselves in weaker and more feverish talk.

> But though not deaf, nor obstinate to find
> Error without excuse upon the side
> Of them who strove against us, more delight
> We took, and let this freely be confessed,
> In painting to ourselves the miseries
> Of royal courts, and that voluptuous life
> Unfeeling, where the man who is of soul
> The meanest thrives the most; where dignity,
> True personal dignity, abideth not;
> A light, a cruel, and vain world cut off
> From the natural inlets of just sentiment,
> From lowly sympathy and chastening truth:
> Where good and evil interchange their names,
> And thirst for bloody spoils abroad is paired
> With vice at home.†

Beaupuy was Wordsworth's instructor in branches of study for which he had until then shown no aptitude. He awakened new interests, gave him social consciousness, clothed for him in garments of majestic association the history of mankind. Henceforth the poet could no

* " Prelude," IX. 321.   † Ibid., 339.

longer regard the chronicles of nations as a mere quarry
for romantic incidents. History, he now saw, was
organic. Heroism was but the eminent outcrop of
deep popular virtues and aspirations.   Creeds and sects
took their place with national customs, as growths
unconsciously implanted and irresistibly evolved.   But
in all this they saw the workings of a destiny, not blind
and aimless, but moving towards a glorious end.

> We summoned up the honourable deeds
> Of ancient Story,
>   *   *   *   *   *
>   and, finally, beheld
> A living confirmation of the whole
> Before us, in a people from the depth
> Of shameful imbecility uprisen,
> Fresh as the morning star.   Elate we looked
> Upon their virtues; saw, in rudest men,
> Self-sacrifice the firmest; generous love,
> And continence of mind, and sense of right,
> Uppermost in the midst of fiercest strife.*

The world has never since offered to generous youth
so wide a prospect. Never again has the future been
so flooded with light, never have distant mountains of
promise beckoned with such strong allurement. From
height to height the promise flashed. It explained the
past, with all its sorrow, now so full of meaning. It
made any sacrifice endurable for the sake of a sure
result. The pathway ahead lay golden in the sunshine.
Not since the earliest days of Christianity had groups of
the purest and strongest men felt so exalted, and whole
communities been so uplifted. Even solitary dreamers
in distant places the thrill of enthusiasm stirred. How
much more, then, were they moved who lived in daily
contact with actors in the mighty drama !†
He compares Beaupuy with Dion, the pupil of Plato,
who headed an expedition under philosophic patronage
against the tyrant of Syracuse. But there is no reason
to think that he had in mind a close parallel between
Beaupuy and the unfortunate Greek hero when, in

* " Prelude," IX. 364.   † *Ibid.*, 390.

1816, he wrote his poem " Dion," for even at that time, in the depths of his political and moral reaction against the Revolution, he could never have intended its last and most significant lines to apply adversely to the friend of his youth:

> Him only pleasure leads, and peace attends,
> Him, only him, a shield of Jove defends,
> Whose means are fair and spotless as his ends.

Poetry, unmindful of moral purposes and public welfare, ever and anon rebelled against his new interests. As they walked side by side through the forest along the Loire, Wordsworth wearied of those " heart-bracing colloquies," and in spite of his real fervour—and that less genuine excitement worked up within himself, as he tells us—he peopled the mysterious glades of those royal demesnes with the heroines of Ariosto and Tasso, saw Angelica upon her palfrey, and Erminia the fair fugitive, rather than the goddess Liberty. He sinned in the eyes of his stern preceptor by sighing for the hushed matin-bell, the extinguished taper, and the displaced cross, when they gazed at the ruins of a convent; he persisted in romancing about pleasure-loving kings and their mistresses, when they caught sight of ancient castles rising above the trees. Thus imagination, he tells us, often mitigated the force of civic prejudice, the bigotry of a youthful patriot's mind. Well would it have been for the over-wrought delegates in Paris if they could have escaped now and then from the fever and glare of the distracted city and let their imaginations rest, even as an interlude, upon quieter scenes; though it is to be doubted whether the sight of Chambord, with its tale of royal vice and extravagance, would have calmed them. But to Wordsworth, who had not to pay for ancient wrongs, those beautiful old palaces gave " many gleams of chivalrous delight." " Yet not the less," he declares, with a return to austerity, " not the less,"

> Hatred of absolute rule, where will of one
> Is law for all, and of that barren pride

> In them who, by immunities unjust,
> Between the sovereign and the people stand,
> His helper and not theirs, laid stronger hold
> Daily upon me, mixed with pity too
> And love; for where hope is, there love will be
> For the abject multitude.*

The one unmistakable note in the pompous harmonies
and crashing discords of the Revolution was hope. He
alone who has hope, who believes in human perfectibility, will have the motive and the courage to love
mankind in spite of all its blemishes. The essence of
Toryism is despair of human nature. The essence of
the Revolutionary or progressive spirit is trust in human
nature. The last sentence of the lines just quoted is
an epitome of that philosophy which animated France
and which made the Revolution a religious movement.
For whether in good or in evil, it was religious. Its
good sprang from unselfish devotion to universal aims,
to impersonal ideals. Its evil came rarely from self-
seeking or littleness, but almost wholly from fanatical
attachment to general principles. Robespierre was as
religious as Mahomet. In Beaupuy an original sweetness
of disposition kept his love for the poor from turning
into hate for their oppressors. He was earnest in his
search for a remedy, but not vindictive. He had no
fear of failure, and could therefore exercise some patience.
He felt sure that most men were with him and that
their united efforts must succeed. Examples of misery
were not wanting, and Beaupuy used them as texts
for discourses which established Wordsworth in his
republican faith.

> When we chanced
> One day to meet a hunger-bitten girl,
> Who crept along fitting her languid gait
> Unto a heifer's motion, by a cord
> Tied to her arm, and picking thus from the lane
> Its sustenance, while the girl with pallid hands
> Was busy knitting in a heartless mood
> Of solitude, and at the sight my friend
> In agitation said, " 'Tis against *that*

---

* " Prelude," IX. 501.

That we are fighting," I with him believed
That a benignant spirit was abroad
Which might not be withstood, that poverty
Abject as this would in a little time
Be found no more, that we should see the earth
Unthwarted in her wish to recompense
The meek, the lowly, patient child of toil,
All institutes for ever blotted out
That legalized exclusion, empty pomp
Abolished, sensual state and cruel power,
Whether by edict of the one or few;
And finally, as sum and crown of all,
Should see the people having a strong hand
In framing their own laws; whence better days
To all mankind.*

It was Beaupuy, also, who told Wordsworth the story of Vaudracour and Julia, as an instance of the bigotry of birth that France was weary of. At least, so we read in " The Prelude." Many years afterwards, Wordsworth said to a friend who was collecting notes on his poems, Miss Isabella Fenwick, that " Vaudracour and Julia " was " faithfully narrated, though with the omission of many pathetic circumstances, from the mouth of a French lady, who had been an eye-and-ear witness of all that was done and said." And he added, using a name which does not occur in the poem: " Many long years after, I was told that Dupligne was then a monk in the Convent of La Trappe." The poem was composed not later than 1804 as an episode in " The Prelude." It was, however, on account of its length, published separately in 1820, with the remark: " The facts are true; no invention as to these has been exercised, as none was needed."

In the same registers at Blois in which I found the

* " Prelude," IX. 509. Curiously enough, Joseph Jekyll, the young English traveller, seventeen years before, had remarked the same evidence of poverty in the country about Blois. He says: " The peasants of this part of France are miserably poor. The girls who herd the cows are always at work with their distaffs, and the cap is a ways clean, and perhaps laced, while the feet are without shoes and stockings." The poor, he declares, lived upon bread and water from Monday till Sunday, and bread was very dear.

motion to admit two Englishmen into the Society of the Friends of the Constitution, on February 3, 1792, I have discovered what appear to be traces of Beaupuy's activity. On January 22 of the same year, it is recorded that " one of our brothers of the 32nd Regiment, an officer, read a very eloquent discourse on political distrust, showing how dangerous it was when it exceeded the limits of that proper watchfulness necessary in all good citizens." The officer's name is almost illegible, but seems to be Beaupuy or Beaupuis. On January 29 he read his speech a second time, and was freshly applauded. An officer of the same regiment, sometimes mentioned as the 32nd, and sometimes under its old name Bassigny, is referred to several times in the next three or four months, but not by name. The club appears to have become attached particularly to Brissot and his faction in Paris, who were moderates.

It is almost necessary to believe that Wordsworth, a lonely young man, must have haunted the daily meetings of the Revolutionary club. They provided entertainment and excitement in a town otherwise dull—too large for rural beauty, too busy with petty retail trade to invite a genial expansion of the soul, a town sunk in a maddening monotony of small comforts. But into this unpromising garden a seed had fallen from the wings of Freedom. A vigorous plant had sprung up, exotic, and yet so well adapted to the soil as to draw to itself the elements of life slumbering round about. There was now one important hour of day and one interesting place. A spirited young man of twenty-one, unless restrained by scruples or prejudices, would naturally avail himself of the opportunity thus offered. Curiosity would induce him to visit the club; sympathy with its objects might easily make him wish to join it. And even if for no other reason than to perfect himself in the French language, he would be attracted to these daily meetings.

Fancy would fain reconstruct the scene: the vaulted church, destitute of altar, shrine, and image, its darkness rendered visible with guttering candles, which cast

" a little glooming light, much like a shade "; the plat-
form draped in red, white, and blue; Bishop Grégoire
in the choir, wearing his violet episcopal vestments to
indicate that, though a Revolutionist, he was a Churchman still; one of those painstaking secretaries at his
side whose handwriting we have been deciphering;
" nos frères," both civil and military, sitting below, and
" nos sœurs " in the gallery, waving each one a copy of
the new patriotic hymn.   Captain Michel Beaupuy,
divested of the haughty air belonging to his birth and
his old training, and clad in the new uniform of a republican regiment, ascends the rostrum and begins
an impassioned speech.   And at the edge of the crowd,
that tall English youth, hanging on his words and
kindling with the double enthusiasm of friendship and
zeal for a great cause, is William Wordsworth !

Wordsworth tells us, in the autobiographical memoranda, that he was still at Blois when the King was
dethroned—August 10, 1792.   We cannot doubt that,
at the time, he rejoiced in this event, in spite of the
massacre of the Swiss Guards which accompanied it.
The Duke of Brunswick had, on July 26, issued an
insolent manifesto, declaring that he was coming, in the
name of the kings of Europe, to restore Louis XVI. to
authority.   Maddened by this declaration, and goaded
by Danton, Marat, and Robespierre, who saw their
opportunity to establish a republic, the people of Paris,
together with large delegations from all parts of the
country, invaded the Tuileries, slaughtered eight hundred
of the King's defenders, and drove him to take refuge
in the hall of the Legislative Assembly, whence he was
sent to prison.   On August 25 news reached Paris that
the Prussians had entered Longwy.   Next came reports
that Verdun had fallen, that it had been treacherously
surrendered, that the enemy were within one hundred
and fifty miles of Paris.   At once the unscrupulous
fanatics of the Jacobin Club seized control of the city
government and sent a band of hired assassins to the
prisons.   In five days, from the 2nd to the 6th of September, more than nine hundred helpless men, women,

and children, were butchered. The madness spread
to Versailles, Rheims, Meaux, Lyons, and Orleans,
where Wordsworth was at the time, as he tells us in the
autobiographical memoranda.

Beaupuy had already, before the beginning of August,
accompanied his regiment into Lower Alsace. The
friends had parted, never to meet again. Wordsworth,
years afterwards, heard and believed a false report of
Beaupuy's death in the war of the Vendée, and wrote,
in " The Prelude ":*

> He perished fighting, in supreme command,
> Upon the borders of the unhappy Loire,
> For liberty, against deluded men,
> His fellow-countrymen; and yet most blessed
> In this, that he the fate of later times
> Lived not to see, nor what we now behold,
> Who have as ardent hearts as he had then.

It is true that Beaupuy was spared the sight of France
ruled by an emperor, which is what Wordsworth saw
with horror in 1804 when he wrote these lines. But
he did not die fighting against the Vendean Royalists.
The report probably originated in the fact that he was
severely wounded at the battle of Château-Gonthier,
October 27, 1793, when commanding the advance-guard
of the Army of the West. He had meanwhile shared
the glory and the persecutions of the Army of Mayence,
victorious on the Rhine, calumniated on the Seine. His
advancement had been rapid. Of mature age, though
retaining the cheerfulness and vivacity of youth, un-
equalled for daring, noted even in the republican army
as a man of strong convictions, he had survived the
jealousy of the Jacobins, in spite of his noble birth and
eminent achievements. Within a year after Wordsworth left France, his soldier hero was a general of
division. His life was too busy and communications
were too much interrupted to admit of correspondence
between the friends, and Wordsworth never knew of
his distinguished career as chief of staff of the Army

* Book IX., line 424.

of the West and general in the army of the Rhine and Moselle. He was killed in battle, October 19, 1797, and buried near Neuf-Brisach, east of Colmar.

From his journal, it is apparent that he was impul-. sive and sincere, self-confident but competent. After a scene that reminds one of some brave passage in the " Iliad," in which he snatches a sword from a Prussian officer and personally causes the retreat of two battalions of the enemy, he concludes: " This affair proves the superiority true Republicans will always have over the satellites of despots !" He never lost an opportunity to sow the good seed. At parleys with hostile outposts, during negotiations with German officers, in conversations with prisoners, he was careful to let fall a word in season, and has recorded the occasions. " I have," he writes, " never neglected these chances. I have seriously performed the oath of my apostleship whenever possible. I have always tried to tear away the thick veil of blindness from the eyes of these Germans. They are not made for freedom, I know; but, after all, some grains, I hope, will sprout."

Besides such preliminary work as Wordsworth may have done on " Vaudracour and Julia," it is not known that he wrote any poetry at Blois and Orleans, except " Descriptive Sketches." Much of the greater part of this poem was composed during his walks on the banks of the Loire, in the years 1791, 1792, and the dates are confirmed in his own handwriting on the margin of a copy which was kindly lent to me by Professor George Herbert Palmer, of Harvard University. As we shall see, this poem reflects the principles and feelings that he describes in " The Prelude " as having been his at that time. He was careful, later, to moderate some of its language. In the first edition the author's sympathy with the Revolutionary tendency is unmistakable, and it is this early version that students of Wordsworth should read, rather than the expurgated text. A letter directing his brother Richard how to send him a sum of money concludes as follows, and fixes a date after which he left Blois to return to Orleans:

" BLOIS,
" *September* 3.

" DEAR BROTHER,
" . . . I look forward to the time of seeing you,
Wilkinson, and my other friends, with pleasure.   I am
very happy you have got into chambers, as I shall
perhaps be obliged to stay a few weeks in town about
my publication; you will, I hope, with Wilkinson's permission, find me a place for a bed.   Give Wilkinson my
best compts.   I have apologies to make for not having
written to him, as also to almost all my other friends—
I rely on their indulgence.   I shall be in town during the
course of the month of October.   Adieu, Adieu; you will
send me the money immediately.
                                      " W. WORDSWORTH."

[Post mark: BLOIS *Se* 10.92
Addressed to MR. WORDSWORTH.
        A. PARKINS, Esq.,
        G. P. OFF.,
        LONDON, ANGLETERRE.

Endorsed by   ⎫   10 *Septr.* 1792.   ⎫ Letter
RICH. WORDSWORTH ⎪   W. WORDSWORTH   ⎪ from Blois
                 ⎬   to   ⎬ about
                 ⎭   RD. WORDSWORTH.   ⎭ money.]

Wordsworth did not carry out his intention of returning to London in October.   It seems likely that he spent
part at least of that month at Orleans.   In a passage
of " Descriptive Sketches," beginning at line 740 in the
original edition, with the apostrophe to the country of
the Loire,

> And thou ! fair favoured region ! which my soul
> Shall love, till Life has broke her golden bowl,

he describes the " October clouds," and the exquisite
description with which the tenth book of " The Prelude "
opens, of the " beautiful and silent day " on which he
bade farewell to the gliding Loire, recalls October with
its " many-coloured woods."
    He must have rejoiced when the good news came of
the defeat of the Prussians at Valmy, on September 20.
Goethe was with the invaders.   France had attracted
those two great poets from neighbouring lands, but
how differently !   Goethe, middle-aged, rich in achieve-

ments and honours, a pensioner of an old-fashioned
court, came to observe, to criticize, to judge, the insane
struggles of the French; Wordsworth, little more than
a boy, free of foot, open-minded, thoughtless of his own
advancement, and glowing with generous hopes for
mankind—the English poet has every advantage romance
can confer.

The day after the battle of Valmy the Revolution
entered upon its third legislative stage, with the opening
of the Convention. At once the Republic was declared.
Even in 1804 the poet still felt the stir of exultation,
when he narrated the repulse of the invading host:

> Presumptuous cloud, on whose black front was written
> The tender mercies of the dismal wind.*

Rash men, the princes of the north had seen their
quarry turn into avengers from whose wrath they fled
in terror.

> Disappointment and dismay
> Remained for all whose fancies had run wild
> With evil expectations; confidence
> And perfect triumph for the better cause.†

Cheered, he tells us, with hope that the crimes of early
September were but ephemeral monsters, and elate
with confidence in the Republic, Wordsworth returned
to the " fierce Metropolis." With ardour hitherto un-
felt, he ranged over the city, visiting the scenes of
recent note, passing the prison where lay the dethroned
monarch, walking through the half-ruined palace of the
Tuileries, dazed by what he saw, and unable to conceive
its meaning. But that night the sense of danger leaped
upon him from out the dark: he remembered what Paris
could do. St. Bartholomew, the September massacres,
and what next? He saw the Terror striding out of
future time. " That night," he writes,

> I felt most deeply in what world I was,
> What ground I trod on, and what air I breathed.
> High was my room and lonely, near the roof
> Of a large mansion or hotel, a lodge
> That would have pleased me in more quiet times;

---

* " Prelude," X. 13.   † Ibid., 27.

Nor was it wholly without pleasure then.
With unextinguished taper I kept watch,
Reading at intervals; the fear gone by
Pressed on me almost like a fear to come.
I thought of those September massacres,
Divided from me by one little month,
Saw them and touched: the rest was conjured up
From tragic fictions or true history,
Remembrances and dim admonishments.
The horse is taught his manège, and no star
Of wildest course but treads back his own steps;
For the spent hurricane the air provides
As fierce a successor; the tide retreats
But to return out of its hiding-place
In the great deep; all things have second birth;
The earthquake is not satisfied at once;
And in this way I wrought upon myself,
Until I seemed to hear a voice that cried,
To the whole city, " Sleep no more."　The trance
Fled with the voice to which it had given birth;
But vainly comments of a calmer mind
Promised soft peace and sweet forgetfulness.
The place, all hushed and silent as it was,
Appeared unfit for the repose of night,
Defenceless as a wood where tigers roam.*

Next day these direful presentiments no doubt
vanished or faded in the brightness of dawn.　He went
forth eagerly through the still unawakened streets to
the centre of excitement, the long arcades of the Palais
Royal.　Here the daily throng was already shouting,
and above the general noise he heard the shrill cries of
hawkers, " Denunciation of the crimes of Maximilian
Robespierre."　And into his hand they thrust printed
copies of the speech in which Louvet, the Girondist, had
essayed to overthrow the Jacobin leader on October 29.
From the futility of this charge Wordsworth foresaw
that liberty and life and death would soon lie in the
hands of those who ruled the capital; he clearly saw the
issue and who were the real combatants:

* " Prelude," X. 63.　Though I quote this passage here, I believe the
feelings expressed in it are more likely to have been experienced by Words
worth ten or eleven months later during a visit which I think he made to
Paris in October, 1793, and of which I shall try to present some evidence
in a later chapter.

> The indecision on their part whose aim
> Seemed best, and the straightforward path of those
> Who in attack or in defence were strong
> Through their impiety.*

Yet did he not for a moment lose trust that all would end well. He had no fear for the ultimate safety of France; what distressed him was delay and her loss of opportunity to do a work of honour, a work that should attract and enamour the nations of the world. And, in a startling passage, he avows that he dreamed—or did he really form a plan?—of offering his life to the cause. Leader or sacrifice, it mattered not which, he would give himself to France. From the solidity of his character we are bound to infer that he would never have mentioned these thoughts had they not been more than passing fancies. They must have taken firm consistency in his mind, and perhaps have grown into active purposes. Modesty struggles with a desire to tell the truth in these deeply-considered lines. He avows that he was urged by a heroic impulse, but gives the credit to Reason working irresistibly through him. He tells us that he thought of means of opposing the Jacobin power, and of remedies; and among them this:

> An insignificant stranger and obscure,
> And one, moreover, little graced with power
> Of eloquence even in my native speech,
> And all unfit for tumult or intrigue,
> Yet would I at this time with willing heart
> Have undertaken for a cause so great
> Service however dangerous. I revolved,
> How much the destiny of Man had still
> Hung upon single persons; that there was,
> Transcendent to all local patrimony,
> One nature, as there is one sun in heaven;
> That objects, even as they are great, thereby
> Do come within the reach of humblest eyes;
> That Man is only weak through his mistrust
> And want of hope where evidence divine
> Proclaims to him that hope should be most sure;
> Nor did the inexperience of my youth
> Preclude conviction, that a spirit strong

---

* " Prelude," X. 130.

In hope, and trained to noble aspirations,
A spirit thoroughly faithful to itself,
Is for Society's unreasoning herd
A domineering instinct.*

These are the lessons of Beaupuy; applied by a young foreigner to himself, they are the reflections of a hero. Had Wordsworth followed his impulse, it is not impossible that an instinct of command, of which he professed himself conscious, might have led him to some act of melancholy renown.   He had great self-control, tenacity, courage, enthusiasm, and depth of conviction.   These qualities would have been recognized and honoured, perhaps with a martyr's death.   Whatever we may imagine as to the possible consequences, there can be no doubt about the perfect sincerity of the disclosure. It probably understates rather than exaggerates the pitch of his ambition.

Then, as he wrote originally in a passage of " The Prelude " which he afterwards altered, he declares:

In this frame of mind
Reluctantly to England I returned,
Compelled by nothing less than absolute want
Of funds for my support, else, well assured
That I both was and must be of small worth,
No better than an alien in the Land,
I doubtless should have made a common cause
With some who perished, haply perished too,
A poor mistaken and bewildered offering.

His nephew, in the " Memoirs," says: " If he had remained longer in the French capital, he would, in all probability, have fallen a victim among the Brissotins, with whom he was intimately connected." This last phrase can hardly have been written at random.   With whom, among the section of the Girondists who followed Brissot's leadership, was the poet intimately connected ?   Affairs in France were more interesting than ever, shortly before the close of the year 1792, and there was as yet no danger for Englishmen there.   The Republican army was everywhere victorious.   On November 18

* " Prelude," X. 148.

the Convention passed a motion declaring that the French Republic desired the liberty of all other nations and would assist them to gain it. This decree, and still more the declaration that the River Scheldt, which was previously kept closed by treaty in the interest of London, was free to the commerce of the world, and an order to Dumouriez to invade Holland, were of course provocations to the British Government, but war was still not declared. December was filled with preliminaries for the King's trial and with the trial itself. He was beheaded on January 21. Before that date Wordsworth had left Paris, and on the first of February France declared war against England.

Naturally enough, Dorothy Wordsworth suffered some anxiety on her brother's account, as he was absent much longer than she had expected. As early as May 6, 1792, she expressed in a letter to Jane Pollard, only a small fragment of which has been published, her hope of seeing William in London, on her way from Forncett to Windsor in July:

" William is still in France, and I begin to wish he was in England. He assures me, however, that he is perfectly safe, but as we hear daily accounts of insurrections and broils, I cannot be quite easy, though I think he is wise enough to get out of the way of danger."

In a letter from Windsor, postmarked October 19, 1792, she says: " My brother William is still in France." On December 15, at Orleans, Anne Caroline, daughter of William Wordsworth and Marie Anne Vallon, was baptized, having been born that same day. Her father, who was absent, was represented by a proxy and acknowledged her over his signature, which the clerk set down as "William Wordwodsth, anglais."

CHAPTER VI

A REVOLUTIONIST IN ENGLAND

THE poet dismissed the next three years in one sentence of his autobiographical memoranda:

" I came home before the execution of the King, and passed the subsequent time among my friends in London and elsewhere, till I settled with my only sister at Racedown in Dorsetshire, in the year 1796." [Really 1795.]

Yet this period of his life was full of consequence for him. It was his time of storm and stress. Largely because of what he underwent between 1792 and 1796 he became one of the voices of his age. Much of the interest and value of his poetry depends upon our knowing its less immediate meaning, its political and philosophical import. If his own account of these critical formative years is provokingly meagre, all other accounts are scanty enough. Our chief dependence is upon a series of letters to his friend Mathews. " The Prelude " itself, hitherto full of significant detail, passes rapidly and vaguely over the time that followed his return from France. Of course, " The Excursion " is an elaborate commentary on his inner life during those years, but our appreciation of " The Excursion " is enhanced by every item of knowledge concerning his goings and comings, his plans and efforts. " The Excursion " is scarcely less autobiographical than " The Prelude." It is the most profound and sensitive comment literature has made upon the most tremendous social upheaval of modern times. And its depth, its truth, its feeling, are due to the fact that it reflects the sympathy and repulsion of a passionate soul who had lived what he wrote. Yet one reason why this great poem has failed, as it undoubtedly has failed, to make

an impression on many readers who thoroughly enjoy
" The Prelude," is that the poet had been too reticent.

Wordsworth's position on returning to England, and
for nearly three years afterwards, was extremely uncomfortable. He had no home, and was obliged to live
with friends and relatives. He had no profession, and
was less inclined than ever to become a clergyman, thus
disappointing his family. His principles were abhorrent
to them. He was a republican. He was not orthodox.
He led an unsettled life. His uncles were irritated by
his conduct. There is nothing to prove that he had
much to do with his brother Richard, who was established as a solicitor in London. Christopher was at
Cambridge, and John at sea. But his sister's faith in
him never faltered. Her enthusiasm for his character,
her romantic interest in his doings, never grew less. He
did not visit her on his return. In her letter of August
30, 1793, to Jane Pollard, she says: " It is nearly three
years since my brother and I parted. It will be exactly
three years when we meet again." The passage in her
letter of June 16, 1793, where she writes: " It was in
winter (at Christmas) that he was last at Forncett,"
refers to the vacation in 1790-91, just before he took his
degree. Still cherishing the idea that he was to enter
the ranks of the clergy, she fondly pictured herself
living with him at last in their own little parsonage.
Comparing Christopher with William, she writes on
February 16, with her gift of discrimination:

" He is like William, with the same traits in his
character, but less highly touched. He is not so ardent
in any of his pursuits, but is attached to the same ones
which have so irresistible an influence over William that
they deprive him of the power of chaining his attention
to others discordant with his feelings."

These are words which paint a portrait. His qualities
highly touched, his ardour, his impatience with uncongenial pursuits, are marks of a poetic temperament.
Miss Pollard may not have been interested in these
effusions, but how charming is the writer's confidence

that nothing which concerns her wonderful brother can be tedious ! Christopher, she continues, " is steady and sincere in his attachments," and then she makes haste to add :

" William has both these virtues in an eminent degree; and a sort of violence, if I may so term it, which demonstrates itself every day, when the objects of his affection are present with him, in a thousand almost imperceptible attentions to their wishes, in a sort of restless watchfulness which I know not how to describe, a tenderness that never sleeps, and at the same time such a delicacy of manner as I have observed in few men."

Then she gives free rein to her fancy, depicting the life with William for which she longed :

" I look forward to the happiness of receiving you in my little parsonage. I hope you will spend at least a year with me. I have laid the particular scheme of happiness for each season. When I think of winter, I hasten to furnish our little parlour. I close the shutters, set out the tea-table, brighten the fire. When our refreshment is ended, I produce our work, and William brings his book to our table, and contributes at once to our instruction and amusement; and, at intervals, we lay aside the book, and each hazard observations on what has been read, without the fear of ridicule or censure. We talk over past days. We do not sigh for any pleasures beyond our humble habitation,—' the central place of all our joys.' With such romantic dreams I amuse my fancy during many an hour which would otherwise pass heavily along; for kind as are my uncle and aunt, much as I love my cousins, I cannot help heaving many a sigh at the reflection that I have passed one-and-twenty years of my life, and that the first six years only of that time were spent in the enjoyment of the same pleasures that were enjoyed by my brothers, and that I was then too young to be sensible of the blessing. We have been endeared to each other by early misfortune. We in the same moment lost a father, a mother, a home. We have been equally deprived of our patrimony by the cruel hand of lordly tyranny. These afflictions have all contributed to unite us closer by the bonds of affection, notwithstanding we have been compelled to spend our youth far asunder."

Immediately upon arriving in England, Wordsworth busied himself with preparing for the press his first volume of poetry, " Descriptive Sketches," which was printed very early in 1793 and followed immediately by a second slim volume entitled " An Evening Walk." The numerous errors in both books, and Miss Wordsworth's expression of regret that her brother had not shown his poems to some friend for criticism before publication, prove that they were printed in haste.

In a letter to Jane Pollard dated February 16, Miss Wordsworth, after a pathetic complaint that she is still separated from her brothers, says:

" By this time you have doubtless seen my brother William's poems. . . . The scenes which he describes have been viewed with a poet's eye, and are pourtrayed with a poet's pencil, and the poems contain many passages exquisitely beautiful; but they also contain many faults, the chief of which is obscurity, and a too frequent use of some particular expressions and uncommon words."

And she mentions " viewless " and " moveless," the former of which occurs four times in " Descriptive Sketches," and once in " An Evening Walk," and the latter once in " Descriptive Sketches," and twice in " An Evening Walk "—in the original editions, of course.

" I regret exceedingly," she continues, " that he did not submit these works to the inspection of some friend before their publication, and he also joins with me in this regret. Their faults are such as a young poet was most likely to fall into, and least likely to discover, and what the suggestions of a friend would easily have made him see and at once correct. It is, however, an error he will never fall into again, as he is well aware that he would have gained considerably more credit if the blemishes of which I speak had been corrected. My brother Kit and I, while he was at Forncett, amused ourselves by analyzing every line, and prepared a very bulky criticism, which he was to transmit to William as soon as he could have added to it the remarks of a Cambridge friend."

It is possible that this friend was Coleridge. In Christopher Wordsworth's diary, under date of Tuesday, November 5, 1793, occurs the following delightful entry:

" Roused about nine o'clock by Bilsborrow and Le-Grice with a proposal to become member of a literary society: the members they mentioned as having already come into the plan Coleridge, *Jes.*, Satterthwaite, Rough, and themselves, *Trin. C.*, and Franklin, *Pembroke.* . . . Got all into a box [at a coffee-house] and (having met with the Monthly Review of my Brother's Poems), entered into a good deal of literary and critical conversation on Dr. Darwin, Miss Seward, Mrs. Smith, Bowles, and my Brother. Coleridge spoke of the esteem in which my Brother was holden by a society at Exeter,* of which Downman and Hole were members, as did Bilsborrow (as he had before told me) of his repute with Dr. Darwin, Miss Seward, etc., etc., at Derby. Coleridge talked Greek, Max. Tyrius he told us, and spouted out of Bowles."

William Bowles and Erasmus Darwin were poets held in high esteem at that time. Bowles occupied the exalted post in Coleridge's mind which Wordsworth was to fill later. With all allowance for Coleridge's readiness to take fire, he cannot be charged with want of discernment in his literary enthusiasms. It means much that he should have perceived in Wordsworth's earliest notes the qualities of freshness and naturalness which he felt in Bowles. As the quotation from Christopher's diary shows, the first impact of Wordsworth's spirit upon Coleridge, an occurrence memorable in the history of poetry and of criticism, probably took place before the autumn of 1793. Coleridge visited his family at Ottery St. Mary in the long vacation of that year. Passing through Exeter, he may have heard the " society " of which he spoke expressing their esteem of Wordsworth's poetry, or, as is far more likely, he may

* Mr. Thomas Hutchinson, editor of the Oxford " Wordsworth," discovered that a literary society of twelve members was founded at Exeter in 1786 by Hugh Downman and Jackson, the organist of the cathedral, and that a volume of the essays and verses read at the weekly meetings was published in 1796.

have carried one of the volumes with him from London
or Cambridge, and " spouted " the lines of a strange
new poet to a wondering provincial audience, himself
creating, and perhaps retaining exclusive possession
of, the enthusiasm. He tells us in the " Biographia
Literaria " that during his first Cambridge vacation he
" assisted a friend in a contribution for a literary society
in Devonshire."

The two poems which so stirred Coleridge were subjected by Wordsworth to much revision in later editions.
This is unfortunate, for their intrinsic merit is at least
equalled by their value as a record of his early powers.
In considering them, I shall therefore refer always to
the editions of 1793. M. Legouis, who has applied to
the study of these two poems his truly wonderful
knowledge of our literature, and has traced to many
diverse sources their diction, their turns of thought,
their allusions, however faint, says that " An Evening
Walk " belongs, as regards the style of its composition,
to Wordsworth's Cambridge days. This is doubtless
true. The poem carries us back, indeed, to Hawkshead.
Not only its subject, but its substance in detail, recalls
the sleeping lakes and cloud-capped hills of Cumberland.
It yields no evidence of foreign travel or of interest in
public affairs. Its curiously compounded literary flavour
could never have been concocted in France, where its
author must have been almost wholly deprived of
English books. For there is scarcely any other poem
in our language so artificially constructed, so full of
echoes from older writings. It contains every device
of the most extreme " poetic licence," every contrivance
by which poets of the descriptive school, from Denham
to Goldsmith, rendered their own labour light and the
task of their readers heavy. Personification, inversion,
ellipsis, apostrophe, periphrasis, and all the unnatural
pomp of a specially reserved rhetoric, abound in these
few hundred lines. The mere diction is far less artificial
than the grammar, and very frequently the plain and
appropriate word is used with a certain naïve courage.
But the sentences are constructed in ways sanctioned

neither by common practice nor by the venerable usage of great poets. Spenser is less loose, Milton less complex, Shakespeare less broken. The young author showed a rare audacity, or perhaps one should say ignorance of danger, in the length and unsparing fulness of his phrase. He was determined, evidently, to express his thoughts at whatever cost. It is unjust to his great predecessors to hint that their example excuses his excess. In diction, and in diction only, is he indebted to them. Reminiscences of Shakespeare, and particularly of Milton, run like a sweet undertone through the whole poem. Some of the best things in " An Evening Walk " are echoes of " Comus," which has ever been a mine of precious phrases and charming images. Wordsworth himself, in footnotes in the original edition, acknowledged his indebtedness for words, phrases, and images, to Spenser, to Tasso, to the French poet Rosset, to Thomson, to Beattie, to Young, to Burns, to Greenwood, author of a " Poem on Shooting," and to Clark, author of " A Survey of the Lakes." Various quotations are encrusted in " An Evening Walk," among them one from Collins. The most beautiful, and one might have said, the most Wordsworthian lines in the poem,

> The song of mountain streams, unheard by day,
> Now scarcely heard, beguiles my homeward way,

were taken without acknowledgment from Dr. John Brown's (1715-1766) Dedication to Mr. Romney of Cumberland's " Ode to the Sun." Many years afterwards, in his " Guide to the Lakes," Wordsworth quotes with praise the passage from Brown's poem, ending as follows :

> Nor voice, nor sound, broke on the deep serene;
> But the soft murmur of swift-gushing rills,
> Forth issuing from the mountain's distant steep,
> (Unheard till now, and now scarce heard) proclaim'd
> All things at rest, and imag'd the still voice
> Of quiet, whispering in the ear of night.

Though written in heroic couplets, the poem is not remarkable for point and vigour. Indeed, being descriptive, such a semblance of point and vigour as the versification necessarily produces tends to break the pictures into a series of short glimpses of equal length. If the author had, at the time he began his poem, been acquainted with the best models which had recently appeared, with Cowper's " Task " (1785), for example, or at least if he had appreciated them, he would scarcely have chosen the heroic couplet as a medium of description.

Has the poem, then, no distinction ? Is it in no way superior to other descriptive compositions of that time, in no way indicative of the birth of an original mind ? Remembering the enthusiasm of Coleridge, we can do no less than look below the diction and the versification for some deeper quality. And here we find an occasional directness of observation, an occasional freshness of energy, which are indeed worthy of note. The poem is scarcely more than a series of ill-connected pictures, but these pictures, one feels, are records of real sensations. This is the beginning of naturalness. No one could doubt that the writer had seen most of the things he described. And the episode of the mother with her starving children, which was evidently imagined, not remembered, charms by another quality which pervades the poem—namely, a sort of moral fervour. It is quite likely that this passage, which may be readily detached from its context, was written after Wordsworth's return from France. It reveals an interest in the victims of war keener than he would have felt before that time. The fact that all the pictures are scenes from humble life only reminds us of the democratic simplicity of his early days. Coleridge must, I think, have felt the startling power of imagination in the word " tremulous," when the poem speaks of

> the roar
> That stuns the tremulous cliffs of high Lodore.

He must have realized how faithful was the poet's effort to reproduce a natural scene, with its peculiar

atmosphere and even its movement, in the following lines:

> When in the south, the wan noon brooding still,
> Breathed a pale steam around the glaring hill,
> And shades of deep embattled clouds were seen
> Spotting the northern cliffs with lights between,

and the rest of the passage. The " subtle sunbeams "
that shine in " the dark-brown bason " of the water-
brook would arrest his eye, when perchance he had just
smiled at the author's conveyance of Milton's epithet
" huddling " from " Comus." Perhaps in his native
Devonshire he may have witnessed some equivalent for
the way the wise sheep-dogs of the Lake country are
directed from a distance by their masters, which Wordsworth describes in plain language, with only one inversion, one abbreviation, one substitution of an adjective
for an adverb, and one obscure term:

> Waving his hat, the shepherd in the vale
> Directs his winding dog the cliffs to scale,
> That, barking busy 'mid the glittering rocks,
> Hunts, where he points, the intercepted flocks.

The description of the swans, especially that of the
female, who " in a mother's care, her beauty's pride
forgets," is worthy of a place in almost any bucolic
poem, and fairly triumphs over the cruel restrictions
of the rhymed couplet. In the account of the soldier's
widow, one is struck by the line,

> On cold blue nights, in hut or straw-built shed,

which strangely resembles the lines of Burns's " First
Epistle to Davie, a Brother Poet ":

> To lie in kilns and barns at e'en
> When banes are crazed, and bluid is thin,
> Is, doubtless, great distress !

and by the poor woman's first-born child being called,
in a phrase worthy of Dante, " her elder grief." It is
hardly possible that Wordsworth was the first poet to
speak of a boat moving slowly over rippling water as a

" talking boat," but I do not remember to have seen
the expression elsewhere.   His line,

> The tremulous sob of the complaining owl,

exactly hits the plaintive note of that misunderstood
bird.   The couplet,

> Fair Spirits are abroad; in sportive chase
> Brushing with lucid wands the water's face,

is what Wordsworth himself would have termed an
expression of fancy, not of imagination.   It is highly
artificial, but how charming, how like our elder poets !
Finally, Coleridge could *not* have understood, but
Dorothy would read through brimming tears the heart-
felt petition of the poet for a humble home,

> Where we, my friend, to golden days shall rise,
> Till our small share of hardly-paining sighs
> (For sighs will ever trouble human breath)
> Creep hush'd into the tranquil breast of Death.

This was what she longed for, and these lines bore to
her the private message and signature of her brother.

" Descriptive Sketches " had a quite different origin
from that of " An Evening Walk."   It was conceived
later, and drawn from sources more widely scattered
and less intimately known.   It dates in no sense from
an earlier occasion than the vacation journey with Jones
on the Continent.   Its general plan is very simple.   We
have first a passage commending foot-travel, then an
extremely brief summary in eight lines of the march
through France, followed by a series of loosely connected pictures—the Grande Chartreuse, the Lake of
Como, a storm in the Alps, other Swiss scenes—and
finally the praise of poverty, simplicity, liberty, and
republicanism.   Many of the same extravagances of
diction which amaze the reader of " An Evening Walk "
mar the second work also.   There is, however, less
borrowing from other poets.   The sentence-structure
is even more arbitrary and confused.   The musical
effects are, naturally, more ambitious and more varied,
though many blemishes may be detected by any sensi-

tive ear.   The " picturesque," a term which Wordsworth scornfully rejected, but which is the only one
really applicable to his chief efforts in this piece, is
achieved by violence, but it is achieved.   There are
many striking scenes, and some which charm by their
completeness and inner harmony.   In " An Evening
Walk " the human element was supplied by the soldier's
widow and her children, by an occasional shepherd or
swain, and chiefly by personifying every object and
idea mentioned.   In " Descriptive Sketches " the widow
reappears as a gipsy of the Grisons, with her babe,
wandering over the mountains in a storm by night.
We have alluring maidens, whose charms were much
reduced in later editions.   Personification is still carried
to excess; and in the second half of the poem a new
element, scarcely foreshadowed at all in " An Evening
Walk," appears and dominates the work.   This is the
cause of Man as Man, and to see how it swept the poet
on a new current away from his original design, we must
read, not the softened conclusion in late editions, but
the lines as they were first printed.

   To consider once more for a moment the workmanship of the poem, it must be admitted that in general
composition or ordering of parts it lacks unity; and
although I think M. Legouis sometimes strains a point
in attempting to show that this or that word or phrase
was borrowed, there can be no doubt that he has con-
victed Wordsworth of astonishing verbal dependence
upon poetic tradition, and, indeed, of having chosen bad
models and exceeded their faults.   Furthermore, not
even by making allowance for the poet's youth and
exuberance can we escape being astounded by the
depths of his obscurity and the heights of his audacity.
Can anyone represent to himself " Silence, on her night
of wing "?   Can anyone read without a smile, in the
account of the riots and gunfire at the Grande Chartreuse,

> The thundering tube the aged angler hears,
> And swells the groaning torrent with his tears ?

The full enormity of the following lines is withheld from
a reverent reader of Wordsworth until dogged syntax

insists that " his " can have no other antecedent than
" infant Rhine." " Shall we," the poet writes,

> led where Via-Mala's chasms confine
> Th' indignant waters of the infant Rhine,
> Bend o'er th' abyss ?—the else impervious gloom
> His burning eyes with fearful light illume.

Describing a chamois-hunter cut off from retreat by
slippery rocks, he imparts a singular piece of information with an outrageous figure of speech:

> To wet the peak's impracticable sides
> He opens of his feet the sanguine tides,
> Weak and more weak the issuing current eyes
> Lapp'd by the panting tongue of thirsty skies.

A tone more formal and dogmatic than any yet
prompted by his native independence begins to show
itself in the second half of the poem. A corresponding
change in style appears. The following lines might
have been written by the hand of Pope recalled to life
for the purpose of condensing into maxims the philosophy
of Rousseau:

> Once Man entirely free, alone and wild,
> Was bless'd as free—for he was Nature's child.
> He, all superior but his God disdain'd,
> Walk'd none restraining, and by none restrain'd,
> Confess'd no law but what his reason taught,
> Did all he wish'd, and wish'd but what he ought.

From this he proceeds to celebrate the ancient victories
of the Swiss over the Austrians, and thence comes to
depict the " homely pleasures," the contentment, and
the hardships of the mountaineers.

I think it has never been remarked that the poem
contains a distinct confession of religious unbelief. Yet
this is plainly the meaning of four lines which conclude
the passage describing a pilgrimage to the shrine of
Einsiedeln. Addressing the credulous worshippers, he
cries:

> Without one hope her written griefs to blot,
> Save in the land where all things are forgot,
> My heart, alive to transports long unknown,
> Half wishes your delusion were its own.

Humane aspirations begin to crowd upon the images of nature with which till now he has been content. The mention of Chamonix makes him remember that Savoy is not free, and political enslavement, he knows, means poverty.

With a truer understanding of political economy than those possess who argue that the extravagance of the rich gives employment to the poor, he perceives that luxury in one place entails misery in another:

> In the wide range of many a weary round,
> Still have my pilgrim feet unfailing found,
> As despot courts their blaze of gems display,
> Ev'n by the secret cottage far away
> The lily of domestic joy decay;
> While Freedom's farthest hamlets blessings share,
> Found still beneath her smile, and only there.
> The casement shade more luscious woodbine binds,
> And to the door a neater pathway winds,
> At early morn the careful housewife, led
> To cull her dinner from its garden bed,
> Of weedless herbs a healthier prospect sees,
> While hum with busier joy her happy bees;
> In brighter rows her table wealth aspires,
> And laugh with merrier blaze her evening fires;
> Her infant's cheeks with fresher roses glow,
> And wilder graces sport around their brow;
> By clearer taper lit a cleanlier board
> Receives at supper hour her tempting hoard;
> The chamber hearth with fresher boughs is spread,
> And whiter is the hospitable bed.

Turning to the valley of the Loire, with an affectionate outcry,

> And thou ! fair favoured region ! which my soul
> Shall love, till Life has broke her golden bowl,

he declares that nature is more beautiful in that land since Freedom has made its fields and skies her peculiar care. Though war is about to commence, yet may that land rejoice, for new virtues are springing even from war's flames:

> Nature, as in her prime, her virgin reign
> Begins, and Love and Truth compose her train;
> With pulseless hand, and fix'd unwearied gaze,
> Unbreathing Justice her still beam surveys.

Even Consumption shall cease to ravage a land that enjoys the blessings of Liberty. As this poem was published after the September massacres, after Wordsworth had seen with his own eyes the Jacobin party locked in a grip of implacable frenzy with the moderates of the Assembly, after the King had been executed, there can be no question of the firmness of his republicanism and of his nerves. The final apostrophe, beginning

> Oh give, great God, to Freedom's waves to ride
> Sublime o'er Conquest, Avarice, and Pride,

is feverish and almost incoherent, but a clear and unmistakable denunciation of the coalition of kings against France rings out in the lines:

> And grant that every sceptred child of clay,
> Who cries, presumptuous, " Here their tides shall stay,"
> Swept in their anger from th' affrighted shore,
> With all his creatures sink—to rise no more.

In taking leave of this singular poem, let us recall the cordial but discriminating words of Coleridge in the " Biographia Literaria ":

" During the last year of my residence at Cambridge, I became acquainted with Mr. Wordsworth's first publications, entitled Descriptive Sketches; and seldom, if ever, was the emergence of an original poetic genius above the literary horizon more evidently announced. In the form, style, and manner of the whole poem and in the structure of the particular lines and periods, there is an harshness and an acerbity connected and combined with words and images all aglow, which might recall those products of the vegetable world, where gorgeous blossoms rise out of the hard and thorny rind and shell, within which the rich fruit was elaborating. The language was not only peculiar and strong, but at times knotty and contorted, as by its own impatient strength; while the novelty and struggling crowd of images, acting in conjunction with the difficulties of the style, demanded always a greater closeness of attention than poetry (at all events, than descriptive poetry) has a right to claim. It not seldom, therefore, justified the complaint of obscurity."

Wordsworth's life in 1793 is shrouded with a degree of mystery that is itself mysterious. A poet in his twenty-fourth year is not likely to live without warm friends and curious acquaintances, is not likely to withdraw from social scenes or to be a niggardly correspondent. Yet not a single letter of the young republican, dating from this year, has ever been printed—except the draft of a public epistle, which we shall consider later. Four of his sister's letters to Jane Pollard—or, rather, fragments of them—written in this year have been published, and in his old age the poet made a few references to this time in notes to his poems. Evidently his relatives not only disapproved of him then, but continued long afterwards to do their utmost to cover with oblivion the season of his unripeness. Later, he too joined the conspiracy against the memory of his youthful self. It has been lightly assumed that he lived while in London with his brother Richard, but I know of nothing to prove this. His income could not have been more than enough for a most frugal existence.

On Sunday morning, June 16, 1793, his sister wrote to Miss Pollard : " I cannot foresee the day of my felicity, the day on which I am once more to find a home under the same roof as my brother. All is still obscure and dark." She pleads for sympathy with her " little schemes of felicity," her " scenes of happiness, happiness arising from the exercise of the social affections in retirement and rural quiet." She says she often hears from her dear brother William. " I am very anxious about him just now," she adds, " as he has not yet got an employment. He is looking out, and wishing for the opportunity of engaging himself as tutor to some young gentleman, an office for which he is peculiarly well qualified. Oh, Jane, the last time we were together he won my affection to a degree which I cannot describe, his attentions to me were such as the most sensible of mortals must have been touched with; there was no pleasure that he would not have given up with joy for half an hour's conversation with me. It was in winter at Christmas that he was last at Forncett." She describes her joys on that memorable occasion, which was at the close of 1790. By her brother's advice, probably, and for his sake, she is now studying French, " fagging it tolerably hard," she says. It is a melancholy fact that not until the next autumn or winter after his return from France did he see his adorable sister. Her passion fed on patience, which nourished it for a sustained and lofty flight. It is through her eyes chiefly that we see him at this time. Her anxiety is equalled only by her confidence. Does he hold with those atrocious French ? No truer Englishman exists ! Can it be true he is a heretic ? Why, he is her brother William, and the charge needs no further refutation ! Is he idle and un-productive ? The finest and rarest qualities, she is cer-tain, lie ready for employment in his rich nature if only he has a chance to teach. How eagerly she catches at his assent, in the last lines of " An Evening Walk," to her long-cherished hope that they might live together in a cottage of their own ! She even includes Miss Pollard in her dream of felicity :

" Why are you not seated with me ? and my dear William, why is he not here also ? I could almost fancy that I see you both near me. I hear you point out a spot where, if we could erect a little cottage and call it our own, we could be the happiest of human beings. I see my brother fired with the idea of leading his sister to such a retreat as I fancy, ever ready at our call, hastening to assist us in painting. Our parlour is in a moment furnished; our garden is adorned by magic; the roses and honeysuckles spring at our command; the wood behind the house lifts its head, furnishing us with a winter's shelter and a summer's noonday shade. My dear friend, I trust that ere long you will be, without the aid of imagination, the companion of my walks, and my dear William may be of our party. He is now going upon a tour to the West of England, along with a gentleman who was formerly a schoolfellow, a man of fortune, who is to bear all the expense of the journey, and only requests the favour of William's company, as he is averse to the idea of going alone. As William has not the prospect of any immediate employment, I think he cannot pursue a better scheme. He is perfectly at liberty to quit this companion as soon as anything more advantageous offers."

Then she bursts into an ecstatic strain, in full accord with her most loving nature, and justified, no doubt, by qualities in her brother known as yet to her alone:

" But it is enough to say that I am likely to have the happiness of introducing you to my beloved brother. You must forgive me for talking so much of him; my affection hurries me on, and makes me forget that you cannot be so much interested in the subject as I am. You do not know him; you do not know how amiable he is. Perhaps you reply, ' But I know how blinded you are.' Well, my dearest, I plead guilty at once; I *must* be blind; he cannot be so pleasing as my fondness makes him. I am willing to allow that half the virtues with which I fancy him endowed are the creation of my love; but surely I may be excused! He was never tired of comforting his sister; he never left her in anger; he always met her with joy; he preferred her society to every other pleasure—or rather, when we were so happy as to be within each other's reach, he had no pleasure when we were compelled to be divided. Do not, then, expect too much from this brother of whom I have delighted so to talk to you. In the first place, you must be with him more than once before he will be perfectly easy in conversation. In the second place, his person is not in his favour—at least, I should think not; but I soon ceased to discover this—nay, I almost thought that the opinion which I had formed was erroneous. He is, however, certainly rather plain, though otherwise has an extremely thoughtful countenance; but when he speaks it is often lighted up by a smile which I think very pleasing. But enough, he is my brother; why should I describe him? I shall be launching again into panegyric."

She returns with undaunted persistence to her plans for a meeting with him:

" My brother's tour will not be completed till October, at which time they [*i.e.*, William and William Calvert, the young man with whom he was to travel] will perhaps make a stand in North Wales, from whence he can very conveniently take a trip to Halifax. It is more than two years and a half since we last saw each other, and so ardent is our desire for a meeting that we are determined upon procuring to ourselves this happiness, if it were even to be purchased at the price of a journey across the kingdom; but from North Wales into York-shire the distance is nothing.   If, therefore, my brother does not meet with any employment, which is likely to fix him before I go to Halifax, we shall certainly meet there; but, if he should be engaged, we are determined to see each other at Forncett.

" If my brother makes an engagement which will take him out of England or confine him to one spot for any length of time, then he is determined to come and see me at Forncett, if it be but for a day, though he has never received an invitation from my uncle, and though he can have no possible inducement but the pleasure of seeing me.   You must know that this favourite brother of mine happens to be no favourite with any of his near relations, except his brothers, by whom he is adored— I mean by John and Christopher, for Richard's disposi-tion and his are totally different, and though they never have any quarrels, yet there is not that · friendship between them which can only exist where two hearts are found to sympathize with each other in all their griefs and joys.   I have not time or room to explain to you the foundation of the prejudices of my two uncles against my dear William; the subject is an unpleasant one for a letter; it will employ us more agreeably in conversation.   Then, though I must confess that he has been somewhat to blame, yet I think I shall prove to you that the excuse might have been found in his natural disposition.

> In truth he was a strange and wayward wight,
> Fond of each gentle, etc., etc.

That verse of Beattie's ' Minstrel ' always reminds me of him, and indeed the whole character of Edwin resembles much what William was when I first knew him after my leaving Halifax.

> And oft he traced the uplands to survey,
> When o'er the sky advanced the kindling dawn,
> The crimson cloud, blue main and mountain gray,
> And lake dim gleaming on the dusky lawn,
> Far to the west the long long vale withdrawn.

I have been much disappointed that my uncle has not invited William to Forncett, but he is no favourite with him.   Alas !   Alas !"

Was ever the fraternal relation endowed with more romantic glamour ? Was there ever a more ardent worship of a brother by a sister ? It never failed, and the companionship of a lifetime was maintained at this high pitch, if not of expression, yet of intense feeling.

Her brother, in writing to her, broke through the formal style which often served as a necessary check to the violence of his emotions. Dorothy proudly transcribes two passages from his letters.

" The first," she explains, " is from the letter he wrote in answer to mine, informing him of my certainty of visiting Halifax. He says: ' Now, my dearest friend, how much do I wish that each emotion of pleasure or pain that visits your heart should excite a similar pleasure or a similar pain within me, by that sympathy which will almost identify us when we have stolen to our little cottage. I am determined to see you as soon as ever I have entered into an engagement. Immediately I will write to my uncle, and tell him that I cannot think of going anywhere before I have been with you. Whatever answer he gives me, I certainly will make a point of once more mingling my transports with yours. Alas ! my dear sister, how soon must this happiness expire; yet there are moments worth ages.' . . . In another letter, in which he informs me of his intention to accept his friend Calvert's offer, he says, ' It will be easy for me to see you at Halifax. Oh, my dear, dear sister ! with what transport shall I again meet you ! with what rapture shall I again wear out the day in your sight ! So eager is my desire to see you, that all obstacles vanish. I see you in a moment running, or rather flying to my arms.'"

Wordsworth's biographers have had little to say about the breach which existed at this time between him and his uncles. The facts appear to be, however, that Dr. Cookson refused to let him visit Dorothy at Forncett, and that his supply of money was so greatly reduced as to make travelling impossible. Poor Dorothy's day of felicity was not to come quite as soon as she expected. She lost her purse, containing six guineas, which she had saved for her visit to Halifax. This was more than made up, however, by generous gifts from her brother Richard

and her uncle Crackanthorpe, of whom she now began
to entertain a better opinion, saying that he had been
influenced against her only by his wife, a proud and
selfish woman.　But her plan was upset by Calvert's
horse, or, as we shall presently see, by an adventure of
which she was kept in ignorance till its dangers were
over.　It seems that the young men began their journey
late in the summer.　They had spent some time in the
Isle of Wight, and were probably at or near Salisbury,
on their way to Wales, when the animal dragged them
and their carriage into a ditch.　The vehicle was ruined.
Calvert rode off north on the steed, and the poet, after
wandering for two days over Salisbury Plain, had no
other resource but to hasten to the home of his old
friend Robert Jones in North Wales.　He went by way
of Bath and Bristol to the banks of the " silvan Wye,"
whence he proceeded on foot.　It was on this journey
that he met, within the area of Goodrich Castle, the little
girl whom he made the heroine of " We are Seven,"
although he did not write the poem at that time.　Five
years later he passed that way again, reposed under the
same " dark sycamore," saw again the same hedgerows
and the same farms, " green to the very door."　If anyone still holds the view that Wordsworth, for two or
three years after his return from France, suffered a
dulling of sensibilities, an obscuration of spirits, was too
sombre, too much absorbed in uncongenial politics to
feel the thrill of nature, and that his poetic faculties
were not reawakened until the soothing influence of his
sister restored him to a more easy-going frame of mind,
to optimism and peace —if anyone still holds this view,
which was set forth in the " Memoirs," and has been
very commonly held, what can he say of the passage in
" Lines composed a Few Miles above Tintern Abbey,"
which describes, though disclaiming the attempt, what
his feelings were in 1793 ?

> Like a roe
> I bounded o'er the mountains, by the sides
> Of the deep rivers, and the lonely streams,
> Wherever nature led: more like a man

> Flying from something that he dreads than one
> Who sought the thing he loved.　For nature then
> (The coarser pleasures of my boyish days,
> And their glad animal movements all gone by),
> To me was all in all.—I cannot paint
> What then I was.　The sounding cataract
> Haunted me like a passion: the tall rock,
> The mountain, and the deep and gloomy wood,
> Their colours and their forms, were then to me
> An appetite; a feeling and a love,
> That had no need of a remoter charm,
> By thought supplied, nor any interest
> Unborrowed from the eye.—That time is passed,
> And all its aching joys are now no more,
> And all its dizzy raptures.

Yet it must be admitted that these high spirits were a rebound from a state of dejection in which he had been plunged a few days before.　It was on Salisbury Plain that he had in part conceived the melancholy tale which now bears the title " Guilt and Sorrow."　And his sad thoughts there were due to reflecting on the probable mission of the British fleet which he had seen from the Isle of Wight.　In the Advertisement prefixed to the above-mentioned poem in 1842 he wrote:

" During the latter part of the summer of 1793, having passed a month in the Isle of Wight, in view of the fleet which was then preparing for sea off Portsmouth at the commencement of the war, I left the place with melancholy forebodings.　The American war was still fresh in memory.　The struggle which was beginning, and which many thought would be brought to a speedy close by the irresistible arms of Great Britain being added to those of the allies, I was assured in my own mind would be of long continuance, and productive of distress and misery beyond all possible calculation. This conviction was pressed upon me from having been a witness, during a long residence in revolutionary France, of the spirit which prevailed in that country."

Far less cautious is his language in " The Prelude," which was written much earlier, and reproduces more faithfully his original emotion:

When the proud fleet that bears the red-cross flag
In that unworthy service was prepared
To mingle, I beheld the vessels lie,
A brood of gallant creatures, on the deep;
I saw them in their rest, a sojourner
Through a whole month of calm and glassy days
In that delightful island which protects
Their place of convocation—there I heard,
Each evening, pacing by the still sea-shore,
A monitory sound that never failed,—
The sunset cannon.   While the orb went down
In the tranquillity of nature, came
That voice, ill requiem ! seldom heard by me
Without a spirit overcast by dark
Imaginations, sense of woes to come,
Sorrow for humankind, and pain of heart.*

The joy with which he took refuge in nature's bosom, when he found himself alone and far from every suggestion of discord, on the banks of the sweet inland river, contrasted strongly with the civic care which had oppressed him ever since his return from France. He had come home, " a patriot of the world." Rural England, erewhile, he tells us, his " tuneful haunt," seemed unsuited to his mood. He felt more in harmony with the general stir of the great city, where public questions were in the air. And though he took but a languid interest in the anti-slavery movement, which was then receiving one of those checks that only served to increase the zeal of its friends, this indifference was due to his conviction that if the French Revolution prospered, slavery, that " most rotten branch of human shame," would vanish with a host of other evils. As high as was his trust, so low was his despair, when his own country, which he had heard Frenchmen praise for her love of liberty, declared war upon the land of his hopes:

What, then, were my emotions, when in arms
Britain put forth her free-born strength in league,
Oh, pity and shame ! with those confederate Powers !

His moral nature, he says, had received no shock down to that very moment. All else had been progress; this was revolution. The order of his attachments was in-

* " Prelude," X. 314.

verted.   Old loyalty to native land, instead of becoming
merged in a more comprehensive allegiance to human
welfare, was found to be a principle of evil.   In what
must have been the bitterest sort of triumph he rejoiced,
" yea, exulted," he tells us, when Englishmen were over-
thrown by thousands, left without glory on the field, or
driven to shameful flight.   When in church prayers were
offered up or praises for English victories, he sat silent,
and

> Fed on the day of vengeance yet to come.

This is a state of mind to which the best of men have
been driven, and will, with the advance of civilization,
be more frequently driven, when placed in a similar
plight.   Accustomed to nourish their patriotism on
hopes of peace, justice, and mercy, they feel only disappointment and dismay when their country takes what
they regard as a backward step.   The excitations to war,
which awaken what the multitudes call patriotism, put
their love of country to the severest strain.   Nowhere
shall we find a more vivid account of the moral distress
which the minority have to endure when their country,
against their principles, goes to arms, than the one
Wordsworth wrote in the tenth book of " The Prelude ":

> Oh ! much have they to account for, who could tear
> By violence, at one decisive rent,
> From the best youth in England their dear pride,
> Their joy, in England.*

And this, too, he says, at a time

> In which apostasy from ancient faith
> Seemed but conversion to a higher creed.

As news came from France, bad enough in itself, and
always rendered more fearful in the telling, his spirits
drooped, and he was obliged to use all his philosophy to
maintain the wider outlook.   How much easier it would
have been to accept the popular and national prejudice,
to admit that his hopes in man had been vain, to let his
heart beat with the fever of warlike passion !   The
early months of 1793 brought almost nothing but dis-

* " Prelude," X. 299.

heartening stories. After the expulsion of his friends, the Girondists, from the Convention, accounts of their arrest, one by one, reached him either through the newspapers or through private letters. He must have shared the view of all competent French observers, that the Jacobins derived their direful power from public fear of the coalition. Thus he must have held England in part responsible for their atrocities. Deep as was his horror for the fanatics in Paris, he hated bitterly the foreign enemies of France:

> It was a lamentable time for man,
> Whether a hope had e'er been his or not;
> A woeful time for them whose hopes survived
> The shock; most woeful for those few who still
> Were flattered, and had trust in human kind:
> They had the deepest feeling of the grief.
> Meanwhile the Invaders fared as they deserved:
> The Herculean Commonwealth had put forth her arms,
> And throttled with an infant godhead's might
> The snakes about her cradle; that was well,
> And as it should be; yet no cure for them
> Whose souls were sick with pain of what would be
> Hereafter brought in charge against mankind.*

At this point we have to consider a startling suggestion. It is possible, and, indeed, from all evidence now accessible it is probable, that Wordsworth returned to Paris in the autumn of 1793. What courage, audacity, skill, and cunning such an act must have required! Motives for it are not far to seek. His conscience and his natural affections drove him to respond to the touching appeals of Annette, and he may have still entertained the fond hope of adding his efforts to those of the moderate Revolutionists and thus helping to save " the good old cause." The facts, if this attractive conjecture is true at all, would be somewhat as follows. Annette had been begging him to return and marry her, writing as if she fully expected him to do so and knew that he was making plans to come, though at the same time forgiving his delay because the danger of

---

* His satisfaction in the defeat of the Allies continued at least till 1805, when the tenth book of " The Prelude " was written, and he never afterwards saw fit to alter these words.

being arrested as a spy was very great.* The war
between England and the French republic had begun
in a hesitating manner, and communications between the
two countries were not yet closed.   Letters occasionally
got through, and there are many instances of British
subjects entering France and remaining there in 1793.
On May 31 the Girondists or moderate deputies were
expelled from the Convention by the Jacobins.   Many
of them, escaping from Paris to Western Normandy,
became the centre of an insurrection against these
extremists.   The insurgent forces held part of the sea-
coast and established secret connections with the British.
By the end of August it was possible, however perilous,
for an Englishman who spoke French well and was
acquainted with some of the Girondist leaders to land
near Caen and proceed through the loosely drawn lines
of the two factional armies to Paris.   We find Wordsworth hovering around Portsmouth late in the summer
with a rich and generous young friend, William Calvert,
and although he made an excursion into the valley of
the Wye and his sister expected him to visit his old
comrade Jones in North Wales, he may have returned to
Portsmouth and crossed to France, having been provided
with money by Calvert.   Arriving in Paris, he would
find the political situation much worse than it was nine
months before.   Of his Girondist friends, some had fled,
others were in prison.   Then, rather than in the preceding year, would he have had those night fears which he
describes in lines 63-93 already quoted from Book X.
of " The Prelude."   Finding that he faced almost inevitable death by remaining in Paris, being unable to
reach Blois, and having witnessed the horrid spectacle
of an execution on October 7, when the head of Gorsas,
one of the Girondist deputies, fell on the scaffold, Wordsworth made his way home, baffled in his bold adventure.
    The main piece of positive evidence that this episode

* See " William Wordsworth and Annette Vallon," by Émile Legouis,
1922, especially pages 124-133, which contain letters from Annette to both
William and Dorothy, written in March, 1793, and intercepted by the
French police.

actually occurred is a statement by Thomas Carlyle in
his " Reminiscences," that Wordsworth, in 1840, told
him he had witnessed the execution of Gorsas.   Negative
evidence in favour of belief is the absence of any record
to show that Wordsworth was in England or Wales in
the autumn of that year.

His sufferings after this vain but gallant attempt were
intense and protracted.   His days were melancholy,
his nights miserable.   For months and years after that
fatal summer and autumn he rarely slept without seeing
horrible visions, of victims on the scaffold and of dungeons
" where the dust was laid with tears."   In his dreams
he was entangled in long orations, striving to clear himself before unjust tribunals, and treacherously deserted.
The stage of these horrid scenes was familiar to him.
He had known some of the actors.   His hallucinations
were echoes of the dreadful nights he had spent in
Paris, not, one feels, in the comparatively safe and
hope-inspiring months of November and December,
1792, but during the Terror.   The gentle forms of
nature had won his worship in boyhood.   Now pity
and sorrow, the handmaids of his second love, the love
of man, exacted a " different ritual "—tears and groans
and ghastly dreams.   For consolation there came to him,
he reverently dared to think, something like the spirit
that must have supported the ancient prophets when
they denounced the doom of God upon a guilty city.
It was the thought that nature was not to blame, that
the ideals of democracy were not to blame:

> When a taunt
> Was taken up by scoffers in their pride,
> Saying, " Behold the harvest that we reap
> From popular government and equality,"
> I clearly saw that neither these nor aught
> Of wild belief engrafted on their names
> By false philosophy had caused the woe,
> But a terrific reservoir of guilt
> And ignorance filled up from age to age,
> That could no longer hold its loathsome charge,
> But burst and spread in deluge through the land.*

* " Prelude," X. 469.

Thus unshaken in the citadel of his faith, though sorely harassed in the outworks of social relations and practical life, he came through that most trying year.

He was not by any means the only person in England who was perplexed by the conflict of loyalties.   Many were afflicted, though none perhaps so acutely as he was, partly because of his fine sensibilities, and partly because he had left his heart behind in France.   History has scarcely done justice to the depth and extent of the moral support which the Revolutionary movement received in Great Britain between the opening of the American War and the proclamation of the French Empire in 1804, and especially between 1789 and 1794. Lost causes are too soon forgotten, though sometimes the strongest threads in the web of life are those that lie unseen below the surface.   There can hardly be any doubt now that at the opening of the war with France Englishmen of finest sympathies and clearest reason were for the most part opposed to the action of their Government.   Some were theoretical republicans, others merely liberal, others opposed to war on any account. It is not surprising that popular prejudice in war-time nicknamed them all Jacobins.

Wordsworth's connection with the English " Jacobins," with the most extreme element opposed to the war and actively agitating in favour of making England a republic, was much closer than has been generally admitted.   In the first place, he appears to have associated himself very soon after his return from France with other young men of radical opinions.   We have a hint of this in " The Prelude," when, referring to the declaration of war, he says:

> Not in my single self alone I found,
> But in the minds of all ingenuous youth,
> Change and subversion from that hour.

It is not without significance that " An Evening Walk " and " Descriptive Sketches " should have been printed for Joseph Johnson.   He was the publisher of Dr. Priestley, Horne Tooke, and Mary Wollstonecraft.   His shop was a favourite meeting-place of republicans and free-thinkers. Paine and Godwin frequented it, and so, for a time, did William Blake, though his religious persuasions were of a very different nature from theirs. Johnson published *The Analytical Review*, which had been founded in 1788. He was hospitable and generous, a man of broad literary culture and philanthropic views. Wordsworth almost certainly met Godwin and Horne Tooke at Johnson's table or in his shop.

Nothing outside of " The Prelude " throws more light on Wordsworth's character and the convictions of his early manhood than a paper he wrote in reply to an attack upon the principles of the French Revolution, by a celebrated Church dignitary, Richard Watson, Bishop of Llandaff. Early in 1793 this interesting and versatile man published a sermon he had preached a long while before, on " The Wisdom and Goodness of God in having made both Rich and Poor," drawing consolation—for the rich—from the text: " The rich and poor meet together; the Lord is the Maker of them all." He had been moved to prescribe this anodyne to the sufferings of the people because he observed a spirit of unrest among them and of unwillingness to engage in a war, the burden of which would, as usual, fall most heavily upon the labouring class. Without exhibiting so much romantic sensibility at the execution of Louis XVI. as Burke displayed, he still was shocked at that event, and, writing a political appendix to his sermon, dated four days after the fatal 21st of January, had them printed together. The appendix is a defence of the British Constitution, with strictures on French affairs.

The chief points in the Bishop's exhortation are as follows: He declares that a republic is of all forms of government the one he most dislikes, because it is most oppressive to the bulk of the people, who live in it under the tyranny of their equals. He is shocked beyond coherent utterance by the execution of a king. He maintains that the greatest freedom that can be enjoyed by man in a state of civil society is afforded to every individual by the British Constitution. He argues, on grounds of expedience, in favour of monarchy. He defends aristocratic institutions. He deprecates the use of the Press " when employed to infuse into the minds of the lowest orders of the community disparaging ideas concerning the constitution of their country." Failing utterly to perceive that the doctrine of equality means equality of opportunity and absence of privilege, and not merely equality before the law, he wanders off into platitudes about equal division of land, the poor laws, and the charity of the rich. The poor are not so very badly off, he thinks, and there are hospitals, relief funds, etc., which would not exist if all men were on a level.

Wordsworth, who appears to have been acquainted with Bishop Watson's previous character for liberal views, felt the unpleasant inconsistency between that character and the spirit of this pamphlet. Coming home from France full of the importance of the struggle there going on, and impressed with the high principles which animated not only the best, but some of the most extreme and dangerous Revolutionists, he resolved to lose no time before following the example of Beaupuy and " performing the oath of his apostleship." The English in general appeared to him sunk in apathy. If he could not sacrifice himself with his Girondist friends in France, he could at least join the little band of English martyrs. He wrote a long reply to Bishop Watson, which was not printed till 1876. I doubt if he even sent a copy of it to the Bishop, who makes no mention of it in his " Anecdotes." The manuscript is carefully written in Wordsworth's own hand, and the title he prefixed to it is, " A Letter to the Bishop of Llandaff on the Extraordinary Avowal of his Political Opinions, contained in the Appendix to his late Sermon: by a Republican." There is no date. Considering that it was written by a young man of twenty-three, or even making no such allowance, this tract deserves to rank with the writings of Burke, Paine, and Mackintosh, as one of the most philosophical treatises occasioned in England by the Revolutionary movement. It goes as far below the surface of human nature as Burke's " Reflections," and is only less eloquent than that great work. " The Age of Reason " is scarcely more pungent and audacious, and Mackintosh's " Vindiciæ Gallicæ " is far less vigorous. From the point of view of immediate public benefit, it is a pity it was not printed and widely circulated as a counterblast, not only to Bishop Watson, but to Burke. What the effect upon Wordsworth's career of such an overt step would have been may be easily conjectured. The slow ripening of the next ten years would have been rendered impossible. He would have been hurried by the pressure of outside opinion into positions from which he could hardly have retired by the aid of reason and feeling alone. The violence of his passionate nature would have been let loose. His reserve would have been broken, his pride offended, his independence lost.

The young author avows that his spirit will not meet with the Bishop's approval, " for it is a republican spirit." He confesses that he is little touched by the death of Louis XVI., of whose guilt he is fully persuaded. In stern and judicial terms, which contrast boldly with the misplaced pathos of Burke, he says : " At a period big with the fate of the human race I am sorry that you attach so much importance to the personal sufferings of the late royal martyr, and that an anxiety for the issue of the present convulsions should not have prevented you from joining in the idle cry of modish lamentation which has resounded from the Court to the cottage." He himself regrets that sombre event only because it took place without regular legal process, and because the poor King, by the nature of his unnatural position above other men, had been " precluded from attaining even a moderate knowledge of common life, and from feeling a particular share in the interests of mankind. . . . Any other sorrow for the death of Louis is irrational and weak." He even excuses, or explains, the other executions which had shocked Watson, by asserting that Liberty is unfortunately " obliged to borrow the very arms of Despotism to overthrow him, and, in order

to reign in peace, must establish herself by violence."
" She deplores such stern necessity," he continues, in a
sentence which might have been borrowed from Robespierre, " but the safety of the people, her supreme law,
is her consolation."

He defends the appropriation of Church property by
the French nation, charging the higher clergy with vice,
jobbery, and hypocrisy. Then, beginning to argue on
the main subject, the superiority of an equalitarian
republic over a monarchy and a system of privilege, he
indulges in much strong and sarcastic language. Curiously modern is his exposition of the principles of the
referendum, but his distrust of long terms of office
brings us back to the eighteenth century. He attacks
the British penal code, pleads in favour of giving much
executive power to the legislature, condemns the hereditary principle, and, in a sentence which might be taken
as a summary of Shakespeare's English history-plays,
declares : " The office of kings is a trial to which human
virtue is not equal."   A legislator, he says, being aware
" that the extremes of poverty and riches have a necessary tendency to corrupt the human heart, will banish
from his code all laws such as the unnatural monster of
primogeniture," and such as encourage associations
against labour, and, indeed, all monopolies and distinctions unfavourable to the poor. He makes the very
keen observation that law-makers " have unjustly left
unprotected that most important part of property, not
less real because it has no material existence, that
which ought to enable the labourer to provide food for
himself and his family."   He calls for " wise and salutary
regulations cour.teracting that inequality among mankind which proceeds from the present *fixed* dispropor-
tion of their possessions."   He objects to nobility on
several grounds, one of which is that " it has a necessary
tendency to dishonour labour."   He advocates manhood franchise, declaring that " if there is a single man
in Great Britain who has no suffrage in the election of a
representative, the will of the society of which he is a
member is not generally expressed ; he is a Helot in

that society." He attacks Burke for endeavouring to
rivet the present to a dead past. He rallies the Bishop
on having deserted the cause of parliamentary reform,
and charges him in terrible indignation with having " no
wish to dispel an infatuation which is now giving up to
the sword so large a portion of the poor, and consigning
the rest to the more slow and painful consumption of
want." The letter ends abruptly, in the middle of a
sentence.

In trying to decide which of the two controversialists
has the better of the argument, much will, of course,
depend upon the reader's point of view. Watson's
opinions are sober, not to say stale. They are those of a
man who looks backward rather than forward. What
has been and is, will probably continue. He is a pessi-
mist when he regards human nature, an optimist when
he estimates human institutions. Wordsworth, on the
other hand, looks at things in precisely the opposite
way. With him, as with all revolutionists, the salient
and blessed fact in life is the possibility of indefinite
progress. Light breaks upon him out of the future,
and he turns his face cheerfully towards the light. In
comparison with the infinite aptitudes of man, the
pregnant powers of his divine nature, how fragmentary
and imperfect are his laws, his social order, and all his
works! There is nothing sacred about institutions
except their value to living men; but man is sacred. It
is absurd to trace this faith to Rousseau, as if it had
never been held before he uttered it. No general advance in civilization has been made except in the
strength it confers. It springs in every healthy young
heart. And Wordsworth's noble pamphlet, in its
buoyant eloquence, its fearless logic, its trust in the
supremacy of goodness, is splendidly youthful. One
would rather live in his ideal world than in the ideal
world of his antagonist. And one would rather be the
writer of his burning plea for a forlorn hope than the
staid and disillusioned apologist of the British Constitution. Wordsworth never wrote anything more creditable to his heart, and, except Burke's " Reflections,"

the literature of the time furnishes no other treatise at once so lively, so acute, and so profound.

It is no wonder Wordsworth's family rejected him. To his uncles it was plain that he shared the views of infidels and traitors. Priestley, Price, and Paine, were the bugbears of " well-disposed " people, who then, as ever, made no mistake in associating orthodox standards of religion with safe and settled political principles. No historical work gives a strong enough description of the struggle then going on in England; but from the pages of reviews, such as *The Gentleman's Magazine*, it is possible to realize how wide apart the two sides were, and how extremely critical was the situation. The Revolutionists were able and active, though relatively not numerous, of course. Their opponents, with the example of France before their eyes, watched them at every turn.

CHAPTER VII

PHILANTHROPIC PLANS

FORTUNATELY for the young poet's artistic development, "Descriptive Sketches" and "An Evening Walk" were unfavourably criticized. Few persons except his sister and his still undiscovered friend Samuel Taylor Coleridge took the trouble to read them, and still fewer liked them. Their unnatural diction and contorted syntax, their affectations and absurdities, were too much even for the perverted taste of that age, while the honest attempts at originality which Coleridge perceived in them were regarded by others as ridiculous. Partly in consequence of adverse criticism, but much more because the change in his social philosophy demanded a corresponding change of artistic method, Wordsworth's style now underwent a complete and momentous transformation. The result is perceptible in "Guilt and Sorrow," a poem which dates chiefly from 1793 and 1794. Some of it— a part, that is, of the Female Vagrant's story—was composed at least two years earlier. The whole, which was completed before the close of 1794, although not published until 1842, seems not to have been much altered. "The Female Vagrant," corresponding to thirty of the seventy-four stanzas which the entire work contains, was published in "Lyrical Ballads" in 1798.

"Guilt and Sorrow" is in almost every respect a great advance over "An Evening Walk" and "Descriptive Sketches." The poet turns from the description of nature, in which he had not excelled Thomson or equalled Cowper, and attempts the more difficult work of narration. The story is entirely of his own invention or discovery. It did not come to him recommended by tradition or romantic glamour. He increases the difficulty of telling it by employing the Spenserian stanza, thus multiplying rhymes and imposing on himself the task of keeping up the interest and movement of the whole tale while preserving the metrical unity of every nine lines. Notwithstanding his use of this highly artificial measure, whose associations suggest loose sentence-structure and the extreme of poetic licence, he has avoided both. The language is plain, the liberties taken are few and innocent, as compared with his previously published poems. The most noticeable improvement is in the diction. There are almost no inappropriate words, almost none of the terms exclusively employed in verse. It is very important to observe that, before he had ever seen Coleridge, conjointly with whom he formulated his theory of poetic diction, and from whom he received welcome encouragement, Wordsworth was already employing the language of everyday life in narrative poetry. Nor is there anything to indicate that he had in mind the examples of Cowper and Crabbe.

As might have been expected from the general direction of his thoughts, the poem deals with humble life. So, indeed, did the earlier ones, whenever human figures appeared in them; but here it is not healthy mountaineers and happy milkmaids, enlivening the scene in harmony with beautiful nature. We have, instead, the victims of social wrong, outcasts from the world, sunk in fortune below the level of contented poverty. Moreover, Wordsworth's immediate preoccupation with the political questions of the day gives the poem its aim and force. It is, in its way, as truly a tract for the times as his Reply to Bishop Watson. The ravages of war among the poor, raising prices, unsettling employment, causing the horrors of forced conscription, with the breaking up of families and impelling of innocent people towards legalized murder, are portrayed in a startling light. There is no relief, no suggestion that the glory of England or the elevation of great captains furnishes compensation for these wars. The evil is probed unflinchingly. It is not fair to say, as some have said, that the young poet hugged his grief because he had at this time an unwholesome fondness for melancholy. It rather seems that he wrote as he did for the noble reason that his mind was filled with sorrow for others, that he had no thought of self, that he was not blinded by false appearances of national splendour, and that he knew where to look for wider and vastly more important interests. Following the lead of his first biographer, students of his life have too generally spoken of the sombre mood out of which this poem grew as something to be regretted, or at least condoned. He never was more truly a poet in the sense of having a prophetic insight into the life of his times and marking out the course of progress, than when he perceived the need of equality and the absolutely unmitigated evil of war. It is to be noticed also that in this poem poor and uneducated persons are represented naturally. They are the objects neither of sentimental affectation nor of contemptuous caricature. They do not speak in dialect, but in plain English. Their emotions are not represented as the peculiar passions of a class, but as human feelings. Above all, they preserve their dignity. Not their poverty and lack of education was what he saw in them, but qualities of mind and heart which are all the more admirable because they withstand every disadvantage. This remained Wordsworth's permanent attitude, and is throughout one of the great distinctions of his poetry.

Some of the incidents of " Guilt and Sorrow," particularly the story of the soldier's widow, had been narrated to him years before by a woman who had suffered as she suffers. The rest had suggested itself to him as he rambled over Salisbury Plain after separating from Calvert. The sight of Stonehenge had made him think of the horrors of war in pagan times, and reflect how awful they are still, and how they fall more upon the poor than upon others. A summary of the poem would fail to reproduce its intense earnestness, its simplicity, and tragic power. In execution no less than in design, it is immeasurably above the rank of *juvenilia* in which it was once classified, and its value is strikingly

enhanced for him who reads it soon after reading the
Reply to Bishop Watson.   Two lines at least have become
celebrated—those in which the unhappy woman, after
losing her husband and children in America during the
War of Independence, and returning to England in
destitution, cries:

> And homeless near a thousand homes I stood,
> And near a thousand tables pined and wanted food.

The political situation in 1793 and 1794, because it
was due to the conflict between two philosophies, which
themselves grew out of two permanent aspects of human
nature, continued to absorb Wordsworth's interest, pre-
venting him from fixing himself in any profession.   No
similar crisis has affected England since, and to find a
parallel we must go back to the middle of the seven-
teenth century.   Without some conception of its mag-
nitude, we shall utterly fail to understand the course of
our poet's outer life, and still more the current of his
deepest opinions and feelings.   To perceive how intense
was the passion, it is not enough to read the speeches
of Pitt and Burke's " Reflections," with the replies made
by their most eminent antagonists, by Fox and Sheridan,
by Mackintosh and Erskine.   It is not enough to study
Godwin's " Political Justice " and Paine's " Rights of
Man."   It is necessary also to know how extensive was
the small-fire amid the crash of this big artillery.   The
Press teemed with sermons and pamphlets for and
against the French Revolution, the doctrine of innate
rights, the theory of equality, the plea for a reform of
the British Constitution.   Several societies existed for
propagating radical views, and at least one for combating them.   The public ferment was widespread.   A
small but not inconsiderable number in England and
Scotland persisted in demanding reforms in spite of the
reflected odium cast upon all advocates of change by
the unhappy condition of France.   As is usually the
case, this movement was confined almost entirely to the
more enlightened class of artisans and to professional
men—in other words, to persons who depended more

than others upon their own faculties. They were for
the most part Dissenters, and of course Whigs. The
Whig party in the House of Commons was very small,
seldom mustering on a division more than sixty votes.
Fox and Sheridan, Whitbread, Grey, and Wilberforce,
were among its most prominent leaders.

Three elements were mingled in the public panic, as
doubtless they were also mingled in the efforts of " seditious persons." These were political theory, economic
theory, and religious belief. Sympathy with France
was considered to imply disloyalty, a levelling tendency,
and infidelity to the Christian religion. From Burke
himself down to the lowest informer this view was held
or professed by nearly all the friends of King, Property,
and Church. " The property of France does not govern
it," was said by Burke in condemnation of that country.

" The body of the people," he declared, " must not
find the principles of natural subordination by art rooted
out of their minds. They must respect that property
of which they must not partake. They must labour to
obtain what by labour can be obtained; and when they
find, as they commonly do, the success disproportioned
to the endeavour, they must be taught their consolation
in the final proportions of eternal justice. Of this consolation whoever deprives them deadens their industry
and strikes at the root of all acquisition, as of all consolation."

Whether this discouraging conclusion, to which his
attachment to established order brought even so humane
a man as Burke, be necessary or not, we can be sure that
the young author of " Guilt and Sorrow " must have
read it with vehement disapproval. Fortunately, he
had gone too far to be caught by the inhuman and
blasphemous use of theology in support of oppressive
institutions implied in this reference to " eternal justice."

It seemed futile for the friends of any reform to
struggle against a public alarmed by fears of plots, or
against a majority in Parliament who were more or less
eager for war. Fox's motion for repeal of the Test and
Corporation Acts, imposing political and social disabili-

ties on Dissenters, was lost in 1790, and the number of his supporters fell from 105 on that occasion, to 63 when he brought in a similar measure two years later. Pitt and Burke, who had once been friends of electoral reform, now thought such subjects inopportune. The Habeas Corpus Act was suspended. Barracks were erected all over the country. Spies and informers were employed by Government. The army and navy were enormously increased. Prices went up. Poverty and unemployment were appalling. The only gleam of comfort was the abolition of the slave-trade, which was at length carried by Wilberforce, Fox, and their friends, against stolid opposition. Speakers and writers on the Tory side, and advocates in courts of law, openly professed that the British Constitution did not admit of representative government, and that men of wealth alone should have the suffrage.

To anticipate a little, the suspicion of Government and the panic of the great majority of the people in England and Scotland resulted at last in the arraignment, on the charge of high-treason, of Thomas Hardy, John Horne Tooke, a preacher and politician, Thomas Holcroft, a dramatist, John Thelwall, a professional agitator, and five other persons. Their cases were practically disposed of with the acquittal of Hardy on November 5, 1794, and of Horne Tooke shortly afterwards. The prisoners were defended by Thomas Erskine, whose speeches did much to counteract the alarmist tendencies fostered by those who favoured the war. The strength of the opposition was shown to be much greater than men supposed, by the widespread sympathy manifested for the prisoners, and by the vast crowds that welcomed them on their release. There can be no doubt now that a very considerable number of British subjects were on their side, ranging all the way from extreme revolutionists to moderate reformers, and it is evident that the opinions of this body cannot justly be all traced to Thomas Paine and Rousseau. They were much too diversified, and many of them too natural and inevitable, to be thus narrowed down. Some of them,

indeed, flow, and have always flowed, as an undercur-
rent, among the less happy and privileged elements of
every community, or among its most enlightened members. History tends to overlook or misjudge movements which do not appear to have a successful issue,
but minority reports often represent views the most
just and the most brave. The trials of Hardy, Horne
Tooke, Thelwall, and their fellows, were the culminating
point of the anti-Jacobin panic. Holcroft, as we shall
see, became soon afterwards, if indeed he was not at
that time, an acquaintance of Wordsworth and Coleridge, and with Thelwall they were later on terms of
considerable intimacy.

Meanwhile, it appears that lack of means prevented
Wordsworth from returning to the intellectual excitement of London, and lack of an invitation kept him
away from Forncett. In a letter to William Mathews,
which is dated February 17 [1794] he gives his address
as " Mr. Rawson's, Mill-house, near Halifax." " I am
now staying," he says, " with a gentleman who married
a relation of mine [his cousin, Miss Threlkeld], with
whom my sister was brought up." And then follows the
momentous statement which marks an epoch in his
life and Dorothy's, the beginning of many happy years :
" My sister is under the same roof with me, and, indeed,
it was to see her that I came into this country." The
hope long deferred had been realized at last. Their
meeting at Halifax had been like the objective of a long
campaign. How many plans, how many sacrifices, how
many delays, had preceded this reunion ! Three long
years had passed since their last meeting, in the Christmas holidays of 1790-91. His only home was in her
heart. Travel, independence, battling with the strong
and dangerous currents of the world's life, had left him
unsatisfied. Her faithful soul had been kept alive
chiefly by hope that this day might come. Her quick
apprehension, her genius for observing nature and the
little events of life, her rare fidelity of expression, these
qualities in which she was surpassed by no woman of
her time, wanted purpose and outlet until then; and it

is plain that, although he might have deepened the line he had already chosen and become a great reflective poet, a master of earnest satire, he would never, without the daily companionship of his sister, have found that " joy in widest commonalty spread " which is the life-blood of his poetry. They were never again separated for more than a few weeks at a time until his death.

But though this great step towards a settlement had been taken, Wordsworth was still far from having found a means of livelihood. " I have done nothing," he writes, " and still continue to do nothing. What is to become of me I know not. I cannot bow down my mind to take orders; and as for the law, I have neither strength of mind, purse, or constitution to engage in that pursuit." He renounces the idea of taking his Master of Arts degree, as being too expensive. He inquires of Mathews, who is travelling in Mediterranean countries, whether " the principles of free government have any advocates in Portugal; or is Liberty a sound, of which they have never heard ?" He says he has read no Spanish for three years, and little Italian, but of French he esteems himself a tolerable master. " My Italian studies," he says, " I am going to resume immediately, as it is my intention to instruct my sister in that language."

Richard Wordsworth, their father's elder brother, was collector of the port of Whitehaven, and thither, after a long visit together near Halifax, the happy pair travelled by coach. The distance is about one hundred miles. How long they remained there is not known, but it appears that William Calvert offered them rooms in a farmhouse, called Windy Brow, belonging to him, near Keswick. It stood on the southern side of Latrigg, a steep hill that rises from the River Greta, and commanded a comprehensive view of Derwentwater and the mountains that encircle both lake and town. They entered the district by way of Kendal.

" I walked," writes Dorothy triumphantly, " with my brother at my side, from Kendal to Grasmere eighteen miles, and afterwards from Grasmere to Kes-

wick, fifteen miles, through the most delightful country
that was ever seen. We are now at a farm-house, about
half a mile from Keswick. When I came, I intended to
stay only a few days; but the country is so delightful,
and, above all, I have so full an enjoyment of my
brother's company, that I have determined to stay a
few weeks longer. After I leave Windy Brow, I shall
proceed to Whitehaven."

In an undated letter to Miss Pollard, she dilates on
the beauty of the landscape and the good manners and
good sense of the tenant-farming family that occupied
Windy Brow. She still exults in her new-found freedom, and is determined it shall last as long as possible:

" You would hear from my aunt of my wonderful
powers in the way of walking, and of my safe arrival at
Grasmere. At Keswick I still remain. I have been so
much delighted with the people of this house, with its
situation, with the cheapness of living, and above all
with the opportunity which I have of enjoying my
brother's company, that, although on my arrival I only
talked of staying a few days, I have already been here
above a fortnight, and intend staying still a few weeks
longer, perhaps three or four. . . . We have a neat
parlour to ourselves which Mr. Calvert has fitted up
for his own use, and the lodging-rooms are very comfortable. Till my brother gets some employment he
will lodge here. Mr. Calvert is not now at Windy Brow,
as you will suppose. We please ourselves in calculating
from our present expenses for how very small a sum we
could live. We find our own food. Our breakfast and
supper are of milk, and our dinner chiefly of potatoes,
and we drink no tea."

But her aunt, Mrs. Crackanthorpe, of Newbiggin,
had views of her own, which were also the views of the
world, or the elderly and respectable part of the world,
as to the propriety of living gipsy-fashion. Long walks,
indeed, and spending several weeks in a farmhouse belonging to the young and wealthy Mr. Calvert ! She
communicated these ideas, and apparently in rather
pungent terms, to her niece, counting perhaps on the
submissiveness which had perforce been shown hitherto

by that young lady.   But the same spirit that prompted
the Reply to Bishop Watson flames up in Dorothy's
answer of April 21, 1794, and it is quite likely that her
independence was charged against the French or Tom
Paine and the Americans.   She takes refuge proudly
under the shadow of her brother's name:

" I affirm that I consider the character and virtues of
my brother as sufficient protection; and besides I am
convinced that there is no place in the world in which
a good and virtuous young woman would be more likely
to continue good and virtuous than under the roof of
these honest, worthy, uncorrupted people: so that any
guardianship beyond theirs I should think altogether
unnecessary.   I cannot pass unnoticed that part of your
letter in which you speak of my ' rambling about the
country on foot.'   So far from considering this as a
matter of condemnation, I rather thought it would have
given my friends pleasure to hear that I had courage to
make use of the strength with which nature has endowed me, when it not only procured me infinitely more
pleasure than I should have received from sitting in a
post chaise, but was also the means of saving me at
least thirty shillings."

She mentions as her greatest inducement the society
of her brother:

" I am now twenty-two years of age, and such have
been the circumstances of my life that I may be said to
have enjoyed his company only for a very few months.
An opportunity now presents itself of obtaining this
satisfaction, an opportunity which I could not see pass
from me without unspeakable pain.   I have regained
all the knowledge I had of the French language some
years ago, and have added considerably to it.   I have
now begun Italian, of which I expect to have soon
gained a sufficient knowledge to receive much entertainment and advantage from it."

She accepts the invitation of her aunt and uncle to
visit them on her return from Whitehaven.

The beautiful poem " Louisa " and the lines " To a
Young Lady who had been Reproached for taking Long
Walks in the Country " may well have been composed

at this time, and the latter in consequence of Mrs. Crackanthorpe's admonition.   It is well known that Wordsworth in a number of poems addressed his sister under other names than her own.   " Dear Child of Nature, let them rail !" is appropriate to her and to the occasion.   Later, when she was definitely settled in life with him, there could have been no one who would feel authorized to " reproach " her.   Wordsworth, in extreme old age, gave an inconsistent account of the dates of both poems, attributing them to 1803 and to 1805, and saying that they were " composed at the same time and on the same view."   Yet the second of them was printed in *The Morning Post* newspaper on February 12, 1802.   Moreover, the expression " Lapland night " is one which he used in a letter in 1791.   The internal connection between the two poems was once closer than it now appears to be.   When " Louisa " was first revised, in the edition of 1836, it began :

> Though by a sickly taste betrayed,
> Some will dispraise the lovely Maid,
> With fearless pride I say ;

though this reading disappeared in the edition of 1845. One is almost persuaded that this was an allusion to Mrs. Crackanthorpe's sense of propriety.   All other editions give a very different reading.   Curiously enough, the peculiar form of stanza used in these two poems is the same as that of " Three years she grew in sun and shower "; and what was printed as the second stanza of " Louisa," in the editions from 1807 to 1843, looks as if it had originally belonged to this lovely nameless piece, which the poet printed as having been composed in the Harz Forest in 1799.   It reads :

> And she hath smiles to earth unknown ;
> Smiles that with motion of their own
> Do spread, and sink, and rise ;
> That come and go with endless play,
> And ever, as they pass away,
> Are hidden in her eyes.

It is a metre the poet rarely used.   One stanza of his translation of the Vicomte de Ségur's French Verses,

1795, the pieces mentioned, " Ruth," 1799, one stanza
of " The Waterfall and the Eglantine," 1800, and six
other poems scattered along between 1814 and 1831,
are the only instances. All these facts incline me to
think that the verses " Louisa " and " To a Young
Lady " were composed long before 1802. Whether
they affect the date and subject of " Three years she
grew " is another matter.

Four long letters from Wordsworth in the North to
William Mathews in London, written at long intervals
between May 23, 1794, and January 10, 1795, present
him in a new and rather surprising light. To no other
correspondent, so far as we know, did he ever write with
so little reserve. The subject this time is a plan of
editing a magazine in the Metropolis, or, in case that
cannot be done, of finding a place on some newspaper.
He is afraid of venturing to London, on account of the
expense. He thinks of remaining in the North and
sending his contributions by post. Mathews and another
young man are to attend to the business in town.
Wordsworth himself, and Mathews, too, as he supposes,
are too poor to advance any money towards carrying
out the scheme, but perhaps this might be got over, he
boyishly says, if they could be sure of the patronage of
the public. He wishes Mathews distinctly to understand what his political sentiments are, as the plan
cannot proceed unless the editors agree on this subject.
In such a work as they have in mind, " it will be
impossible not to inculcate principles of government
and forms of social order of one kind or another."
His confession of political faith is brief and unequi-
vocal :

" I solemnly affirm that in no writings of mine will I
ever admit of any sentiments which can have the least
tendency to induce my readers to suppose that the
doctrines which are now enforced by banishment, im-
prisonment, etc., etc., are other than pregnant with
every species of misery. You know perhaps already
that I am of that odious class of men called democrats,
and of that class I shall for ever continue."

He proposes to contribute essays on Morals and Politics, besides critical remarks upon Poetry, Painting, Gardening, " and other subjects of amusement." He declares that all the periodicals with which he is acquainted, except one or two, " appear to be written to maintain the existence of prejudice and to disseminate error," and to such purposes he will not prostitute his pen. He has plenty of leisure, and is only correcting and adding to his published poems, which he had " huddled up " and sent imperfect into the world with great reluctance.

" But," he continues, " as I had done nothing by which to distinguish myself at the University, I thought these little things might show that I could do something. They have been treated with unmerited contempt by some of the periodical publications, and others have spoken in higher terms of them than they deserve. I have another poem, written last summer, ready for the press, though I certainly should not publish it unless I hoped to derive from it some pecuniary recompense."

And he begs Mathews to look in at Johnson's, the publisher's, " and ask him if he ever sells any of those poems."

Writing again from Whitehaven in June, he says he has read with great pleasure the explicit avowal of Mathew's " political sentiments," and in return will set forth his own in more detail.

" I disapprove," he declares, " of monarchical and aristocratical governments, however modified. Hereditary distinctions, and privileged orders of every species, I think must necessarily counteract the progress of human improvement: hence it follows that I am not amongst the admirers of the British Constitution."

Two causes are at work, he says, subverting the Constitution: first, the bad conduct of men in power; and second, " the changes of opinion respecting matters of government which within these few years have rapidly taken place in the minds of speculative men." To hasten these changes, he says, " I would give every

additional energy in my power," though he adds: " I
recoil from the bare idea of a Revolution." Then, as
if to give Mathews a specimen of what the country
editor of the proposed magazine was capable of, he rises
heavily to a flight of eloquence in a manner already long
out of fashion. There is a magisterial air in all Wordsworth's prose, except his shortest and most familiar
letters. On more than one occasion the style attains
real majesty. On many others, we must confess, it is
affectedly pompous, owing very likely to the fact that
he was imitating Milton and other seventeenth-century
controversialists. His political programme is vague.
He has hardly got beyond sentiment and declamation.
He mentions no definite reform which he wishes to see
established, except granting complete liberty of the Press.

" On this subject," he concludes, " I think I have
said enough, if it be not necessary to add that, when I
observe the people should be enlightened upon the subject of politics, I severely condemn all inflammatory
addresses to the passions of men, even when it is intended to direct those passions to a good purpose. I
know that the multitude walk in darkness. I would
put into each man's hand a lantern to guide him, and
not have him set out upon his journey depending for
illumination on abortive flashes of lightning or the
coruscations of transitory meteors."

From this dizzy height the young enthusiast descends
to particulars. He proposes as the name of their
periodical, *The Philanthropist, a Monthly Miscellany*,
gravely remarking: " This title, I think, would be
noticed. It includes everything that can instruct and
amuse mankind." He goes on buoyantly to sketch the
several departments of the magazine, insisting that the
pages allotted to verse should be filled from new poetical
publications of merit, and such old ones as are not generally known. As to subscribers, he expresses himself
hopefully, but warns Mathews that " amongst the partisans of this war and of the suspension of the Habeas
Corpus Act, amongst the mighty class of selfish alarm-
ists," they would find no friends. " We must then look

for protection entirely amongst the dispassionate advocates of liberty and discussion." The clergy, he is sure, will turn from them. But from young men at the universities, from Dissenters, and perhaps in Ireland, they will receive support. As to money, he has not a single sixpence to advance, and he must remain in the country. A friend, he says, has offered him a share of his income, which puts him under the obligation of trying to be of some little service to his fellow-men. It was well for him and for his fellow-men to all time that he did not plunge into the soul-consuming trade of journalism. It is interesting, however, that he thought seriously of doing so, and under all his odd verbiage one may easily perceive a brave and enterprising spirit. Boyish zest and manly foresight here meet and mingle strangely. He begs Mathews to answer him " as soon as possible, and at great length." His own letter covers nearly eight printed pages, and ends with the stately assurance: " I am, with great respect and esteem, your fellow-labourer and friend, W. WORDSWORTH."

After such a bold challenge, it is amusing to turn to Wordsworth's letter to Mathews, headed Keswick, November 7, 1794, and read: " The more nearly we approached the time fixed for action, the more strongly was I persuaded that we should decline the field. I was not, therefore, either much surprised or mortified at the contents of your letter." The scheme has been abandoned, and Mathews has taken a position on some London newspaper. Wordsworth wants to know what it is like, with the idea of seeking a similar post. " I begin to wish much to be in Town," he says, and adds very sensibly, " Cataracts and mountains are good occasional society, but they will not do for constant companions." In January, 1795, he takes up again the topic of journalism in London, admitting his total ignorance of what qualifications are required. He is sure he could not make a good parliamentary reporter, having neither strength of memory, quickness of penmanship, nor rapidity of composition, and being subject to violent headaches.

" One thing, however, I can boast," he says, " and on that one thing I rely, extreme frugality. . . . You say a newspaper would be glad of me; do you think you could insure me employment in that way on terms similar to your own ? I mean also in an opposition paper, for really I cannot, in conscience and in principle, abet in the smallest degree the measures pursued by the present Ministry."

A little light from another quarter is thrown upon these journalistic projects by a passage in Charles Mathew's " Memoirs." He tells us that his brother added to the income allowed him by his father by contributing to *The Oracle* and *The World*, and for a time was parliamentary reporter to these and other newspapers. Boaden, the enthusiastic admirer and subsequently the biographer of the Kembles, edited *The Oracle*, and Charles Mathews himself was for a little while editor of *The Thespian*, a periodical entirely devoted to the drama.

It is a pity that so little is known about one who evidently was Wordsworth's most intimate friend at this interesting period of his life. Inference based upon only one side of their correspondence enables one to assert, with considerable confidence, that Mathews was a rebel against religious authority, and that community of feeling on this subject was one of the bonds between the young men. They had been contemporaries at Cambridge, they saw something of each other afterwards in London, they both refused to obey the wishes of their families and study for the ministry. A letter from Mathews to his brother, dated Barbados, June 5, 1801, confirms the conjecture that religious independence was a very serious concern with him. He writes:

" . . . Tell Eliza [his brother's wife] from me that I sincerely wish her well in body and mind; but that to secure the latter from disease she must carefully watch that the seeds of superstition, which some one has plentifully sown in her heart, do not bring forth the fruit it generally does, illiberality of sentiment and that worst of all fiends, religious bigotry. The whole history of mankind is but a relation of the fatal and mischievous effects of this diabolical tyrant who has uniformly preyed upon the enlightened few that have dared to lift up their heads against the oppressor of their afflicted brethren, and has gnawed the very vitals of social existence. There is no part of the globe that is not even now groaning beneath her baneful pressure; and whatever form she assumes, she still arrogates to herself the claim of infallibility, and her votaries, of whatever sect they may be, damn by wholesale all the rest of the world. A freedom from superstition is the first blessing we can enjoy. Religion in some shape seems necessary to political existence. The wise man laughs at the follies of the vulgar, and in the pure contemplation of a benevolent Author of all Beings finds that happiness which others in vain look for amid the load of trumpery and ceremonies with which they think the Creator is gratified. If He can be gratified by an exertion of feeble mortals, it must be when they imitate His perfection by mutual benevolence and kindness. That you may long enjoy these blessings is the sincere prayer of your brother and friend, W. MATHEWS."*

Whereupon Charles Mathews's second wife, who edited his " Memoirs," comments as follows:

" With the above remarks the writer's early experience had something to do; and his feelings naturally took alarm at a mistaken tendency, evident to all who knew the amiable person to whom he alludes. Mr. William Mathews had in his boyhood felt the gloom and rigours of fanaticism beneath his father's roof, where he had ceased to reside for some years, although he frequently visited it, and was on the most affectionate terms with all his family, who might be said to idolize him. But in these visits he resisted with all the energies of his strong mind every after-association with the ignorant and illiberal portion of his father's ' brethren.' "

Meanwhile—to be as vague as possible, for the exact time is not known—Wordsworth had found means of being directly serviceable to a fellow-being, and was faithfully performing his duty. His friend William Calvert and a younger brother, Raisley, were sons of the steward of the Duke of Norfolk, who owned a large

* " Memoirs of Charles Mathews."

estate at Greystoke, four miles from Penrith. They
had considerable independent means. William, as we
have seen, owned Windy Brow. It was evidently one
of these brothers, probably the younger, who offered
Wordsworth a share of his income. Raisley was dying
of consumption, and Wordsworth remained with him
to comfort and entertain him, probably all through the
summer and autumn of 1794. On October 1 he wrote
to William Calvert from Keswick, suggesting that by
a little economy the latter might help Raisley to go to
Lisbon for his health, and offering to accompany him.

" Reflecting," he says, " that his return is uncertain,
your brother requests me to inform you that he has
drawn out his will, which he means to get executed in
London. The purport of his will is to leave you all his
property, real and personal, chargeable with a legacy of
£600 to me, in case that on inquiry into the state of our
affairs in London he should think it advisable to do so.
It is at my request that this information is communicated to you, and I have no doubt but that you will do
both him and myself the justice to hear this mark of his
approbation without your good opinion of either of us
being at all diminished by it."

It would appear that inquiry into the affairs of the
Wordsworth heirs showed that their lawsuit against the
Earl of Lonsdale was going badly; for Raisley Calvert,
who died at Penrith in January, 1795, left Wordsworth
£900.

This legacy from a young man who judged highly of
Wordsworth's powers must not only have released him
from the fear of want, but have made him renew his
dedication to that art which thus far had proved almost
too stubborn for him. In a letter to Mathews, written
just before this event, Wordsworth admits that, although
he had had sufficient time on his hands to write a folio
volume, he had been undergoing much uneasiness of
mind. " My poor friend," he says, " is barely alive . . .
but he may linger on for some days." Politics and the
success of Mathews's newspaper appear to have been his
only other interests. His sister had been obliged to leave

him and return to Halifax. But for the dying gift of
Raisley Calvert, bestowed with so much insight, the
cottage they dreamed of might have been still a dream
for many years. Without some degree of independence,
and without the constant society of Dorothy, the years of
fruitfulness could not have come for Wordsworth. The
£900 made an immense difference in his prospects, and
we may well believe that his hope of writing poetry
revived in him at once. The money meant even more
to his sister than to him. Before the summer of 1795
was over, their plans were made. In September she was
still at Millhouse, near Halifax. Where and how her
brother spent his time after the death of Raisley Calvert,
there is very little to show. I believe he returned to
London and remained there trying in vain to write.
In her letter of September 2, 1795, to Jane Pollard, who
by this time had become Mrs. Marshall, Miss Wordsworth,
referring to her brother, says: " Living in the unsettled
way in which he has hitherto lived in London is altogether
unfavourable to mental exertion."

CHAPTER VIII

THE GODWIN CIRCLE

FROM January to September, 1795, Wordsworth is as completely lost to sight as if he had been locked up in Newgate or had returned to France. There is a gap of sixteen months in the published letters of his sister, and of nearly eleven months in his own. This is very strange, for not only had he a large family connection of educated persons, and not only was he already the author of two volumes of verse, but his character was energetic, and his ambitions inclined him towards public life. Yet in passing over this period, almost all that his first biographer remarks is:

" He had a good deal of Stoical pride, mingled with not a little Pelagian self-confidence. Having an inadequate perception of the necessity of divine grace, he placed his hopes where they could not stand; and did not place them where, if placed, they could not fall. He sought for ideal perfectibility where he could not but meet with real frailty, and did not look for peace where alone it could be found."

It is not known where he was or how employed outwardly; but one may safely infer something of his mood and the direction of his thoughts during those veiled months, for when he reappears there is a new firmness in his tone, as of one who has made renunciations, and thereby taken a step towards finding himself. He is confirmed in his disapproval of the war, and his feelings now seem more solidly based on philosophical principles. Sufficient proof of this assertion will be found in " The Borderers," composed in 1795-96, the thirteenth book of " The Prelude," and his letters to Francis Wrangham and Mathews immediately after the long silence. Furthermore, in the " Lines left upon a

179

Seat in a Yew-tree " there is heard a note which is quite rare in Wordsworth's poetry, a note of personal resentment for the world's neglect, its failure to appreciate him and his ideals. Although he told Miss Fenwick that they were composed in part at school at Hawkshead, it is impossible to believe that their actual turn, their indwelling sentiment, and their best qualities, can be traced farther back than 1795. In no other of his early poems do we find a line so characteristic of Wordsworth in his maturity, so certainly indicative of great poetic genius, as the last of these three:

> Yet, if the wind breathe soft, the curling waves,
> That break against the shore, shall lull thy mind
> By one soft impulse saved from vacancy.

None of his poems written before 1795 contains a line equal in magical felicity to

> The stone-chat, or the glancing sand-piper.

To have uttered that particular combination of sounds was to have made a fresh advance in English versification, although, strange to say, Wordsworth changed it in the edition of 1815, thereby drawing a protest from Charles Lamb. The passage of this poem which, under cover of allusion to an imaginary person already dead, is probably autobiographical, and gives us a picture of Wordsworth in 1795, is as follows:

> He was one who owned
> No common soul.   In youth by science nursed,
> And led by nature into a wild scene
> Of lofty hopes, he to the world went forth
> A favoured Being, knowing no desire
> Which genius did not hallow; 'gainst the taint
> Of dissolute tongues, and jealousy, and hate,
> And scorn,—against all enemies prepared,
> All but neglect.   The world, for so it thought,
> Owed him no service; wherefore he at once
> With indignation turned himself away,
> And with the food of pride sustained his soul
> In solitude.

This is no less than an epitome of his life before his reunion with Dorothy and his meeting with Coleridge, the brother of his soul.   The strain is Byronic.   Shelley, too, sounded a like complaint.   Wordsworth was too strong, and also, it must be said, he became too happy, to linger in such a mood.

He rose above it by establishing his life, for a time, upon the principles of William Godwin.   This is a fact which no biographer of the poet has ventured to deny, though many attempts have been made to minimize its importance.   I am acquainted with no account of Wordsworth's life that does justice to the strength and attractiveness of the philosophy upon which he disciplined his powerful reasoning faculties, and to which he gave a brave and stubborn allegiance from his twenty-third to his twenty-ninth year.   When one considers how, in the lives of nearly all poets, the third decade stands preeminent as a formative and productive period, it seems impossible to exaggerate the value of Godwin's ideas to Wordsworth.   And Wordsworth is admitted to be a great philosophical poet.   Yet all his biographers have termed Godwin's system " preposterous."   Wordsworth, even when he renounced it, fully appreciated its compulsive appeal.   And for at least three or four years it claimed both his intellectual assent and his active support.   He went to great lengths.   If Wordsworth had published his Reply to Bishop Watson, he would have been liable to prosecution on a charge of sedition.   It is amazing that Godwin escaped being imprisoned or exiled for his " Enquiry concerning Political Justice."   But books have their fates, and this remarkable treatise has fared ill, for it was from the beginning covered with obloquy, and probably no literary or philosophical work of equal value has been so little read in proportion to its merit.   Such is the force of organized prejudice.   Also, the price was three guineas. The " patriotic " party were not content with crushing the democratic movement; they did their best to smother even the memory of it.   Not only did they promptly check overt acts of a revolutionary tendency; they entered into a century-long conspiracy to suppress a number of noble intellectual works.   Contemptuous disapproval was the means employed, and it succeeded. The share of Godwin's " Political Justice " in the thought of the nineteenth century has been inconsiderable, if we set aside its influence on Wordsworth and Shelley and the Utilitarian school of philosophy. This, however, is no inconsiderable exception.

Wordsworth, in the years we are considering, was a disciple of Godwin. This did not mean the acceptance of his master's political theory alone, but of his system as a whole. Godwin has this much at least in common with Locke, that his philosophy is integral. It is rigorously deduced from a few chief principles. Thus its ethics cannot be held separately from its metaphysics, nor can its politics be detached from its psychology. Although the largest and the soundest part of the " Political Justice " is devoted to ethical and political considerations, which can hardly be distinguished from each other, as it is his dearest purpose to show they should not be, Godwin insists on their dependence on his doctrine of knowledge and will. He is a determinist, and the only weak element of his book is the thinness of his argument for necessity. The many pleas in favour of free-will which suggest themselves even to philosophers, as well as to ordinary thinkers, he almost wholly fails to take into account. Equally dogmatic, though not so audacious, because more widely shared, is his belief that experience is the source of all knowledge. " Nothing can be more incontrovertible," he asserts, " than that we do not bring pre-established ideas into the world with us." Justice, he contends, is the whole duty of man. And it seems that his criterion of justice is the greatest good of the greatest number: " utility, as it regards percipient beings, is the only basis of moral and political truth." Reason is the only organ whereby men can discover what is just : " to a rational being there can," he says, " be but one rule of conduct, justice, and one mode of ascertaining that rule, the exercise of his understanding."

Intuition and every form of mystical illumination, together with all authority, whether of numbers, an-

tiquity, institutions, or " inspired words," are calmly
set aside. Morality is a matter of knowledge: " the
most essential part of virtue consists in the incessantly
seeking to inform ourselves more accurately upon the
subject of utility and right." He affirms these principles unhesitatingly, and as if they must, of course, be
admitted by every thinking person to whom they are
stated separately, each in its own strength. But he
himself supplies in his practical illustrations difficulties
which might not have occurred to a less acute mind,
and which a less honest mind would not have raised.
It was upon these examples that his opponents seized.
For instance, since man is a moral being and all his
actions are either just or unjust, he has no rights—*i.e.*,
no moral options—but only duties. And therefore there
is no place for deeds of gratitude, for pardon, for partiality to friends or kindred, for vindictive punishment.
Moreover, a promise has no sanctity, and an oath is an
abomination; because " an individual surrenders the
best attribute of man the moment he resolves to adhere
to certain fixed principles for reasons not now present
to his mind, but which formerly were." Marriage,
accordingly, falls under his disapproval, in so far as it
is a relation maintained solely in virtue of a promise.
Creeds and similar fixed affirmations of belief lose their
binding power, for, he says, " If I cease from the habit
of being able to recall this evidence [that upon which
the validity of a tenet depends], my belief is no longer a
perception, but a prejudice." Some of these principles
are to be found distinctly echoed in Wordsworth's
" Borderers." Both that tragedy and the slightly
earlier poem " Guilt and Sorrow " indicate that he was
also imbued with Godwin's doctrine that " under the
system of necessity the ideas of guilt, crime, desert, and
accountableness, have no place." Godwin declares that,
since the will is not free, " the assassin cannot help the
murder he commits any more than the dagger." Punishment, therefore, should be limited to restraining the
criminal from repeating his act of injustice.

It is evident that a society holding such views must

reject all but the barest essentials of government. Accordingly, Godwin insists that " government is an evil, an usurpation upon the private judgment and individual conscience of mankind." This would seem to be downright anarchism, and it must be said of Godwin, as Edward Caird said of Rousseau :*

" His method is always determined by the individualistic prejudices of his time. In morals, in politics, and in religion alike, he goes back from the complex to the simple; and for him the simple is always the purely individual, the subject apart from the object, the man apart from society. He does not see that in this way he is gradually emptying consciousness of all its contents, and that of the abstract individual at which he must finally arrive nothing can be said."

But there can be no doubt that much of the constructive thought which found expression in early British Liberalism and in the Constitution of the United States followed this line. To many practical statesmen, as well as to Rousseau and Godwin, it seemed that the sole function of government was to secure liberty of action to the individual. Wordsworth was prepared for Godwin's uncompromising enunciation of this principle by his previous acceptance of Rousseau's doctrine that every individual is by nature independent. Godwin never shrank from rigorous deduction, and uttered his thought as clearly as he conceived it. Stated less dogmatically, the same idea, of course, is latent in the writings of the American Federalists and in Bentham and J. S. Mill. All these political theorists, having an eye to practice, checked themselves halfway. But many Continental writers, of whom Tolstoi is the best known, have gone as far as Godwin. Nor was Godwin himself afraid to be called an anarchist. " Where anarchy," he says, " has slain its hundreds, despotism has sacrificed millions upon millions." And it cannot be said that he had not present in his mind the full meaning of the term when he thus wrote, for " Political

* " Essays on Literature."

Justice " was published in 1793, the preface being dated
January 7 of that year.   It is doubtful whether Wordsworth or many other of Godwin's disciples possessed
enough confidence in abstract reasoning to follow him
to this extreme conclusion.   They gave an eager assent,
however, to the less incisive and more practical statement that government, as actually existing, " reverses
the genuine propensities of mind, and, instead of suffering us to look forward, teaches us to look backward
for perfection; it prompts us to seek the public welfare,
not in innovation and improvement, but in a timid
reverence."   The pure word of the Revolution, a creed
to which the young Wordsworth clung with passionate
fervour, is condensed in a few articles.   They lie more
or less scattered in Godwin's " Enquiry."   The first
concerns prophecy: " To conceive an order of society
totally different from that which is now before our
eyes, and to judge of the advantages that would accrue
from its institution, are the prerogatives only of a few
favoured minds."   The second concerns prerogative:
" They are the higher orders of society that find, or
imagine they find, their advantage in injustice, and are
eager to invent arguments for its defence."   The third
concerns the wisdom of common people: " The vulgar
have no such interest, and submit to the reign of injustice
from habit only and the want of reflection. . . . A
very short period is enough for them to imbibe the sentiments of patriotism and liberty."   The fourth concerns
property: " My neighbour has just as much right to put
an end to my existence with dagger or poison as to deny
me that pecuniary assistance without which I must
starve, or as to deny me that assistance without which
my intellectual attainments or my moral exertions will
be materially injured."   The fifth concerns priests:
" Their prosperity depends upon the reception of particular opinions in the world; they must therefore be
enemies to freedom of inquiry; they must have a bias
upon their minds impressed by something different from
the force of evidence."   Every one of these articles is
affirmed by Wordsworth, either graphically in his early

poems, or dogmatically in his Reply to Bishop Watson, or
by implication in his letters to Mathews.

To say that Godwin was lacking in historical feeling
is putting the case too negatively. It is more correct to
say that he chose not to be hampered by history. He
regarded the present with keen perceptive powers, and
looked to the future. The absence of a background in
his picture of human destiny is not due to shallowness
of literary culture, but to a deliberate theory. He was
one of the last, and certainly the clearest, of the philosophers of the Enlightenment in the eighteenth century.
And his method, as regards the use of history, is precisely the method of that whole great movement.

A peculiarity of his own, however, is that he relies
altogether upon his individual judgment, and not at all
upon the collective judgment of his fellow-men, which
he mistrusts because it has been institutionally organized,
and thus clogged with the weight of selfish advantages.
And even in his own case he trusts, or professes to trust,
only his perceptive and logical powers, and not at all his
affections. He has, however, by no means succeeded
in shutting out every emotional influence. To take
him at his word in this respect is to do him an injustice.
His principles are not cold-drawn. There is no fire
more intense than the flame of pure intelligence. It is
not conceivable that, without the tremor of inward
burning, a man possessed as Godwin was, with a sense
of responsibility, could write: " The doctrine of the
injustice of accumulated property has been the foundation of all religious morality." The philosophy of the
Enlightenment may well have been too difficult, too
sheer, for minds accustomed to beaten tracks in the broad
vales of thought, but it was not wanting in emotional
splendour.

There was an appeal to high-souled youth in his apparently quiet statement: " It is in the nature of things
impossible that the man who has determined with himself never to utter the truths he knows should be an
intrepid and indefatigable thinker. The link that binds
together the inward and the outer man is indissoluble;

and he that is not bold in speech will never be ardent and unprejudiced in enquiry." The voice of Burke, pleading for reverence towards the past, utters no call more eloquent and none so inspiring as this. German idealism, to be introduced into England presently by Coleridge, will teach perhaps a more aspiring ambition, but none so sane. Romanticism, more alluring to the artist, will lack something of this moral dignity. Not till Emerson comes, and after him the new leaders of scientific research, will that clear tone be heard again.

Godwinism soon fell into deep and undeserved disrepute. This was not due wholly to its peculiar features, some of which were beyond the comprehension of pragmatical minds, and others objectionable on the very grounds of practical utility to which Godwin sought to refer his thinking. It was due chiefly to the inherent unattractiveness of the whole philosophy of the Enlightenment, and to the inauspicious character of the times. Pure rationalism can perhaps never be expected to win the favour of more than a small minority, even among reflective men. Its voice is in no age altogether silent, but the echoes nearly always come back mingled with alien notes, the note of Classicism, the note of Transcendentalism, the note of Romanticism.

That Godwin's system did, through Bentham and Mill, for a while at all events, and in a limited degree, *faire école*, is indeed remarkable. The age, moreover, was not propitious. The passion of patriotism, lately starved by the disapproval with which thoughtful Englishmen viewed the conduct of their government before and during the American War and throughout the period of State trials between its disastrous conclusion and the opening of the new French War in 1793, the impatient desire to justify England's past and her present course, made men very intolerant of Godwin's imperturbable criticism. This was no time, they thought, for reform. Wordsworth, one of the first, as he was the greatest of its converts, adhered to the Godwinian system for six years. He met the passion of the hour with his own deep inward passion. He conquered love

of country with love of mankind.   He rebuked with a
reasoned hatred of war the elemental instincts of a
people in arms.   For six years his tenacious and inwardly energetic nature held fast its own religion.   Well
for him was it that prudence bade him keep to himself
his perilous thoughts.   Men were fined, imprisoned, and
deported, for remarks no more seditious and far less
explicit than his Reply to Bishop Watson.   He was
unable or unwilling, before Coleridge furnished him
with a more supple dialectic than his own, to take advantage of the obvious defects of Godwinism, its in-
attention to human history, its blindness to the natural
world, its indifference to the many irrational cravings
of mankind.   It is significant that both Goethe and
Wordsworth, the greatest poets who crossed the thresh-
old of the nineteenth century, were for a time votaries
in the temple of rationalism, a temple nobly bare and
generously open whether for entrance or egress, and
that neither of them could compel himself to remain.

It is well known that in the character of the Solitary,
in " The Excursion," Wordsworth has combined traits
of several persons who had aroused his interest.   The
character was designed to represent a Godwinian, as the
poet conceived of such a person in 1814.   In the note
dictated to Miss Fenwick in 1843, he speaks of the Solitary
as follows:

" A character suitable to my purpose, the elements of
which I drew from several persons with whom I had
been connected, and who fell under my observation,
during frequent residences in London at the beginning
of the French Revolution.   The chief of these was, one
may *now* say, a Mr. Fawcett, a preacher at a dissenting
meeting-house at the Old Jewry.   It happened to me
several times to be one of his congregation through my
connection with Mr. Nicholson of Cateaton Street, who
at that time, when I had not many acquaintances in
London, used often to invite me to dine with him on
Sundays; and I took that opportunity (Mr. N. being a
dissenter) of going to hear Fawcett, who was an able
and eloquent man.   He published a poem on war, which
had a good deal of merit, and made me think more about

him than I should otherwise have done. But his Christianity was never very deeply rooted; and, like many others in those times of like showy talents, he had not strength of character to withstand the effects of the French Revolution, and of the wild and lax opinions which had done so much towards producing it, and far more in carrying it forward in its extremes. Poor Fawcett, I have been told, became pretty much such a person as I have described; and early disappeared from the stage, having fallen into habits of intemperance, which I have heard (though I will not answer for the fact) hastened his death."

Poor Fawcett indeed, if this were all. But the aged poet's reminiscences should never be accepted without scrutiny, except in regard to his own emotional life, and happily we are able to piece together, from other sources, a much more favourable account of this person. A patient search has failed to discover anything derogatory to his character, and the gossip about him which Wordsworth heard is only an instance of the way in which men's reputations were assailed by those who took for granted that heterodox opinions must of necessity spring from a wicked heart and end in an evil life. The Rev. Joseph Fawcett was between thirty-five and forty years old in 1795, and had been preaching on Sunday evenings in a Dissenting church in the Old Jewry since about 1783. He preached to large intelligent audiences, upon whom he left an impression of originality and power. Among his hearers were Mrs. Siddons, the Kembles, Holcroft, the actor and dramatist, and perhaps also the comedian Charles Mathews, a brother of Wordsworth's most intimate friend. He left the ministry in 1795, and published in that year two volumes of sermons and a poem on " The Art of War," printed for J. Johnson. Of this generous and humane effusion a critic in *The Gentleman's Magazine* for June, 1795, judged far less favourably than Wordsworth, but deigned nevertheless to remark: " Mr. F. deserves commendation for awakening the milder feelings, and his expression will be pardoned for his sentiments." Two years later Fawcett published another long poem,

" The Art of Poetry," and in 1798 appeared his collected
" Poems," including both " The Art of War," now
entitled " Civilized War," and " The Art of Poetry,"
this volume also being printed for Johnson. In the
preface the author says of himself :

" However humble a place in the scale of poetical
excellence his readers shall ultimately allot him, it will
ever be a source of proud satisfaction to him to remember
that the first poetical effort he submitted to the public
eye was neither a simple attempt to amuse the fancy nor
to soothe the heart, but an indignant endeavour to tear
away the splendid disguise which it has been the business
of poets in all nations and ages to throw over the most
odious and deformed of all the practices by which the
annals of what is called civilized society have been dis-
graced."

The poem is a noble piece of work and shows an
enlightened spirit. In " A War Elegy," which follows,
Fawcett, like Wordsworth and Coleridge, illustrates
the evils of war with a concrete instance. In his poem
" On Visiting the Gardens of Ermenonville," he pays
a hearty tribute to Rousseau. In the Advertisement to
his " Ode on the Commemoration of the French Revolution, in the Champ de Mars, July 14, 1792," he declares
that he witnessed the ceremonies described.

His character as a Godwinian is plainly stamped
upon his " Sermons delivered at the Sunday Evening
Lectures for the Winter Season, at the Old Jewry," as
may be seen from some of the titles, as, for example,
" Right and Wrong Judgment the Origin of Virtue and
Vice." Another, entitled " Christianity vindicated in
not particularly inculcating Friendship and Patriotism,"
is a truly great and brave sermon, in which he says .

" Friendship and Patriotism, so far as they stand distinguished from general humanity and philanthropy, so
far as we consider only what is *peculiar* to them, although
the more passionate operations of them may have captivated the popular imagination, yet if examined with a
cool and sober eye will appear not to possess, strictly
speaking, any moral beauty, and therefore not to have
merited a place among the precepts of him who came to

inculcate simply pure religion and morality upon mankind. . . . Social virtue consists not in the love of this
or the other individual or body of individuals, but in
the love of man."

Another sermon, " On the Respect that is Due to all
Men," is thoroughly equalitarian.

Among Fawcett's poems there is one, consisting of
seven stanzas, entitled " Louisa: a Song." Wordsworth had it in memory, and was probably alluding to
it consciously, when he wrote his own verses beginning
" I met Louisa in the shade." Fawcett's first stanza is—

> As with Louisa late I sat,
> In yonder secret grove,
> How fondly did each bosom beat,
> And pour its tale of love !

Fawcett's " War Elegies " were published in 1801,
three years before his death. The writer of his obituary
in *The Gentleman's Magazine* dismissed him from life
somewhat contemptuously as " an eccentric character,"
and referred slightingly to his works as being full of the
" spirit of invention and bombast." But from Fawcett's
inventive spirit so original a thinker as William Godwin
had received some of his most striking ideas. He had
known Fawcett for nearly twenty years before the date
of " Political Justice," and declared him to be one of
the four principal oral instructors to whom he felt his
mind indebted for improvement, the others being
Thomas Holcroft, George Dyson, and Samuel Taylor
Coleridge. " Mr. Fawcett's modes of thinking," he
wrote, " made a great impression upon me, as he was
almost the first man I had ever been acquainted with
who carried with him the semblance of original genius."*
One of Fawcett's favourite topics, Godwin declared, " was
a declamation against the domestic affections, a principle
which admirably coincided with the dogmas of Jonathan
Edwards, whose works I had read a short time before."
What Godwin means when he refers in this cool way to
the domestic affections will not appear monstrous to

* C. Kegan Paul, " William Godwin, his Friends and Contemporaries,"
1896.

anyone who has read " Political Justice." When he asks
the old question, " Who is my mother, or my brethren ?"
and gives the old and startling answer, he makes the
sound inference, which weak mortality is very slow to
accept, that domestic ties can never excuse unjust discrimination. No one who has read Godwin's heart-
broken letters after the death of his wife can have any
doubt that his own domestic affections, in spite of.his
austere habits of seclusion, were pure and strong.

The influence of Godwin on Wordsworth and Coleridge
has never been satisfactorily explained or sufficiently
emphasized. In his account of his life in 1794, he says:
" It was in the close of this year that I first met with
Samuel Taylor Coleridge, my acquaintance with whom
was ripened in the year 1800 into a high degree of affectionate intimacy." It appears that he knew Wordsworth in 1798. He wrote of them in that year: " They
are both extraordinary men, and both reputed men of
genius." But there is every probability that Wordsworth and he had met in 1795 or earlier. The Mr.
Nicholson with whom the young poet was in the habit
of dining on Sundays when in London moved in Godwin's
circle. He is often mentioned in Godwin's diary. He
belonged to a small club, of which Thomas Holcroft and
the actor Shield were members, called the Cannonian,
after its president and founder, Cannon, an elderly
Irishman, of bohemian habits, who was supposed to
be engaged on an edition of Tibullus. At one time,
long before Wordsworth's first visit to London, Nicholson lived in apartments which he rented from Holcroft,
and the two wrote a novel together, which appeared in
1780 as " Alwyn, or the Gentleman Comedian." Mrs.
Siddons's sister, the actress Elizabeth Kemble, afterwards Mrs. Whitelocke, rented lodgings from Holcroft
in the same house. Holcroft's acquaintance with
Godwin began in 1786, and it was he who reviewed
" Political Justice " in *The Monthly Review*, in 1793.
Before that work appeared, Godwin discussed its
principles, " at occasional meetings," with Nicholson,
Holcroft, Joel Barlow the American poet, Mackintosh,

the author of " Vindiciæ Gallicæ," and David Williams, the anonymous author of " Lessons to a Young Prince," an extremely revolutionary book. In Godwin's diary the name of Nicholson occurs several times in brief remarks, such as " Sup at Nicholson's, talk of ideal unity." Similar remarks occur in Holcroft's " Memoirs," showing that he, too, was intimate with Nicholson. Godwin dined frequently at the hospitable board of Johnson, the publisher of " An Evening Walk " and " Descriptive Sketches." Among the persons he met there were Thomas Paine and Mary Wollstonecraft, who was employed by Johnson as a reader and translator. On December 11, 1794, Robert Lovell, the friend of Coleridge and Southey, wrote to Holcroft about their scheme of emigrating to America, and asked to be remembered to Nicholson and Godwin. This was only ten days after Holcroft's discharge from Newgate Prison, having been declared not guilty of the charge of treason for which he had lain committed since October. Nicholson was a teacher of mathematics and natural science, and a writer of books on chemistry. The name of Cateaton Street, where Wordsworth visited him, has disappeared from the map of London. It ran westward from the northern extremity of Old Jewry, and is now called Gresham Street. From Nicholson's house to Fawcett's chapel was only a step. To these curious affiliations may be added the fact that Nicholson was foreign agent for Thomas Wedgwood, the friend and patron of Coleridge, and that Basil Montagu, of whom we shall hear presently in connection with the Wordsworths, was a member of this circle of political and religious radicals.

The most extensive notice of Fawcett by a contemporary is that of William Hazlitt in 1810, which is as follows, and makes a very different impression from that made by Wordsworth's remarks to Miss Fenwick:

" It was he who delivered the Sunday evening lectures at the Old Jewry, which were so popular about twenty years ago. He afterwards retired to Hedgegrove in Hertfordshire. It was here that I first became acquainted with him, and passed some of the pleasantest days of my life. He was the friend of my early youth. He was the first person of literary eminence whom I had then known; and the conversations I had with him on subjects of taste and philosophy (for his taste was as refined as his powers of reasoning were profound and subtle) gave me a delight, such as I can never feel again. The writings of Sterne, Fielding, Cervantes, Richardson, Rousseau, Godwin, Goethe, etc., were the usual subjects of our discourse, and the pleasure I had had in reading these authors seemed more than doubled. Of all the persons I have ever known, he was the most perfectly free from every taint of jealousy or narrowness. Never did a mean or sinister motive come near his heart. He was one of the most enthusiastic admirers of the French Revolution; and I believe that the disappointment of the hopes he had cherished of the freedom and happiness of mankind preyed upon his mind and hastened his death."*

It seems, then, from these bits of evidence, that during his various sojourns in London between January, 1793, and September, 1795, amounting in all to many months, Wordsworth lived in at least occasional connection with a circle that included Godwin, Nicholson, Fawcett, Holcroft, Shield, the Kembles, William Mathews, and perhaps his brother Charles, Johnson the bookseller, Thomas Paine, Mary Wollstonecraft, Robert Lovell, Basil Montagu, and indirectly Coleridge, Southey, and the Wedgwoods. This is not to say that he was acquainted at any one time with all these persons. In those years, however, the entire number were more or less in communication with one another. The influence of Godwin was dominant among them. Some of them were under the ban of public censure for holding democratic principles. They sympathized with the French Revolution; they opposed the war. The centre of political disaffection was to be found somewhere within this circle. More and more, as the Revolution went to extremes, and the military success of France exasperated and consolidated English patriotism, the possession of extreme democratic ideals was narrowed down to members of this group, so far as

* William Hazlitt's " Life of Holcroft," p. 171, London, 1902.

the intellectual society of England was concerned.   The independence of character and the confidence in rational deduction which made them radical in politics had the same effect in religion.   Several of them were professed Unitarians, and active in the propagation of their faith. They were feared and denounced as free-thinkers no less than as levellers.   A very well-defined line was drawn around them.   Wordsworth could not have associated with them without being considered by his family to have definitely taken their side in all respects.   He never maintained a lively intercourse with many acquaintances at once.   If he was at all intimate with the revolutionary group in London, they probably absorbed nearly all his social activity for the time.   And it is plain that whatever use he may have made in " The Excursion " of reminiscences of Fawcett, it was sympathy, not vagrant curiosity, that drew him to the meeting-house in Old Jewry, and a deep intellectual interest that made him a student of Godwin.   Not " The Excursion," nor even " The Prelude," but " Guilt and Sorrow," " The Convict," and " The Borderers," provide the direct reflection of his mood in 1795.

It is possible also that Wordsworth first heard through Holcroft or Godwin, early in 1795, of the arrangements being made between Coleridge, Southey, Lovell, and one or two other young men, to migrate to America and establish a philosophical community.*   As we have seen,

* Some of the stages of this enterprise are to be seen in Southey's correspondence, beginning with the Easter Sunday, 1793, when he tramped away from Oxford with Milton's " Defence " in his knapsack, wishing he had the pen of Rousseau.   In a letter to W. H. Bedford, written at Bristol, November 13, 1793, he mentions, as a mere speculation, going to America. On December 14, and again later in the month, he refers to the project, in letters to G. Bedford.   Coleridge came over to Oxford in June, 1794, and met Southey, who wrote to Grosvenor Bedford an enthusiastic account of his new acquaintance, June 12.   Cuthbert Southey, in Vol. I., p. 211, of Southey's " Letters," gives the names of the proposed company as including Southey, Robert Lovell, George Burnett of Balliol, Robert Allen of Corpus Christi, Oxford, Edmund Seward of Balliol, and S. T. Coleridge. Later adherents were Favell, Scott, and Le Grice.   Seward died in 1795. The best and most tangible result of the scheme is intimated in Southey's enthusiastic remark to G. Bedford, in a letter from Bristol, February 8, 1795: " Coleridge is writing at the same table; our names are written in the book of destiny on the same page."

Lovell had written about this plan to Holcroft in the preceding December. The idea was not without example. Dr. Priestley's withdrawal from mob violence and calumny in England to the peaceful shores of the Susquehanna was much discussed in the public prints. *The Gentleman's Magazine* for June, 1795, contained the following notice, which would naturally arouse a romantic interest:

" There is a colony established not far from the Susquehanna River, in America, by a class of wealthy Frenchmen, who formerly distinguished themselves in the Constituent Assembly of France, but were prudent enough to retire in time with their families and property; among them are Noailles, Talon, Blacon, Talleyrand, and other of the ci-devant noblesse: they have relinquished their titles, and have domesticated here in the most social manner. Their little settlement is called French Town. The tavern is kept by an officer who was formerly le baron Beaulieu!"

The settlement here referred to was made at Asylum, in what is now Bradford County, Pennsylvania. It was visited in May, 1795, by La Rochefoucauld-Liancourt, who described it minutely in the first volume of his "Voyage en Amérique." He made his way thither, along the Susquehanna, after visiting the home of Dr. Priestley, at Northumberland. Asylum had been established about fifteen months before, on land purchased through the agency of the great proprietors, Morris and Nicholson. Talon and Noailles had come to Pennsylvania by way of England. Among the settlers were M. de Blacons, formerly a deputy to the Constituent from Dauphiné, and M. Colin, formerly M. l'Abbé de Sévigny, Priest-Archdeacon of Toul, who were partners, and kept a store in the wilderness; M. de Montulé, formerly a cavalry captain; M. de Bec de Lièvre, formerly a canon, now a storekeeper; the Messieurs de la Roue, old army officers; M. de Noailles, of San Domingo; M. d'Andelot, of Franche-Comté, an ex-officer; M. du Petit-Thouars, an old naval officer, with a remarkable record for adventure and suffering; and several other ecclesiastics, merchants, and nobles. Thomas Twining, an Englishman, in his " Travels in America," says that he met the Count de Noailles, Count Tilley, and Volney, at the house of Mr. Bingham, in Philadelphia, in 1795; and that he saw walking in Chestnut Street, Philadelphia, " a tall gentleman in a blue coat, pointed out as M. Talleyrand."* There were several French ladies of high rank and good education among the refugees on the Susquehanna, and a spirit of cheerful adventure pervaded the community. There can be scarcely any doubt that our young English collegians had their thoughts directed to America by hearing or reading some account of this colony.

Public interest in Dr. Priestley's settlement at Northumberland in Pennsylvania was very lively. For many years he had been the leader of the English Unitarians, and his name had been associated, whether justly or not, with that of Paine as that of a chief enemy of the British Constitution. Hundreds of attacks upon his religious and political opinions had appeared within the space of half a dozen years, in pamphlets, treatises, satirical poems, and printed sermons. No name appears so frequently as his among the book reviews of *The Gentleman's Magazine* and *The Monthly Review* between 1789 and 1796. His personal character was not spared by enemies both open and secret, though in no respect was its integrity really involved. Learned opponents, especially at Cambridge, were never weary of combining criticism of his chemical theories with charges of theological unsoundness. Now curiosity followed him beyond the Atlantic, while the malignity which had hounded him from England turned in triumph upon those of his way of thinking who remained. The pressure of Conservative opinion was enormous and unrelenting.

The poem " Guilt and Sorrow " contains faint but hardly mistakable traces of Godwin's philosophy and of Fawcett's teaching. It was not published as a whole until 1842, when it had been considerably altered. We

* J. G. Rosengarten, " French Colonists and Exiles in the United States," p. 129.

may judge of the nature of the changes by comparing the thirty stanzas extracted from their setting, and printed in 1798 as " The Female Vagrant," with their final form. Though much of this part was, according to Wordsworth's recollection, composed in 1791 and 1792, the first draft of the entire poem was certainly not completed before 1794, and the work was rehandled in 1795. The action is represented as taking place during the American War. The leading psychological motive of the Sailor's story, which was composed later than the Woman's story, is the same as one which was presently to appear again in " The Borderers "—namely, that " sin and crime are apt to start from their very opposite qualities," a statement to which Godwin would have given his assent, and which is easily recognized as conformable to his view of human nature. Political disaffection shows itself in the fifth and sixth stanzas of " The Female Vagrant " as originally printed, where the legalized oppression of a poor man by his neighbour, a rich land-owner, is feelingly described. This passage was afterwards completely altered, being represented finally by the vague statement :

> But through severe mischance and cruel wrong,
> My father's substance fell into decay.

It is significant that another passage in the thirty stanzas originally printed as " The Female Vagrant " was also softened later into a far less bitter indictment of society. One of the main sources of evil represented in the Woman's story as well as in the Man's is war. In the fragment printed in 1798, the soldiery after whom the poor creature has dragged herself through America are called

> the brood
> That lap (their very nourishment) their brothers' blood.

This was omitted in all editions after 1800, and if similar features once existed in the Sailor's story, as is probable from the fact that a like fate had dragged him from his peaceful home and made him a man of blood against his will, they too have been expunged. There remains only an ironical reference to " social Order's care for wretchedness." As " Guilt and Sorrow " was finally published, it contained not a word against capital punishment, but ends with the poor Sailor's voluntary submission to the law, which avenges in his person a crime for which he has atoned, and the guilt of which has left no stain upon his soul.   Here was ample opportunity to illustrate Godwin's doctrine of the injustice of retributive punishment, and especially of the death penalty.   If the poem originally ended with such an illustration, Wordsworth in 1842 of course would not have let such an ending stand, for he had meanwhile, as if in expiation of former laxity, published fourteen sonnets in favour of capital punishment ! But it is almost inconceivable that the poem in 1794 concluded with this note of acquiescence in the wisdom of an institution which not only Godwin's book, but events in France, had brought in question.   The structural lines of the poem seem to converge towards something which they never reach, some passage of protest and revolt.   Furthermore, in a letter to his friend Francis Wrangham, written November 20, 1795, Wordsworth says that he desired to publish a poem, the object of which " is partly to expose the vices of the penal law, and the calamities of war, as they affect individuals." It expressed his sentiments at that time no less than at an earlier period, for he declared that he had recently made alterations and additions so material that it might be looked on almost as another work.   It is also evident from this letter that the poet had recently been with Wrangham in London, where he had read to his friend the first draft of this poem, and had planned others, of a satirical character, dealing with political questions. It would appear that he delayed realizing Dorothy's dream of a reunion and life in a cottage, in order to try once more to gain a livelihood by direct application of his powers to public affairs.   Perhaps also much time was required to secure and invest the legacy of £900.

CHAPTER IX

DOROTHY

MEANWHILE Dorothy had to exercise patience. She spent the spring and summer and part of the autumn of 1595 near Halifax, with her relative Mrs. Rawson, and was more or less in touch with Jane Pollard, so that apparently no letters passed between them. Besides, the latter was preparing for her marriage with Mr. Marshall, which took place before September 2. On that date we have the first record of a new life about to begin for the long-separated brother and sister, a life destined to be happy for them and memorable for mankind.

" I am now going to tell you," she writes to Mrs. Marshall, " what is for your own eyes and ears alone; I need say no more than this, I am sure, to insure your most careful secrecy. Know then that I am going to live in Dorsetshire. Let me, however, methodically state the whole plan, and then, my dearest Jane, I doubt not you will rejoice in the prospect which at last opens before me of having, at least for a time, a comfortable home and a house of my own. You know the pleasure I have always attached to the idea of home, a blessing which I so early lost (though made up to me as well as the most affectionate care of relatives not positively congenial in pursuits and pleasures could do, and with separate and distinct views)."

Then follows a careful computation of the means which will enable her and William to maintain themselves. The house in which they expect to live belongs, she says, " to a Mr. Pinney, a very rich merchant of Bristol," who has given it up to his son. The latter, who has hitherto kept it open at some expense, has now offered to let William occupy it.

" He is to come occasionally for a few weeks to stay with us, paying for his board. William is at present staying with the Pinneys at Bristol. The house in

Dorsetshire is furnished, and has a garden and orchard. I have great satisfaction in thinking that William will have such opportunities of studying as will be advantageous not only to his mind, but his purse. Living in the unsettled way in which he has hitherto lived in London is altogether unfavourable to mental exertion."

Raisley Calvert's legacy is about to be invested. "William finds that he can get 9 per cent. for the money upon the best security. He means to sink half of it upon my life, which will make me always comfortable and independent."

It is probable that Wordsworth was introduced to the Pinneys by Basil Montagu, at whose house in London he had been recently staying. He left his books there, and wrote to Mathews several weeks later, asking him to have them packed. Montagu, who was of the same age as the poet, had been with him at Cambridge, where he resided till 1795. He was a natural son of the Earl of Sandwich, who acknowledged him and left him a legacy, which, however, failed to reach its destination. Montagu then, in 1795, began to read law, and engaged in literary work. He was assisted later in life by Wordsworth's intimate friend, Francis Wrangham, in his edition of Bacon, and maintained a lifelong friendship with Coleridge and Wordsworth. His opinions were always liberal; in his youth and early manhood they were extremely radical. He is said to have been so zealous a follower of Godwin that at one time he thought seriously of relinquishing the profession of a lawyer on the ground that it was injurious to society. His first wife, whom he married in the year of his graduation, and with whom he kept house in Cambridge while Wordsworth was still at college, died in childbirth, leaving him a son named Edward. This is the boy referred to in an "Anecdote for Fathers," and the lines beginning "It is the first mild day of March." In their letters William and Dorothy call the child Basil. It is to him that she now refers as follows, in estimating their means of livelihood: "I think I told you that Mr. Montagu had a little boy, who, as you will perceive, could not be very

well taken care of, either in his father's chambers, or
under the uncertain management of various friends of
Mr. M., with whom he has frequently stayed.   Lament-
ing this, he proposed to William to allow him £50 a
year for his board, provided I should approve of the
plan."   The motherly instincts of this young woman of
twenty-three, which had already prompted her to keep
a little school for her neighbours' children at Forncett,
must have been gratified with this prospect.   She even
mentions an extension of the idea, for she adds:

" A natural daughter of Mr. Tom Myers (a cousin of
mine whom I dare say you have heard me mention) is
coming over to England by one of the first ships, which
is expected in about a month, to be educated.   She is,
I believe, about three or four years old, and T. Myers'
brother, who has charge of her, has requested that I
should take her under my care.   With these two children, and the produce of Raisley Calvert's legacy, we
shall have an income of at least £170 or £180 per annum.
. . . As for the little girl, I shall feel myself as a mother
to her. . . .   It is a painful idea that one's existence is
of very little use, which I have been always obliged to
feel hitherto. . . .   I shall have to join William at Bristol,
and proceed hence in a chaise with Basil to Racedown; it
is fifty miles.   I have received a very polite invitation
from the Pinneys to stay at their house on my road."

Apparently the little girl did not join them, nor did
Mr. Pinney's thirteen-year-old boy, whom William hoped
to have as a pupil, and it is not likely that their income
was nearly as large as she expected.   But they had the
cares and delights of young Basil's company for several
years, and a realization of this fact helps us to understand many traits in Wordsworth's early poems.   He
keeps child nature constantly in view.   The joyousness,
the wonder, the power of concealment, the susceptibility
to keen and unspeakable grief, the subtle and devious
ways of reasoning, which are some of the strongest traits
of childhood, are felt in many a poem which Wordsworth
wrote before he had observed children of his own.   One
of the deepest peculiarities of his poetry is that it conveys

a sense of having been written, not for children, but with consciousness of how a child thinks.

Miss Wordsworth's letter contains one more remark about her brother, which raises several interesting questions. She says: " By the bye, I must not forget to tell you that he has had the offer of ten guineas for a work which has not taken him much time, and half the profits of a second edition if it should be called for." To what work does this refer? Beyond reasonable doubt to " Guilt and Sorrow." As finally published, this poem contains 666 lines. We have seen that it once had a different ending and a different emphasis. To give a well-proportioned weight to its original " objects," which then were dear to the poet's heart, it must have been longer than it is in its present form. And even were this not the case, the poem would have been long enough for publication in a volume by itself. In the original editions, " An Evening Walk " contained only 430 lines, and " Descriptive Sketches " 813. It is evidently the same work that Wordsworth describes to Wrangham less than three months later in terms which unmistakably refer to " Guilt and Sorrow." He writes of it then as follows: " Have you any interest with the booksellers? I have a poem which I should wish to dispose of, provided I could get anything for it. I recollect reading the first draft of it to you in London." To the same correspondent he writes on March 7, 1796:

" I mean to publish a volume. Could you engage to get rid for me of a dozen copies or more among your numerous acquaintance? The damages — to use a Lancashire phrase—will be four or five shillings per copy. I do not mean to put forth a formal subscription; but could wish, upon my acquaintances and *their* acquaintances, to quarter so many as would insure me from positive loss; further this adventurer wisheth not."

And on the same day Dorothy writes to Mrs. Marshall: " William is going to publish a poem. The Pinneys have taken it to the booksellers." May not the explanation of these various passages be that, while at Bristol towards the end of the summer, Wordsworth

showed what he had written of " Guilt and Sorrow," or
spoke of it, to the enterprising and ambitious publisher
Joseph Cottle; that Cottle made him a tentative or con-
ditional offer; that this was presently withdrawn or not
accepted; that the poet then, as his November letter
shows, thought of finding a London publisher; that
failing in this, he sent it again to Cottle by the Pinneys ?
In any case, his efforts were unsuccessful, though Cottle
in the end did publish the extract known as " The
Female Vagrant " with the other " Lyrical Ballads " in
1798. The fact that Cottle in his " Early Recollections; chiefly relating to the late Samuel Taylor Coleridge," 1837, makes no reference to having met Wordsworth so early as 1795, nor to any negotiations of this
kind, may be explained by his extraordinary vanity
and his well-known lack of scruple about garbling letters
and incidents. The pride of his life was to have been
one of the early friends and helpers of Wordsworth,
Coleridge, and Southey. He was quite capable of sup-
pressing the evidence of a false start with one of them.
Had the offer of ten guineas come from a London publisher, Wordsworth, one is almost forced to think, would
have communicated the fact to Wrangham when touching on the subject of his proposed volume.

It is strange that no record of the first meeting between Wordsworth and Coleridge has come down to us.
Something like the awe that Dante felt when he pondered on the results of the descent of Æneas to the
" immortal world,"

pensando l' alto effetto
Ch' uscir dovea di lui, e 'l chi, e 'l quale,

creeps over one who attempts to weigh the consequences
of that event. It occurred, I believe, somewhat earlier
than has been generally supposed. Bishop Wordsworth
in the " Memoirs " makes no mention of it at all. He
does not introduce Coleridge upon the scene before June,
1797. J. Dykes Campbell, whose authority regarding
facts in the life of Coleridge was unsurpassed, says with
his customary caution, in his " Life of Coleridge ": " The
precise date of the first meeting of Coleridge and Words-

worth has not been ascertained, but a careful examination of all the evidence available, published and unpublished, has all but convinced me that it may have
probably taken place as early as September, 1795."

As we have already seen, Coleridge was an enthusiastic admirer of Wordsworth's poems in November,
1793, when he discussed them with Christopher Wordsworth at Cambridge.   They had many friends in common.   It was known in the London circle which Wordsworth frequented that Coleridge, Southey, and other
young men, were planning to emigrate to America.
Their centre of operations was Bristol.   The plan, which
came to be known as the Pantisocratic Scheme, was
probably conceived in the spring of 1794, and matured,
if the wild scheme could ever be termed mature, during
a visit Coleridge, then a Cambridge undergraduate,
made to Southey at Oxford in the following summer.
The most trustworthy account of it is given in a letter
from Southey to Cottle in 1836, quoted by Campbell in
his " Life of Coleridge ":

" In the summer of 1794 S. T. Coleridge and Hucks
came to Oxford on their way into Wales for a pedestrian
tour.   Then Allen introduced them to me, and the
scheme was talked of, but not by any means determined
on.   It was talked into shape by Burnett and myself,
when, upon the commencement of the long vacation,
we separated from them, they making for Gloucester,
he and I proceeding on foot to Bath.   After some weeks,
S. T. C., returning from his tour, came to Bristol on his
way, and slept there.   Then it was that we resolved
upon going to America, and S. T. C. and I walked into
Somersetshire to see Burnett, and on that journey it
was that he first saw Poole.   He made his engagement
with Miss [Sarah] Fricker on our return from this
journey at my mother's house in Bath, not a little to
my astonishment, because he had talked of being deeply
in love with a certain Mary Evans.   I had previously
been engaged to my poor Edith [Fricker]. . . .   He
remained at Bristol till the close of the vacation [?]—
several weeks.   During that time it was that we talked
of America.   The funds were to be what each could
raise—S. T. C. by the Specimens of the Modern Latin

Poets, for which he had printed proposals, and obtained a respectable list of Cambridge subscribers before I knew him; I, by Joan of Arc, and what else I might publish. I had no . . . other expectation. We hoped to find companions with money."

A much more detailed account, and the earliest of which I have any knowledge, is a letter from Thomas Poole to a Mr. Haskins, written September 20, 1794. Poole was an energetic and wealthy young tanner, of democratic principles, who lived at Nether Stowey, in Somerset, about thirty-five miles from Bristol:

" DEAR SIR,—I received your obliging letter a day or two ago, and will with pleasure give you all the information I can respecting the emigration to America to which you allude. But first, perhaps, you would like to have some idea of the character of the projectors of the scheme. Out of eight whom they informed me were engaged, I have seen but two, and only spent part of one day with them; their names are Coldridge and Southey.

" Coldridge, whom I consider the Principal in the undertaking, and of whom I had heard much before I saw him, is about five-and-twenty, belongs to the University of Cambridge, possesses splendid abilities—he is, I understand, a shining scholar, gained the prize for the Greek verses the first or second year he entered the University, and is now engaged in publishing a selection of the best modern Latin poems with a poetical translation. He speaks with much elegance and energy, and with uncommon facility, but he, as it generally happens to men of his class, feels the justice of Providence in the want of those inferior abilities which are necessary to the rational discharge of the common duties of life. His aberrations from prudence, to use his own expression, have been great; but he now promises to be as sober and rational as his most sober friends could wish. In religion, he is a Unitarian, if not a Deist; on politicks a Democrat, to the utmost extent of the word.

" Southey, who was with him, is of the University of Oxford, a younger man, without the splendid abilities of Coldridge, though possessing much information, particularly metaphysical, and is more violent in his principles than even Coldridge himself. In Religion, shocking to say in a mere Boy as he is, I fear he wavers between Deism and Atheism.

" Thus much for the characters of two of the Emigra-
tors.   Their plan is as follows:
" Twelve gentlemen of good education and liberal
principles are to embark with twelve ladies in April next.
Previous to their leaving this country they are to have
as much intercourse as possible, in order to ascertain
each other's dispositions, and firmly to settle every regu-
lation for the government of their future conduct.   Their
opinion was that they should fix themselves at—I do
not recollect the place, but somewhere in a delightful
part of the new back settlements; that each man should
labour two or three hours in a day, the produce of which
labour would, they imagine, be more than sufficient to
support the colony.   As Adam Smith observes that
there is not above one productive man in twenty, they
argue that if each laboured the twentieth part of time,
it would produce enough to satisfy their wants.   The
produce of their industry is to be laid up in common for
the use of all; and a good library of books is to be collected, and their leisure hours to be spent in study,
liberal discussions, and the education of their children.
A system for the education of their children is laid down,
for which, if this plan at all suits you, I must refer you
to the authors of it.   The regulations relating to the
females strikes them as the most difficult; whether the
marriage contracts shall be dissolved if agreeable to one
or both parties, and many other circumstances, are not
yet determined.   The employments of the women are
to be the care of infant children, and other occupations
suited to their strength; at the same time the greatest
attention is to be paid to the cultivation of their minds.
Every one is to enjoy his own religious and political
opinions, provided they do not encroach on the rules
previously made, which rules, it is unnecessary to add,
must in some measure be regulated by the laws of the
State which includes the district in which they settle.
They calculate that each gentleman providing £125 will
be sufficient to carry the scheme into execution.   Finally,
every individual is at liberty, whenever he pleases, to
withdraw from the society."

By the autumn of 1795 the Pantisocratic dream had
almost faded away.   The adventurers had consumed part
of their energies in writing a drama, " The Fall of Robespierre," which Coleridge, Southey, and Lovell planned,
and the first two wrote.   Coleridge returned to Cam-

bridge, but left college in December without taking his degree. Forgetting both the Susquehanna and his Sarah, he sought out his old schoolmate Charles Lamb, and was enjoying the freedom of bachelorhood and the conveniences of civilization at the Angel tavern or " the little smoky room at the Salutation and Cat," where, as his companion wrote, they " sat together through the winter nights, beguiling the cares of life with Poesy." But Southey went to London to look for him, and brought him back to his lady at Bristol. Here they both, with Burnett, another of the band, lodged together and once more began to think seriously of America. Lovell was the first to take a practical step, by marrying Mary Fricker. Coleridge made a little money by lecturing. Joseph Cottle, himself only twenty-four years old, and a poet, but not a friend of Pantisocracy, helped the comrades to pay their bills by advancing money on poems written and unwritten.

The friendship between Coleridge and Southey became strained before the middle of 1795. It was at this time, I am inclined to think, that Wordsworth met them. Their fortunes were desperate. Their rose-coloured vision had faded away. The great contrast between their characters had begun to show itself. And although they kept their engagements and espoused each of them a Miss Fricker, marriage was no longer a move towards the communal life, with two or three hours a day of farming, on the banks of the Susquehanna. In estimating the likelihood that Wordsworth, if he remained any time at all in Bristol, would encounter this band of young men, several facts must be taken into consideration. They were persons of marked peculiarity. Cottle, in his very natural desire to provide a market for their literary efforts, would be sure to talk about them. Coleridge was " a noticeable man " and gave public lectures. Southey was a native of Bristol and well connected. They were all very young—Southey was twenty-one in August. Their peculiarities of manner, dress, and especially of opinion, must have made them objects of curiosity or alarm to the heavy-going merchants of that rich port, which still profited largely by the slave-trade. The town, including the suburbs, had only about 60,000 inhabitants.

It was in August that Coleridge took a cottage at Clevedon, on the Bristol Channel, about twelve miles south-west of the city. In his volume of Poems published in 1796, the lines entitled " The Eolian Harp " are declared to have been " composed August 20, 1795, at Clevedon, Somersetshire." But as he was not married until October 4, it is not likely that he removed thither before that date. Coleridge's daughter Sara, seeking information as to the time of the first meeting of the poets, received the following answer from Mrs. Wordsworth, November 7, 1845:

" With my husband's tender love to you he bids me say, in reply to a question you have put to him through Miss Fenwick, that he has not as distinct a remembrance as he could wish of the time when he first saw your father and your uncle Southey; but the impression upon his mind is that he first saw them both, and your aunt Edith at the same time, in a lodging in Bristol. This must have been about the year 1795."

Racedown is the name of a farm in Dorsetshire. It lies seven miles back from the shore of the English Channel, to the north-east of Lyme Regis, and is about equally distant from Lyme, Beaminster, Crewkerne, and Chard. A sharp point of Devonshire almost touches it, and Ottery St. Mary in that county, the birthplace of Coleridge, is only twenty-four miles distant. The land lies along the bed of a small watercourse that winds between bold hills. In sheltered parts it is fertile, and vegetation is abundant. But where the ground rises above the common level, the trees are stunted and bend weirdly in one direction, away from the sea. Heavy, flat-topped hills, that look like elephants' brows, push southward as if they still held the ocean at bay. On the highest of them, its immense flank rising from the edge of the Racedown fields, the green ramparts of an ancient " camp " still

overlook the Channel.   From the roads that follow
the trend of the streams glimpses of blue water show
themselves here and there as the valleys open out
southward.   Through these immense funnels the wind
brings the scent and the sound of the sea, and the
place is never quiet, for all its seclusion.   The house
is a stiff, dignified brick building, covered now with grey
plaster.   It looks comfortable, though a little gloomy,
not grand enough to be called a country-seat nor plain
enough to be called a farmhouse.   The country even
now is rather thinly settled.   There are no large villages
near.   Three miles away, at the hamlet of Broadwindsor,
is the ancestral home of the Pinney family.   The owner
of Racedown in 1795 was John Preter, who took the name
of Pinney on succeeding to the estate in 1762.   He was
at one time High Sheriff of Dorset, and had two sons,
John Frederick and Charles, and two daughters.

The Wordsworths went to Racedown in September,
1795.   The next date in connection with their life
there is November 20, when William addressed a letter
to Wrangham from " Racedown Cottage, near Crewkerne."   He was still busy with a task he and Wrangham had undertaken together, which was the composition of satires on public men and measures, in imitation of Juvenal.   Among the objects of derision were
King George, the Prince of Wales, the Duke of Norfolk,
and, doubtless for private reasons, the Earl of Lonsdale.
The specimen lines given in this letter are enough to
make one thankful on many accounts—of which prudence is not the chief—that the rash satirist learned
to suppress his rage.

In another but undated letter to Wrangham from
Racedown containing satirical verses occurs the following passage on the Prince Regent:

> The nation's hope shall show the present time
> As rich in folly as the past in crime.
> Do arts like these a royal mind evince ?
> Are these the studies that beseem a prince ?
> Wedged in with blacklegs at a boxers' show,
> To shout with transport at a knock-down blow—

'Mid knots of grooms, the council of his state,
To scheme and counter-scheme for purse and plate.
Thy ancient honours when shalt thou resume ?
Oh shame, is this thy service' boastful plume ?—
Go, modern Prince ! at Henry's tomb proclaim
Thy rival triumphs, thy Newmarket fame,
There hang thy trophies—bid the jockey's vest,
The whip, the cap, and spurs thy fame attest.

In the letter of November 20 he sends Wrangham
more of his imitations, including a very daring couplet :

Heavens ! who sees majesty in George's face ?
Or looks at Norfolk, and can dream of grace ?

And of this he says :

" The two best verses of this extract were given me
by Southey, a friend of Coleridge's : ' Who sees majesty,'
etc.   He supplied me with another line which I think
worth adopting.   We mention Lord Courtenay : Southey's
verse is, ' Whence have I fallen ? alas ! what have I
done ?' a literal translation of the Courtenay motto,
' Unde lapsus ? quid feci ?' "

It is in this letter also that Wordsworth mentions
" Guilt and Sorrow " :

" I have a poem which I should wish to dispose of
provided I could get anything for it. . . .   Its object
is partly to expose the vices of the penal law, and the
calamities of war as they affect individuals."

We may gain some idea of his poverty and the deep
seclusion of Racedown from the following passage :

" You flattered me with a hope that, by your assistance, I might be supplied with the Morning Chronicle;
have you spoken to the editors about it ?   If it could be
managed, I should be much pleased; as we only see here
a provincial weekly paper, and I cannot afford to have
the Chronicle at my own expense.   I have said nothing
of Racedown.   It is an excellent house and the country
far from unpleasant, but as for society we must manu-
facture it ourselves.   Will you come and help us ?   We
expect Montagu at Christmas, and should be very glad
if you could make it convenient to come along with him.
If not, at all events, we shall hope to see you in the
course of the next summer."

In another letter to Wrangham, apparently of not much later date, he says: "We have neither magazine, review, nor any new publication whatever." He modestly declines to set up as a schoolmaster, saying: "As to your promoting my interest in the way of pupils, upon a review of my own attainments I think there is so little that I am able to teach that this scheme may be suffered to fly quietly away to the paradise of fools."

The two letters contain 158 lines of the satires, but as they stand they scarcely make sense. Their purport, however, is plain enough, and the poet's nephew described them with precision when he wrote: "These specimens exhibit poetical vigour, combined with no little asperity and rancour against the abuses of the time, and the vices of the ruling powers, and the fashionable corruptions of aristocratical society." The most vivid picture in the fragments is that of a subservient Parliament and the mad King:

> So patient Senates quibble by the hour
> And prove with endless tongues a monarch's power,
> Or whet his kingly faculties to chase
> Legions of devils through a keyhole's space.

Wrangham was a prolific author of verse and prose, but I have discovered nothing in his writings which indicates that he ever published his part of this joint production. Wordsworth was even then finding more congenial modes of expression, and it was not to be expected that a man of so little practical experience of public life, and living far, moreover, from the scene of combat, could continue to criticize passing events with the light and yet penetrating touch that satire demands. And so he, too, suppressed his part of this adventure. He was already engaged upon another. He announced to Wrangham: "I have been employed lately in writing a tragedy—the first draft of which is nearly finished." The same letter contains a humorous allusion to Godwin's curious doctrine on the subject of promises, and another profession of poverty. Ten to one, he says, he will not be able to release Wrangham's reply from the post-office unless it is franked. He has been living lately, he gaily says, upon air and the essence of carrots, cabbages, turnips, and other esculent vegetables, not excluding parsley, the produce of his garden.

In another letter to Wrangham, dated March 7 (1796 evidently), he congratulates him, somewhat jocosely, on having been presented to a very rich living, as Rector of Hunmanby, in Yorkshire, and expresses a hope that his friend will now, " like every sensible rich man,". turn his thoughts towards travel. This, we may be sure, is what he would have done himself, for he was always possessed with a love of wandering, and gratified it frequently when his circumstances permitted, and even sometimes when they seemed very unpropitious. He says he does not mean " to drop the Juvenal scheme," and has been working at it that morning. " We have had the two Pinneys with us," he remarks, " John for a month. They left us yesterday, and, as I now feel a return of literary appetite, I mean to take a snack of satire by way of sandwich." Alluding again to Wrangham's promotion and to Montagu's ill-fortune in losing his father's legacy, he says: " I have been engaged an hour and a half this morning in hewing wood and rooting up hedges, and I think it no bad employment to feel ' the penalty of Adam ' in this way. Some of our friends have not been so lucky, witness poor Montagu." In a postscript he adds: " Basil is quite well, *quant au physique, mais pour le moral, il y a bien à craindre.* Among other things, he lies like a little devil."

On March 21, 1796, and this time in a letter to Mathews, he writes:

" I was tolerably industrious in reading, if reading can ever deserve the name of industry, till our good friends the Pinneys came among us; and I have since returned to my books. As to writing, it is out of the question. Not, however, entirely to forget the world, I season my recollection of some of its objects with a little ill-nature—I attempt to write satires; and in all satires, whatever the authors may say, there will be found a spice of malignity."

Years afterwards, in 1807, Wordsworth forbade
Wrangham to publish these verses, alleging with great
solemnity that he had " long since come to a fixed
determination to steer clear of personal satire." Many
reasons had, moreover, by that time made it undesirable
that his name should be mentioned in connection with
the work.

It is amazing how numerous were the ties that bound
Wordsworth's youthful friends to one another. It is
evident that Mathews, too, was acquainted with the
Pinneys, for the poet writes to him:

" I fully expected to hear from you by Azar Pinney
[Azariah is a name that occurs several times in the
Pinney pedigree], and was not a little surprised you
omitted so good an opportunity of sending me the
volume of fugitive poetry."

And then, referring perhaps to the Cannonian Club, to
which Holcroft and some of his friends, as we have seen,
belonged, he continues:

" Pray write to me at length, and give me an account
of your proceedings in the Society, or any other information likely to interest me. Are your members
much increased ? and what is of more consequence, have
you improved I do not ask in the [art] of speaking, but
in the more important one of thinking ?"

The Pinneys probably brought a copy of Southey's
epic poem, " Joan of Arc," which Wordsworth criticizes
severely, in a passage from which I infer that the young
Oxford poet was known personally, and unfavourably,
to Mathews. Montagu has sent a copy of the second
edition of " Political Justice," and the recluse shows his
previous acquaintance with the work by remarking that
he expects to find it much improved. He thinks the
preface badly written. " Give me some news about the
theatre," he begs; " I have attempted to read Holcroft's
Man of Ten Thousand, but such stuff." And after be-
seeching Mathews to come and visit him, he says: " My
sister would be very glad of your assistance in her
Italian studies. She has already gone through half of

Davila,* and yesterday we began Ariosto." From these
few lines of Wordsworth's, and with the knowledge that
he was then composing his tragedy " The Borderers,"
we may form some idea of how he employed himself
during the twenty-two months, more or less, that he
lived at Racedown. There is here no trace whatever of
that mental depression, that clouding of his spiritual
faculties, that moroseness, which we have been so often
told worked a crisis in his life and particularly charac-
terized the early months of his residence in Dorsetshire.
Affecting pictures have again and again been drawn of
a young sufferer, his heart chilled, his intellect sated,
by the sophistries of rationalism, creeping to this lonely
place, and here recovering his faith through the minis-
trations of his sister and the kindly influence of nature.
Some very small degree of truth perhaps there is in these
descriptions. They find a general warrant in certain
passages of " The Prelude " and " The Excursion."
And after the crowding experiences of the preceding
eight years, with their frequent changes of scene, their
homeless wanderings, their generous hopes, and sharp
disappointments, after keen intercourse with men
struggling to establish new and despised systems, after
the distress due to his false step with Annette, after
the miserable life of cities, we might expect to find him
weary and longing for a chance to think out his future
course; but in his letters from Racedown there is of all
this not a word. We see him more cheerful than he
was a year before, in the north, and intellectually more
active; we feel in what he writes to Wrangham and
Mathews an abounding energy, and, above all, a tone
of self-confidence. Moreover, there is here no hint that
he has broken or desired to break with his old connections in London. Politics, the theatre, the books of his
acquaintances, still interest him. He begs eagerly to
be kept informed of what is going on in the world. He
gives absolutely no ground to suppose that he has been

* If this was Davila's " Istoria delle Guerre civili di Francia," an ancient
copy of which was catalogued among Wordsworth's books after his death,
it was rather solid reading for a beginner.

disillusioned with regard to the social and religious views professed by himself and his friends. The causes of his retirement, he gives it to be understood, are poverty and a wish to study. If he was ever to carry out the long-cherished plan of living with his sister, the opportunity of having a large house in the country, rent-free, and in a place where his little income would go farthest, was not to be rejected. The quiet of Racedown gave him a chance to do some extensive reading, which included many works of modern European literature, and especially books of travel. The fact that he was writing a tragedy is no proof that his own mood was tragic.

Perhaps, then, in Dorothy's letters from Racedown we shall find evidence in support of the traditional theory. Perhaps in her simpler though not more open-hearted style, she will reveal his secret grief. But this is not so. She gives a charming and harmonious picture of domestic happiness. They are both busy with their reading and the education of little Basil. Visitors are few. They fare plainly, but pleasantly. They enjoy their big house. The country round about draws them forth on long walks. She is perfectly happy, perfectly in accord with her brother, zealous to have him succeed in his work. There is nothing whatever to suggest that she is trying " to win him back " to something that he has left behind.

Her letters from Racedown to Mrs. Marshall are most engaging. She begins to reveal in them for the first time her extraordinary gift of direct observation and accurate description.. Her remarks on the bringing up of children are very sound for a girl of twenty-three, and the plan she was following in the case of Basil shows that she had some acquaintance with Rousseau's theory. The first letter is dated November 30, and opens with an apology for not writing sooner after her arrival:

" We are now surrounded with winter prospects without doors, and within have only winter occupations, books, solitude, and the fireside; yet I may safely say we are never dull. Basil is a charming boy; he

affords us perpetual entertainment. Do not suppose
from this that we make him our perpetual plaything,
far otherwise. I think that is one of the modes of treatment most likely to ruin a child's temper and character;
but I do not think there is any pleasure more delightful
than that of marking the development of a child's
faculties and observing his little occupations. We
found everything at Racedown much more complete
with respect to household conveniences than I could have
expected. You may judge of this when I tell you that
we have not had to lay out ten shillings on the house.
We were a whole month without a servant, but now we
have got one of the nicest girls I ever saw; she suits us
exactly, and I have all my domestic concerns so arranged
that everything goes on with the utmost regularity. . . .
We walk about two hours every morning. We have
many very pleasant walks about us; and, what is a great
advantage, the roads are of a sandy kind and almost
always dry. We can see the sea 150 or 200 yards from
the door, and, at a little distance, have a very extensive
view terminated by the sea, seen through different
openings of the unequal hills. We have not the warmth
and luxuriance of Devonshire, though there is no want
either of wood or cultivation; but the trees appear to
suffer from the sea-blasts. We have hills which—seen
from a distance—almost take the character of mountains; some cultivated nearly to their summits, others
in a wild state, covered with furze and broom. These
delight me the most, as they remind me of our native
wilds. . . . I have had only one great disappointment
since we came, and that is about the little girl. I lament
it the more, as I am sure if her father knew all the circumstances, he would wish her to be placed under our
care. Mr. Montagu intended being with us a month
ago, but we have not seen him yet. I have the satisfaction of thinking that he will see great improvements
in Basil."

Towards the conclusion of this, her first letter from
Racedown to Mrs. Marshall, Dorothy makes a statement which shows that the ties which bound her brother
to France were by no means yet broken, and that they
were known to her and to her friend: " William has
had a letter from France since we came here. Annette
mentions having despatched half a dozen, none of which

he has received." She has an eye for the condition of the poor country-people about her, which compared unfavourably with that of the Cumberland and Westmorland " statesmen." " The peasants are miserably poor," she writes; " their cottages are shapeless structures of wood and clay : indeed, they are not at all beyond what might be expected in savage life." Appearances at least have much improved since.

In another letter to Mrs. Marshall, written evidently on March 7, 1796, she says :

" We have not seen Mr. Montagu, which disappointed us greatly. . . . The Pinneys have been with us five weeks, one week at Christmas and a month since. They left us yesterday. We all enjoyed ourselves very much. They seemed to relish the pleasures of our fireside in the evening and the excursion of the morning. They are very amiable young men, particularly the elder. He is two and twenty, has a charming countenance, and the sweetest temper I ever observed. He has travelled a good deal in the way of education, been at one of the great schools, and at Oxford, has always had plenty of money to spend. This instead of having spoiled him, or made him conceited, has wrought the pleasantest effects. He is well informed, has an uncommonly good heart, and is very agreeable in conversation. He has no profession. His brother has been brought up a merchant. . . . We have read a good deal while they were with us (for they are fond of reading), but we have not gone on with our usual regularity. When the weather was fine they were out generally all the morning, walking sometimes. Then, I went with them frequently, riding sometimes, hunting, coursing, cleaving wood—a very desirable employment, and what all housekeepers would do well to recommend to the young men of their household in such a cold country as this, for it produces warmth both within and without doors."

Lovers of English poetry may congratulate themselves that this method of employing handsome young visitors did not have the same results at Racedown as on Prospero's enchanted isle. It is pleasant, though rather startling, to think of Dorothy Wordsworth coursing hares and fox-hunting.

" I have not spoken of Basil yet," she continues. " He is my perpetual pleasure, quite metamorphosed from a shivering half-starved plant to a lusty, blooming, fearless boy. He dreads neither cold nor rain. He has played frequently for an hour or two without appearing sensible that the rain was pouring down upon him, or the wind blowing about him. I have had a melancholy letter from Mary Hutchinson. I fear that Margaret is dead before this time. She was then attending her at Sockburn, without the least hope of her recovery. Last year at this time we were all together, and little supposed that any of us was so near death."

She tells of a grand dinner-party they gave while the Pinneys were with them, to which they invited their neighbours : " and very dull it was, except for the entertainment of talking about it before and after." She gives a glimpse of her more serious life :

" I am studying my Italian very hard. I am reading the Fool of Quality, which amuses me exceedingly. Within the last month I have read Tristram Shandy, Brydone's Sicily and Malta, and Moore's Travels in France. I have also read lately Madame Roland's Memoirs and some other French things."

She mentions that her brother and the Pinneys had been at Crewkerne to dinner, and were detained by a fire. In another letter, dated March 19, and postmarked " Crewkerne, Mar. 27, 97," she describes at considerable length their method of managing and teaching little Basil. It all sounds like a page from " Emile."

" We teach him nothing at present," she says, " but what he learns from the evidence of his senses. He has an insatiable curiosity, which we are always careful to satisfy to the best of our ability. It is directed to everything he sees, the sky, the fields, trees, shrubs, corn, the making of tools, carts, etc. He knows his letters, but we have not attempted any further step in the path of *book-learning*. Our grand study has been to make him *happy*, in which we have not been altogether disappointed. . . . We have no punishments, except such as appear to be, so far as we can determine, the immediate consequences that grow out of the offence."

She says that Montagu had come to them unexpectedly, and that he and William had started that morning for Bristol, where they were to spend about a fortnight. A year before—in March, 1796—Coleridge was at Bristol, getting out, with what excitement can be imagined, the first four numbers of *The Watchman*, a periodical miscellany, intended, as the Prospectus declared, " to proclaim the State of the Political Atmosphere, and preserve Freedom and her Friends from the attacks of Robbers and Assassins ! !" In the spring of 1796, while he was " on Watch," as he says, Coleridge wrote to Cottle declaring his intention of giving away a sheet full of sonnets, one to Mrs. Barbauld, one to Wakefield, the radical pamphleteer, one to Dr. Beddoes, one to Wrangham, whom he calls " a college acquaintance of mine, an admirer of me, and a pitier of my principles," one to C. Lamb, one to Wordsworth, etc. Coleridge, Lamb, Wrangham, and Wordsworth ! The lines were already converging. In a long letter to Thelwall, dated May 13, 1796, Coleridge refers unmistakably to Wordsworth, though without naming him. " A very dear friend of mine," he says, " who is, in my opinion, the best poet of the age (I will send you his poem when published), thinks that the lines from 364 to 375 and from 403 to 428 are the best in the volume,—indeed, worth all the rest." Coleridge is referring here to his own book. He continues: " And this man is a republican, and, at least, a *semi*-atheist."

In March, 1797, Wordsworth would be likely to see Coleridge in Bristol, though by this time *The Watchman* had long since ceased to warn the public, and its editor was living at Nether Stowey. He was not the man to stay in a place because he belonged there, and he is known to have been preaching at this time in the Unitarian chapels of Taunton and Bridgwater, and often went to Bristol. It is more surprising that Wordsworth should have left Racedown at this time, for his old friend and future wife, Mary Hutchinson, was visiting his sister.

" You perhaps have heard," the latter writes on March 19, 1797, in her enthusiastic way, " that my friend Mary Hutchinson is staying with me. She is the best girl in the world, and we are as happy as human beings can be, that is," she adds ruefully, " when William is at home; for you cannot imagine how dull we feel, and what a vacuum his loss has occasioned, but this is the first day; to-morrow we shall be better; we feel the change more severely as we have lost both Montagu and him at once. M. is so cheerful and made us so merry that we hardly know how to bear the change. Indeed, William is as cheerful as anybody can be; perhaps you may not think it, but he is the life and soul of the whole house."

She writes with the same girlish simplicity that she is excessively pleased with Mr. Montagu, that he is one of the pleasantest men she ever saw, and so amiable and good that everyone must love him.

It may have been during this visit to Bristol that Wordsworth met Thomas Poole, Coleridge's good angel. The following letter shows that Coleridge visited Wordsworth in June, 1797, at Racedown, and indicates besides that the latter already knew Poole and Cottle. Part of it was printed by Cottle in his " Early Recollections," and again, with a wrong date, in his " Reminiscences." J. Dykes Campbell saw the original, and was led to infer from the sentence about Poole that it seemed " to point to a previous visit or visits to Stowey paid by Wordsworth, or to meetings with Poole at Bristol, of which direct record is lacking." A less cautious reader than Campbell might go further, and surmise that this was not the first time Cottle had been informed that Wordsworth had written a play. When the latter left the two young ladies at Racedown mourning his departure, he probably sacrificed inclination to business, and what business could have appeared to him more urgent than the launching of his tragedy ? Having done all he could in that direction, in March, he would naturally seek to renew his intercourse with Coleridge, and if he had not met Poole before, he would do so then. Coleridge, as we have seen, returned the visit in June. His

letter from Racedown was finally printed by Ernest
Hartley Coleridge, in his " Letters of Samuel Taylor
Coleridge," Vol. I., p. 220.   The probable date, the
editor says, is Thursday, June 8.   He notes that " On
Monday, June 5, Coleridge breakfasted with Dr. Toul-
min, the Unitarian minister at Taunton, and on the
evening of that or the next day he arrived on foot at
Racedown, some forty miles distant."   Omitting three
sentences which have reference only to the forthcoming
volume of poems, which Cottle was printing, it is as
follows :

" June, 1797.

" MY DEAR COTTLE,—I am sojourning for a few days
at Racedown, the mansion of our friend Wordsworth,
who has received Fox's ' Achmed.'   He returns you his
acknowledgments, and presents his kindliest respects to
you.   I shall be home by Friday—not to-morrow—but
the next Friday. . . .   Wordsworth admires my tragedy,
which gives me great hopes.   Wordsworth has written
a tragedy himself.   I speak with heartfelt sincerity, and
(I think) unblinded judgment, when I tell you that I feel
myself *a little man by his side,* and yet do not think myself
the less man than I formerly thought myself.   His drama
is absolutely wonderful.   You know I do not commonly
speak in such abrupt and unmingled phrases, and therefore will the more readily believe me.   There are in the
piece those *profound* touches of the human heart which
I find three or four times in ' The Robbers ' of Schiller,
and often in Shakespeare, but in Wordsworth there are
no *inequalities.*   T. Poole's opinion of Wordsworth is
that he is the greatest man he ever knew; I coincide.
" It is not impossible that in the course of two or
three months I may see you.   God bless you and
" S. T. COLERIDGE."

It would almost appear that the writer, knowing
Cottle's amiable ambition to be the publisher of men of
poetical genius, was trying to inflame his zeal to the
point of undertaking to bring out " The Borderers."   It
will be observed from the first sentence that Cottle and
Wordsworth were already acquainted, though the former
is presumed not to have heard of the tragedy.
There could be no more characteristic introduction of

Coleridge as Wordsworth's generous admirer, enthusiastic critic, and intimate friend than this letter.   Their
paths were drawn together and their destinies united by
the same mysterious power that gave to English poetry
at almost the same moment a Sidney and a Spenser,
and, again, a Marlowe and a Shakespeare.   How much
help they were to be to each other in the coming years !
How they were each to add to the other's poetic vision
and poetic faculty !   How many sorrows they bore in
common and for one another's sake, and how great is
the glory they share !

Half a century later, when Dorothy's mind had given
way under the strain of too much sympathy and thought,
and Coleridge was beyond the touch of infirmity, the
aged survivors of that group recalled vividly the happy
hour when they all four came together for the first time.
Mrs. Wordsworth wrote to Sara Coleridge, November 7,
1845 :

" Your father came afterwards to visit us at Racedown, where I was living with my sister.   We have both
a distinct remembrance of his arrival.   He did not keep
to the high road, but leaped over a high gate and
bounded down the pathless field, by which he cut off
an angle.   We both retain the liveliest possible image
of his appearance at that moment.   My poor sister has
just been speaking of it to me with much feeling and
tenderness."

Were it not for this reminiscence, we should not have
known that Mary Hutchinson spent the whole spring at
Racedown.   She was an eminently cheerful, sensible
person, and her presence at the farmhouse could not
have been consistent with the melancholy with which
an unfounded tradition has invested Wordsworth's residence there.   Compared with the bright, open situation
of Alfoxden, his next home, Racedown might be considered dark, but when we remember how young its
occupants were, and how young all their visitors, fancy
loves to picture them chatting gaily about a wood fire
in their common parlour, " the prettiest little room
that can be," or strolling through the apple orchards,

which were so numerous, Dorothy tells us, that nobody
thought of enclosing them, or climbing through yellow
furze to the broad top of Pilsdon Pen to gaze upon the
English Channel. When Coleridge was there, indoor
delights sufficed. He was a man for the fireside and
long evenings with books and talk.

" You had a great loss in not seeing Coleridge," wrote
Dorothy after his departure. " He is a wonderful man.
His conversation teems with soul, mirth, and spirit.
Then he is so benevolent, so good-tempered and cheerful,
and—like William—interests himself so much about
every little trifle. At first I thought him very plain—
that is, for about three minutes. He is pale and thin,
has a wide mouth, thick lips, and not very good teeth,
longish loose growing half-curling rough black hair. But
if you hear him speak for five minutes you think no
more of them. His eye is large and full, not dark but
grey; such an eye as would receive from a heavy soul
the dullest expression, but it speaks every emotion of
his animated mind. It has more of the ' poet's eye in
a fine frenzy rolling ' than I ever witnessed. He has
fine dark eyebrows, and an overhanging forehead. The
first thing that was read after he came was William's
new poem, The Ruined Cottage, with which he was much
delighted: and after tea he repeated to us two acts
and a half of his tragedy Osorio. The next morning
William read his tragedy The Borderers."

Part of the poem here called " The Ruined Cottage "
is to be found embedded in " The Excursion." It is
the oldest portion of that work—lines 871 to 916 of the
first book. Commenting on the passage in 1843, the
poet says: " All that relates to Margaret and the ruined
cottage, etc., was taken from observations made in the
south-west of England." It shows that he was still
deeply concerned with the evil effects of war. Margaret
is left to grieve amid the ruins of her home because her
husband, hopeless through poverty, has " joined a troup
of soldiers, going to a distant land." Not only the forty-
five lines specified above, but fully half of the book, does
this subject occupy. It is impossible to say how much
of the original poem has been actually retained.

Two other pieces of verse probably written by
Wordsworth at Racedown, or perhaps before he went
there, have come down to us. One, entitled "The
Birth of Love," appeared under Wordsworth's name
in a volume of poems published by Wrangham, and
is a translation of some French lines.* Wordsworth
never reprinted it. Another, "The Convict," appeared
in "Lyrical Ballads," 1798, and was thenceforth
dropped from the poet's editions of his works. The
contrast in execution between these two pieces is very
great. The former has a certain brilliancy, demanded
by the subject-matter, which is clever and conventional.
The latter is laboured and unmusical. It possesses
no other value than its political significance. The poet
compares the sleep of a King—who is presumed to be
necessarily a guilty person—with the horrid dreams of
a convict shut up to brood over his fault:

> When from the dark synod, or blood-reeking field,
> To his chamber the monarch is led,
> All soothers of sense their soft virtue shall yield,
> And quietness pillow his head.

But the poor convict, through tumult and uproar, is
denied even a brief forgetfulness of *his* crimes. The
last stanza, as printed in "Lyrical Ballads," contained
a humane expression which carries us back again to
"Political Justice":

> At thy name though compassion her nature resign,
> Though in virtue's proud mouth thy report be a stain,
> My care, if the arm of the mighty were mine,
> Would plant thee where yet thou might'st blossom again.

M. Legouis remarks that in this "thoroughly Godwinian poem" Wordsworth dramatized "the philosopher's favourite idea for the reformation of the
penal laws"—*i.e.*, transportation as a substitute for
capital punishment. It is altogether to the credit
both of Godwin and his disciple that they felt the folly
and wickedness of the penal code in their time. And

* "L'Education de l'Amour," by the Vicomte de Ségur.

as Milton attained full stature as a poet only after twenty years of attention to public affairs, so we have no reason to regret that Wordsworth for a time gave himself to such questions, even if, as is not at all certain, he thereby delayed the expansion of his poetic powers.

" The Convict " was originally printed in *The Morning Post*, December 14, 1797, and this version shows very emphatically the poet's anti-monarchical principles, his philanthropic purpose, and a very creditable willingness to incur public censure at the bidding of conscience. As poetry, these verses are inferior to the touching lines entitled "The Dungeon," which Coleridge composed about the same time, and which contain the theme of Wordsworth's " Peter Bell.".

RACEDOWN.

CHAPTER X

COLERIDGE

THE life of Samuel Taylor Coleridge is hardly more
remarkable for his genius than for the demonstrations
of generosity which he evoked in other men. It would
be unfair to insinuate that Cottle's practical advice
and frequent loans were prompted solely by self-interest.
If he took pains and even ran risks because he had
faith in Coleridge's powers, one reason was that he
" honoured verse." Although the natural differences
of temperament between Coleridge and Southey, exasperated by their recent approximation, in having
embarked upon the same mad project and married im-
prudently into the same family, had by 1796 resulted
in coolness and dislike, Southey was still faithful to
his ideal of Coleridge. One of the most satisfactory
of these friendships, satisfactory because it gave equal
delight and advantage to both parties and was preserved
by a fine balance of mutual respect, was that between
the poet and Thomas Poole. The story of their relations with each other has been charmingly recounted
in Mrs. Sandford's " Thomas Poole and his Friends,"
one of those biographies for which people who have
passed the meridian of life forsake fiction without a sigh
or a sense of loss.

Poole came to Coleridge's aid at a very critical
moment. The scheme of emigration had fallen through.
Southey had perceived how impracticable it was, and
though his loyal nature compelled him to fulfil his
engagement to Miss Edith Fricker, he had bidden her
farewell at the church door after their marriage and
had gone to Portugal. When he returned, in the
summer of 1796, the project seemed to him wilder
than ever. Nor did Lovell, who had married Mary

Fricker, care to revive it.   Coleridge, who had married
their sister Sara Fricker, perhaps as much out of Pantisocratic enthusiasm as for love, felt woefully deceived
in the loss of his romantic hopes.   He had nerved
himself for a great adventure, of which only the first
step had been taken, and that irretrievable.   As a
preacher and lecturer, he had not been very successful.
He had not kept appointments with his audiences nor
with his own soul.   His friends tried to hold him to
his dates, but no power on earth could make his pen
catch up with his thoughts.   A project for serving as
tutor in a rich family near Derby had failed.   His
magazine, *The Watchman*, had come to an end after
the tenth number, on May 13, 1796.   His first child,
Hartley, was born September 19.   On the same day,
however, he took up the intellectual guardianship of
Charles Lloyd, a young poet, the son of a rich Quaker
of Birmingham, who for nearly a year was to live with
him constantly.   But even with what he earned in this
way and by occasional contributions to London newspapers, Coleridge was submerged in poverty.   Cottle
and other friends made occasional offerings, which
were gratefully accepted.   Superiority to trifles, either
favourable or unfavourable, is a form of magnanimity,
and the great soul of Coleridge shines almost unclouded
in his poems written during this nerve-racking time.
Not the least of his titles to our love is his entire freedom
from the vanity of authorship.   He, who had written
the " Poems on Various Subjects," published by Cottle,
in April, 1796, could be so self-forgetful as to append
this note to the " Lines Written at Shurton Bars ":
" The expression ' green radiance ' is borrowed from
Mr. Wordsworth, a poet whose versification is occasionally harsh and his diction too frequently obscure;
but whom I deem unrivalled among the writers of the
present day in manly sentiment, novel imagery, and
vivid colouring."

He desired to find a cottage in the country, where
he could live more cheaply and with fewer interruptions
than in Bristol, taking with him his wife and child

and his disciple Charles Lloyd. To his other troubles was now, towards the close of 1796, added, the demon Neuralgia. To combat this he unsuspectingly admitted a more terrible demon, Opium, and between the two his distraction was complete. For peace he turned to Thomas Poole. This young man, who was seven years his senior, lived in the village of Nether Stowey, about thirty miles from Bristol. One day in August, 1794, Poole had brought two strangers to call at the house of his uncle, who lived in the neighbouring hamlet of Upper Stowey. His cousin John, who was fresh from Oxford, and kept a diary in Latin, recorded his impressions, which Mrs. Sandford has thus translated:

" About one o'clock Thomas Poole and his brother Richard, Henry Poole, and two young men, friends of his, come in. These two strangers, I understand, had left Cambridge, and had walked nearly all through Wales. One is an undergraduate of Oxford, the other of Cambridge. Each of them is shamefully hot with Democratic rage as regards politics, and both Infidel as to religion. I was extremely indignant. At last, however, about two o'clock, they all go away. . . . About seven o'clock Mr. Reekes comes from Stowey. He is very indignant over the odious and detestable ill-feeling of those two young men, whom he had met at my Uncle Thomas's. They seemed to have shown their sentiments more plainly there than with us. But enough of such matters !"

The strangers, of course, were Southey and Coleridge.

The acquaintance soon ripened into friendship. Coleridge, perhaps in connection with his preaching in the Unitarian chapel at Bridgwater, visited Poole in September, 1795, as is thus recorded, in a diary kept by the latter's cousin Charlotte, under date of the 19th: " Tom Poole has a friend with him of the name of Coleridge: a young man of brilliant understanding, great eloquence, desperate fortune, democratick principles, and entirely led away by the feelings of the moment."

Three weeks later Poole wrote to Coleridge congratulating him on his marriage, and we see that he has

already assumed the tone of counsellor and comforter.
On the very day the last *Watchman* came out, Poole
transmitted to the penniless and discouraged poet
a considerable sum of money which he had collected
as a testimonial, and sent with it a beautiful letter.
That they agreed in politics is shown by Coleridge's
remark in a letter to Poole, March 30, 1796, now in the
British Museum: " Burke's Letter to a Noble Lord
is as contemptible in style as in matter—it is sad
stuff."

To Poole, then, Coleridge naturally turned at the end
of the year, when illness and bad fortune drove him to
seek another home. Poole, with proper caution, described the disadvantages of Nether Stowey and the
cottage there on which Coleridge had set his heart;
but the latter broke into such transports of despair
that nothing more could be urged, and before January 1,
1797, he was settled, uncomfortably enough, in a mean
little house beside the village street. Nether Stowey
lies on the north-eastern slope of the Quantock Hills,
eight or ten miles back from the Bristol Channel, and
may have to-day a population of six or seven hundred.
In Thomas Poole's time it was smaller. It is built in
the form of the letter **Y**. Poole's house, which was
one of the largest in the place, faced the left-hand street,
which leads into the hills towards Upper Stowey. Its
garden ran back almost to the garden of the Coleridge
cottage, which faced the other branch. According to
the poet's estimates, the accuracy of which my own
observation leads me to doubt, he had an acre and a
half of ground behind his cottage, where, before he had
been in the place three weeks, and in the depth of
winter, he wrote: " I raise potatoes and all manner of
vegetables; have an orchard, and shall raise corn (with
the spade) enough for my family. We have two pigs,
and ducks and geese. A cow would not answer to
keep; for we have whatever milk we want from T.
Poole." Not even the memorial tablet which now dig-
nifies the little house can make it other than very plain.
It stands elbow to elbow with other plain little houses.

According to Mrs. Sandford, " in Coleridge's time it would seem to have consisted of two small and rather dark little parlours, one on each side of the front door, looking straight into the street, and a small kitchen behind, wholly destitute of modern conveniences, and where the fire was made on the hearth in the most primitive manner conceivable. There cannot have been more than three or, at most, four bedrooms above." But if his own quarters were cramped, Coleridge had an escape into the more spacious property of Poole, who had room enough and a well-chosen library. Nor was there a bigger heart in the world than Poole's. Poetry and politics were his intellectual passions. He had taught himself and had made others teach him Latin and French. He had reserved four or five hours of his busy day for reading.

Poole took a lively interest in the Revolution. His cousin Charlotte wrote of him in her diary: " I wish he would cease to torment us with his democratick sentiments; but he is never happy until the subject of politicks is introduced, and, as we all differ so much from him, we wish to have no conversation about it." He suffered some petty persecution for giving a copy of " The Rights of Man " to a cabinet-maker, and prevented the excited people of Stowey from burning Tom Paine in effigy. For some years he cherished the hope of making a journey of observation through the Western republic, and he treasured a lock of George Washington's hair which an American friend had given him. He wore his own hair without powder, as a sign of protest against the war-tax on that commodity. Although he inherited considerable property, including a tan-yard, he spent some time as a journeyman tanner on the outskirts of London learning the mechanical details of his trade. He was an embodiment of practical good sense combined with theoretical ability. He wrote the article on Tanning for the third edition of the " Encyclopædia Britannica," introduced improved machinery, managed most of the public and philanthropic affairs of his neighbourhood, fought the slave-

trade, helped to support Coleridge, and was the centre
of the distinguished group who made the obscure hamlet
of Nether Stowey for a time the intellectual capital of
England. All these interests, too, he kept up without detri-
ment to the energetic handling of a large private business.

Coleridge spent the first six months of 1797 at Nether
Stowey revising his " Poems " for a second edition and
writing his tragedy " Osorio." Charles Lloyd was intelligent, attractive, and devoted to his instructor, but
extremely delicate. There was little gardening, after all.
On Sundays Coleridge often walked to Bridgwater, eight
miles away, or to Taunton, somewhat farther, to preach
to the Unitarian congregations there. This sojourn
was one of his few green isles " in the deep wide sea
of misery." The outdoor life was good for his health.
Poole's friendship comforted his soul. There was no
immediate cause for alarm as to the hostile league of
those " two giants, BREAD and CHEESE." His poetic
vein was proving very rich. And best of all, he was
getting out the ore. Altogether, we may treat ourselves to the thought that it was a right happy young
man who, leaping over the gate at Racedown, ran
across the triangular field to salute his brother poet.
It is always a pleasure to think of Coleridge happy.
And his best days henceforth are those spent in the
society of William and Dorothy Wordsworth.

He no doubt gave them a most enthusiastic account
of Nether Stowey. Poole, as we know, was built according to Wordsworth's ideal, an example of what an English
farmer and artisan could become. His attainments,
Wordsworth thought, were, in kind at least, not beyond
the reach of the better sort of Westmorland and Cumberland " statesmen." Coleridge, of course, described
Poole. Probably, too, he dilated on the superior beauty
of the scenery in Somerset. And it is true that the hills
about Racedown are bleak compared with the richly-
wooded heights and combes of the Quantocks, the landscape less open and cheerful, the general air of nature
less warm and opulent. But more attractive than all
his descriptions, there was Coleridge himself. Words-

worth had not hitherto been appreciated; Coleridge caught, interpreted, and approved his every expression. Wordsworth was still in rebellion against Church and State, and had been perhaps wondering in his seclusion whether, after all, there were any other young men quite so extreme as himself. Coleridge made no concealment of his own radical views, which he no doubt clothed with splendour and paraded with pomp. They were both Cambridge men, both poets—though undiscovered by a senseless world—and both writing tragedies. In Dorothy's heart the subtle instincts of pity and womanly solicitude were stirred. She penetrated their guest's disguise, and behind his gay and fluent speech detected his unrest, his anxiety, his self-reproach. At that moment began the long years wherein her first thought, next to William's welfare, ever was how to alleviate Coleridge's suffering.

Nether Stowey is well over thirty miles from Racedown by the roads existing at that time. Yet, having tasted the joys of companionship with the Wordsworths, Coleridge thought nothing of flying back to sip the nectar again and again, and in a letter to Southey written in July, 1797, he says: " I had been on a visit to Wordsworth's at Racedown, near Crewkerne, and I brought him and his sister back with me, and here I have *settled them.*" It is not unlikely that between June 16 and July 2, Wordsworth walked over with Coleridge from Racedown, was captivated by the beauty of the Quantocks, and learned that a good house could be rented on extremely easy terms not far from Coleridge, to whom by this time he was already deeply attached. At any rate, he and his sister came to Nether Stowey on July 2, 1797, apparently with no intention of returning to Dorsetshire.

On this occasion Coleridge drove and Dorothy sat beside him. No doubt they brought the few articles which constituted the Wordsworths' slight *impedimenta,* and of course five-year-old Basil. Coleridge referred to this exploit as proof of his ability to drive a one-horse chaise. The roads, he told Southey, were execrable.

This journey was a fitting close to a month of inter-
mittent and enthusiastic talk, of thrilling discoveries, of
frank disclosures. Their acquaintance ripened quickly
into a relation for which even " friendship " is too cold
a word. The anxieties, the sorrows of Dorothy Wordsworth's life, and perhaps, too, her intensest joys, dated
from that happy time. " My sister," he calls her after
that, and she was brave enough to remain on that foot-
ing through the years to come. We have seen how unrestrained she was in expressing her love for William.
To this other love she grants no stronger phrase than
" dear Col." Not until her mind gave way beneath the
load of sympathy and suppressed emotion, and the light
of her glad youth darkened down to premature old age,
did those about her half understand. " Her health
broken by long walks," indeed ! Why keep up this
fiction, when the truth but testifies to the fulness of
her womanly nature and adds a crowning touch to the
beauty of her character ? She loved Coleridge, and was
able, through long years, not of mere silence and withdrawal, but of close intimacy, to transmute her love into
helpfulness, forgetting self and reverencing every obligation. Did she perchance strengthen her soul, in moments
of extreme trial, with Godwin's law that " man has no
rights, but only duties " ? The story of Dorothy Wordsworth is the tenderest, the purest, the most sacred page
in the annals of poetry. " She never told her love,"
but her sweet innocency never taught her to practise
concealment of it; so that even those who knew her well
were deceived by her frankness into a belief that she
really felt towards Coleridge only a sisterly solicitude
and the affection of an old comrade.

The Wordsworths, not to mention Basil—whom at
this juncture nobody mentions—appear to have been
crowded somehow into that little house in Nether
Stowey, with Coleridge and Mrs. Coleridge, and Hartley
the baby, and Nanny the maid (" simple of heart,
physiognomically handsome, and scientific in vacci-
mulgence "), and to have stayed there the two weeks
beginning with July 2. Coleridge writes to Cottle:

"STOWEY, 1797.

"Wordsworth and his exquisite sister are with me. She is a woman indeed ! in mind, I mean, and heart; for her person is such, that if you expected to see a pretty woman, you would think her rather ordinary; if you expected to see an ordinary woman, you would think her pretty ! but her manners are simple, ardent, impressive. In every motion, her most innocent soul outbeams so brightly, that who saw would say,

> Guilt was a thing impossible in her.

Her information various. Her eye watchful in minutest observation of nature; and her taste, a perfect electrometer. It bends, protrudes, and draws in, at subtlest beauties and most recondite faults. She and W. desire their kindest regards to you.—Your ever affectionate friend, S. T. C."

As if it were not an amazing enough coincidence that three persons of genius should be sheltered under one mean roof, who should arrive from London but Charles Lamb ! Lloyd, be it observed, had had several attacks of melancholia, and was no longer living at Nether Stowey. It was less than a year since the terrible day when Lamb's dear sister Mary, in a fit of insanity, killed her mother, September 22, 1796. Coleridge had for some time been trying to persuade his old schoolfellow to visit him, and, apparently without knowing that the Wordsworths were there, Lamb at last consented to come to Nether Stowey. He arrived on July 7, and stayed until the 14th. In the letter to Southey already cited, Coleridge writes:

"Charles Lamb has been with me for a week. He left me Friday morning. The second day after Wordsworth came to me, dear Sara accidentally emptied a skillet of boiling milk on my foot, which confined me during the whole time of C. Lamb's stay, and still prevents me from all *walks* longer than a furlong. While Wordsworth, his sister, and Charles Lamb were out one evening, sitting in the arbour of T. Poole's garden, which communicates with mine, I composed these lines, with which I am pleased."

Here he inserts the earliest extant and no doubt original draft of his delightful poem, " This Lime-Tree Bower my Prison," one of the sweetest and most tranquil of his compositions. Twice in these lines appears the expression, " my Sister and my Friends." In a copy which he wrote for Lloyd, who had not met the Words-worths, and could better picture the scene without them, he changed this to " my Sara and my friend," and in the printed version, which he prepared after his sad estrangement from Wordsworth, he altered it to " my gentle-hearted Charles." In the prefatory note, be-ginning "In the June of 1797 some long-expected friends paid a visit to the author's cottage," he named the month incorrectly.

It was an extraordinary company that strolled back and forth between Poole's house and the cottage, and climbed up to the ancient British camp, above the village, and wandered through the wooded hills. Country people meeting them stared at their unconventional clothing, and commented on their apparent idleness. Coleridge himself was hardly yet an accepted figure, and all Tom Poole's old radicalism was remembered afresh. Even Mrs. Coleridge was not like other women. We think of her too exclusively as a careworn mother, much concerned with household economy, and are in-clined to forget that she married with the expectation of becoming a Pantisocrat and leading a very different sort of life from most women. Moreover, she too wrote verses. The other three were extraordinary-looking persons. William was tall and gaunt, with a peculiar nervous smile that played about the corners of his mouth. He wore his hair long, straight, and un-powdered, like a Jacobin. Charles Lamb was only twenty-two, and delighted in mystifying people. He and Dorothy, with their dark skin and roving eyes, had a foreign air. They looked enough alike to be members of the same gipsy band.

It is probable that they all, in spite of Coleridge's scalded foot, managed to inspect the property which it was planned that Wordsworth should rent. Lamb

reproached himself with being a rather silent guest.
There was much talk, and Coleridge, beyond question,
did his share; but Lamb can hardly have deserved his
own censure. They were entertained at Poole's, and
one or two other houses. On his return to London,
Lamb wrote to his host:

" I feel improvement in the recollection of many a
casual conversation. The names of Tom Poole, of
Wordsworth and his good Sister, with thine and Sara's,
are become ' familiar in my mouth as household words.'
You would make me very happy, if you think W. has
no objection, by transcribing for me that inscription of
his. I have some scattered sentences ever floating on
my memory, teasing me that I cannot remember more
of it."

This must refer to the " Lines left upon a Seat in a
Yew-Tree."

A pretty clear trace of these conversations remains in
a few sentences of that letter from Coleridge to Southey
which I have already quoted, and which was written
just after Lamb's departure, and we can see in them
the print of Wordsworth's mind. They are perhaps the
earliest witnesses to that understanding between Wordsworth and Coleridge on the subject of poetic diction
which resulted in " Lyrical Ballads," and the critical
works growing out of that venture.

" A young man," he writes, " by strong feelings is
impelled to write on a particular subject, and this is all
his feelings do for him. They set him upon the business
and then they leave him. He has such a high idea of
what poetry ought to be, that he cannot conceive that
such things as his natural emotions may be allowed to
find a place in it; his learning therefore, his fancy, or
rather conceit, and all his powers of buckram are put
on the stretch."

It must have been Wordsworth's natural gifts that
won Coleridge's admiration; certainly not his learning.
The plastic mind of Coleridge respected his guest's
superior power of self-determination, and above all,
perhaps, the quality of spirit which made him regard

his natural emotions with so much reverence that to
dress them in buckram would have been impossible.
" Wordsworth is a very great man," wrote Coleridge to
Southey in this same letter; " the only man to whom
at all times and *in all modes of excellence* I feel myself
inferior."

Alfoxden is a long, low, and very beautiful country-
house, about four miles north-west of Nether Stowey.
It is surrounded by a romantic park, heavily wooded
with noble oaks and beeches, which extends far back
into the Quantock Hills.   The road from Bridgwater and
Stowey passes below the house at the foot of a broad
lawn to the little village of Holford.   The brown waters
of the Bristol Channel bound the view on the north-east.
After the plainness of Nether Stowey, and the strictly
agricultural character of all the country which a traveller
from Bridgwater sees from the road, Alfoxden has a
somewhat grand, though genial air.   It is much larger
than Rydal Mount.   Miss Wordsworth was not exaggerating when she called it a mansion.   Seventy head of
deer fed in the glades around it, and their descendants
give life to the park now.   The place has a warm
and open look, very different from that of Racedown.
But it has been described by an inimitable pen.
Miss Wordsworth and her brother found their way
into the park before they had been two days at Nether
Stowey, and she wrote on July 4:

" There is everything there; sea, woods wild as fancy
ever painted, brooks clear and pebbly as in Cumberland,
villages so romantic; and William and I, in a wander by
ourselves, found out a sequestered waterfall in a dell
formed by steep hills covered with full-grown timber-
trees.   The woods are as fine as those at Lowther, and
the country more romantic; it has the character of the
less grand parts of the neighbourhood of the lakes."

On August 14, writing now from Alfoxden itself, she
says:

" The evening that I wrote to you, William and I had
rambled as far as this house, and pryed into the recesses
of our little brook, but without any more fixed thoughts

upon it than some dreams of happiness in a little cottage
and passing wishes that such a place might be found
out.   We spent a fortnight at Coleridge's: in the course
of that time we heard that this house was to let, applied
for it, and took it.   Our principal inducement was Coleridge's society.   It was a month yesterday since we
came to Alfoxden.

" The house is a large mansion, with furniture enough
for a dozen families like ours.   There is a very excellent
garden, well stocked with vegetables and fruit.   The
garden is at the end of the house, and our favourite
parlour, as at Racedown, looks that way.   In front is a
little court, with grass plot, gravel walk, and shrubs;
the moss roses were in full beauty a month ago.   The
front of the house is to the south, but it is screened from
the sun by a high hill which rises immediately from it.
This hill is beautiful, scattered irregularly and abun-
dantly with trees, and topped with fern, which spreads
a considerable way down it.   The deer dwell here, and
sheep, so that we have a living prospect.   From the
end of the house we have a view of the sea, over a woody
meadow-country; and exactly opposite the window
where I now sit is an immense wood, whose round top
from this point has exactly the appearance of a mighty
dome.   In some parts of this wood there is an under
grove of hollies which are now very beautiful.   In a
glen at the bottom of the wood is the waterfall of which
I spoke, a quarter of a mile from the house.   We are
three miles from Stowey, and not two miles from the
sea.   Wherever we turn we have woods, smooth downs,
and valleys with small brooks running down them,
through green meadows, hardly ever intercepted with
hedgerows, but scattered over with trees.   The hills that
cradle these valleys are either covered with fern and
bilberries or oak woods, which are cut for charcoal.
. . . Walks extend for miles over the hill-tops; the
great beauty of which is their wild simplicity: they are
perfectly smooth, without rocks.   The Tor of Glaston-
bury is before our eyes during more than half of our
walk to Stowey; and in the park wherever we go, keeping about fifteen yards above the house, it makes a part
of our prospect."

Alfoxden belonged to a family named St. Albyn.   A
lease of the property, including house, furniture, gardens,
stables, and coach-house, was signed July 14 by their

tenant, John Bartholomew, and William Wordsworth, and witnessed by Thomas Poole, the rental being only twenty-three pounds, for one year, Bartholomew to pay all rates and taxes, and keep the premises in good tenantable repair. This merely nominal price was due to the fact that the sole object of letting the place at all was to keep the house inhabited during the owner's minority. It may be remarked also that the war had seriously checked the prosperity of the country, and many great families were glad to get anything for their country-seats.

From the letters just quoted, it might seem that when the Wordsworths came to visit Coleridge, they did not dream of renting Alfoxden; yet they appear to have come away from Racedown with bag and baggage, for they took possession of their new place at once. When Miss Wordsworth wrote, " It was a month yesterday since we came to Alfoxden," she probably meant four weeks, which would be July 16. Lamb left Nether Stowey July 14. Poole, of course, was active in securing Alfoxden for Wordsworth. It was probably in the interval between July 14 and 17 that Coleridge wrote to Poole: " I pray you come over if possible by eleven o'clock that we may have Wordsworth's Tragedy read under the trees."

Immediately after Lamb's departure he was succeeded at Nether Stowey by another invited guest. This was John Thelwall, the political agitator, with whom Coleridge had for some months been in frequent correspondence. Coming to Coleridge's house late on July 17, he found that his host was spending the night at Alfoxden. The necessity of " superintending the wash-tub " had brought Mrs. Coleridge home, but next morning she and Thelwall hastened over to Alfoxden, four miles away, in time, as we are told, " to call Samuel and his friend Wordsworth up to breakfast."* Thus began a day which must have remained bright in Thelwall's memory for ever. " We are a most philosophical

* Letter from Thelwall to his wife, dated Alfoxden, July 18, 1797. See Mrs. Sandford's " Thomas Poole and his Friends," I. 232.

party," he declared, " the enthusiastic group consisting of C. and his Sara, W. and his sister, and myself, without any servant, male or female." They rambled through the grounds, exploring its woods and its romantic dell. They " passed sentence on the productions and characters of the age," and gave full vent to their enthusiasm in poetical and philosophic flights. " Citizen John," cried Coleridge, as they gazed at the water tumbling in its dim recess, " this is a fine place to talk treason in." " Nay ! Citizen Samuel," rejoined the tired fighter, " it is rather a place to make a man forget that there is any necessity for treason."*

Though this appears to have been their first meeting, Coleridge and Thelwall had been in correspondence for over a year. In December, 1796, Coleridge had written : " Though *personally* unknown, I really love you, and can count but few human beings whose hand I would welcome with a more hearty grasp of friendship." There is in the British Museum a letter from Thelwall to Coleridge, May 10, 1796, mentioning previous correspondence between them, and referring to a sonnet by Coleridge in Thelwall's honour, containing the words : " Thou, mid thickest fire, Leap'st on the perilous wall." The person thus esteemed by Coleridge was about eight years his senior, a self-made man, who during a youth of poverty, in which he tried several occupations, never ceased to read and to practise composition. He was deeply affected by the French Revolution. He perceived its social significance. As M. Charles Cestre has well said :† " He played a prominent part in the

* Coleridge's " Table Talk," July 26, 1830. Wordsworth's version of this little incident, as recorded in the Fenwick note to his " Anecdote for Fathers," is characteristic of the way in which, in the latter part of his life, he made light of his early connection with radicals like Thelwall : " I remember once when Coleridge, he, and I were seated together upon the turf, on the brink of a stream in the most beautiful part of the most beautiful glen of Alfoxden, Coleridge exclaimed : ' This is a place to reconcile one to all the jarrings and conflicts of the wide world.' ' Nay,' said Thelwall, ' to make one forget them altogether.' " Who can doubt that Coleridge has reported the words correctly ?

† " John Thelwall : a Pioneer of Democracy and Social Reform in England during the French Revolution," p. 13. London, 1906.

first democratic agitation in England, gained great ascendancy over the more educated elements of the labouring class, and cannot but have been powerfully instrumental in awakening the lower orders to the consciousness of their opportunities."

In the height of the reactionary panic in May, 1794, Thelwall was arrested, his house was searched, his library was taken from him and never restored, his writings were scattered, and he was committed to await trial on the flimsiest of testimony.*

He lay for five months untried in the Tower, and for one month in Newgate prison, " in the dead-hole, or charnel-house, where the corpses of such prisoners as died of diseases were placed before the burial."

In spite of the desperate and contemptible measures taken by Government to procure conviction, Thelwall was acquitted of the charge of high treason.   His sufferings only increased his zeal, and on his release, as he was not allowed to speak in public places, he fitted up a lecture-room of his own, where he spoke twice a week to large audiences, expounding the philosophy of the Revolution, and pleading such causes as electoral reform and liberty of assembly.   He published his lectures in a periodical, *The Tribune*, which he owned and edited. After the great mass-meeting of December 7, 1795, in Marylebone Fields, the Government renewed its pressure, his supporters fell away, and he was obliged to give up lecturing.   *The Tribune* was suppressed in April, 1796, but Thelwall continued publishing his doctrines in pamphlets until the close of the year.   He earned a precarious living, and managed to continue his political propaganda, by lecturing in many parts of the country on subjects not immediately revolutionary, such as

---

* Thelwall says: " Every manuscript was seized, upon whatever subject—Poems, Novels, Dramas, Literary and Philosophical Dissertations—all the unfinished labours of ten years' application. Successful or abrotive, it matters not; they were the fruits, the creations of my own industry, and therefore were more *absolutely my property* than the estate of the landed gentleman or the stock-in-trade of the manufacturer. Whether they are worth *sixpence* or *six thousand pounds* is of no consequence."   See Vol. I., p. 90, of *The Tribune*, London, 1795.

Roman history. But his activities became more and
more difficult and unprofitable as the rising war-passion
swept men and parties into the Tory ranks. He was
frequently mobbed, and the magistrates of some of the
towns where he spoke refused to give him protection.
He had few friends left except Coleridge. He was
attracted to the latter not only personally, but for the
rather amusing reason that he conceived of him as one
who had found a way to combine intellectual freedom
with agricultural success. Coleridge, on the other hand,
was interested in Thelwall, not only as a talented and
brave revolutionist, but as an atheist, who might be
converted to more moderate religious views.

Coleridge charged his correspondent with " anti-
religious bigotry." To a man of his argumentative disposition, the task of converting such a person was very
alluring. He himself could so easily see many sides to
all great philosophical questions, that the simple dogmatic Thelwall must have seemed to him a mere child.
He had not found it easy to alter the mood of his other
ew-found friend, Wordsworth, whom he termed " a
semi-atheist." He was proud of having won Charles
Lloyd " to a conviction of the truth of Christianity,
. . . for he had been, if not a deist, yet quite a sceptic."
The half-dozen letters in which he poured out his
heart to Thelwall before meeting him are among the
liveliest and most affectionate Coleridge ever wrote.
Small wonder that the persecuted and discouraged
agitator sought at last to enjoy his presence and
see if there was any chance of settling in his neighbourhood.

The world has long ago forgotten, if it ever indeed
admitted, that Thelwall was a poet. Yet he was the
author of much verse. Its quality is below mediocrity;
but the subjects he chose and the nature of his attempt
are not without significance to a student of Wordsworth.
The plan of Thelwall's " Peripatetic " is similar in its
mechanism to that of " The Excursion," and it is
perhaps not too fanciful to think that in " Michael "
we have a reminiscence of Thelwall's poem, " On Leaving

the Bottoms of Gloucestershire, August, 1797," in which
he thus describes the cottages of weavers :

> Industry,
> Even from the dawning to the western ray,
> And oft by midnight taper, patient plies
> Her task assiduous; and the day with songs,
> The night with many an earth-star, far descried,
> By the lone traveller, cheers amid her toil.

Thelwall and Wordsworth agreed perfectly in their
opposition to war and their belief that the poor of
England were oppressed.   Thelwall was one of the first
observers to sound a warning against the dangers of
the industrial movement just beginning, which tended to
attract the population into large centres and to exploit
children's labour.   He raised his voice against

> the unwieldy pride
> Of Factory overgrown, when Opulence,
> Dispeopling the neat cottage, crowds his walls
> (Made pestilent by congregated lungs
> And lewd association) with a race
> Of infant slaves, brok'n timely to the yoke
> Of unremitting drudgery.

All that rendered Thelwall interesting to Coleridge,
Wordsworth, and Thomas Poole, made him an object
of horror to other people in the Stowey neighbourhood.
Poole's cousin Charlotte wrote in her diary :

"*July* 23, 1797.—We are shocked to hear that Mr.
Thelwall has spent some time at Stowey this week
with Mr. Coleridge, and consequently with Tom Poole.
Alfoxton House is taken by one of the fraternity, and
Woodlands by another.   To what are we coming ?"

The chief offender had left Nether Stowey by July 27,
for on that date, being his birthday, he wrote some
verses at the neighbouring town of Bridgwater.   They
were composed, as their title informs us, "during a long
Excursion in quest of a peaceful Retreat," and contain
a pathetic expression of hope that the recent pleasant
days may sometime be renewed :

Ah ! 'twould be sweet, beneath the neighb'ring thatch,
In philosophic amity to dwell,
Inditing moral verse, or tale, or theme,
Gay or instructive; and it would be sweet
With kindly interchange of mutual aid
To delve our little garden plots, the while
Sweet converse flow'd, suspending oft the arm
And half-driven spade, while, eager, one propounds,
And listens one, weighing each pregnant word,
And pondering fit reply, that may untwist
The knotty point—perchance, of import high—
Of moral Truth, of Causes infinite,
Created Power, or uncreated Worlds
Eternal and uncaus'd ! or whatsoe'er
Of Metaphysic, or of Ethic Lore,
The Mind, with curious subtlety, pursues—
Agreeing or dissenting—sweet alike,
When wisdom, and not Victory, the end. . . .

There is a letter from Coleridge to John Chubb, of Bridgwater, written in 1797 or 1798, on the subject of Thelwall's difficulty in finding a place where he could live unmolested. Mr. Chubb, who appears to have been an estate-agent, is urged to find a cottage for Thelwall somewhere within five or six miles of Stowey.

" He has found by experience," writes the sympathetic poet, " that neither his own health or that of his wife and children can be preserved in London; and were it otherwise, yet his income is inadequate to maintain him there. He is therefore under the necessity of fixing his residence in the country. But, by his particular exertions in the propagation of those principles which we hold sacred and of the highest importance, he has become, as you well know, particularly unpopular, through every part of the kingdom—in every part of the kingdom, therefore, some odium and inconvenience must be incurred by those who should be instrumental in procuring him a cottage there—but are Truth and Liberty of so little importance that we owe no sacrifice to them ?"

Thelwall desired to take a house at Nether Stowey, and settle there permanently with his wife and children, but Coleridge, in the autumn, warned him not to come. Without Poole's help it would be impossible, he says, and " to such interference on his part there are insuper-

able difficulties." " The whole malignity of the Aristocrats," he continues, " will converge to him, as to one
point. His tranquillity will be perpetually interrupted;
his business and his credit hampered and distressed by
vexatious calumnies; the ties of relationship weakened,
perhaps broken; and, lastly, his poor old mother made
miserable." Then from what follows we have the information that Wordsworth at the time of his coming
had been regarded as a dangerous man:

" Very great odium Tom Poole incurred by bringing
me here; my peaceable manners, and known attachment
to Christianity, had almost worn it away, when Wordsworth came, and he, likewise by T. Poole's agency,
settled here. You cannot conceive the tumult, calumnies, and apparatus of threatened persecutions, which
the event has occasioned round about us. If *you*, too,
should come, I am afraid that even riots, and dangerous
riots, might be the consequence. Either of us separately would perhaps be tolerated; but *all three* together
—what can it be less than plot and damned conspiracy ?
—a school for the propagation of Demagogy and
Atheism ?"

In another letter, of about the same time, he says:

" I am sad at heart about you on many accounts, but
chiefly anxious for this present business. The aristocrats seem to persecute *even Wordsworth*. But we will at
least not yield without a struggle; and if I cannot get you
near me, it shall not be for want of a trial on my part."

We have here a reference to a fact which gives one some
idea of the state of the public mind. Coleridge, un-
supported by other testimony, might be suspected of
exaggerating very mild alarms into something more
considerable. But it is known that someone in the
neighbourhood sent word to the authorities that dis-
affected persons were gathering about Nether Stowey,
and a Government spy was sent down to observe them.
Mrs. St. Albyn, the mother of the heir to Alfoxden, was
invoked to look into Wordsworth's case. She repri-
manded her tenant or agent, Bartholomew, for having
let the house to him, and notice was given the poet to

quit the place on the expiration of his term, which would
be the next June. Poole, who had to bear the responsibility, shouldered his part of the blame right manfully,
and wrote a letter of explanation to the incensed
" aristocrat," but in vain. The important parts of his
letter to Mrs. St. Albyn are as follows:

" MADAM,—I have heard that Mr. Bartholomew of
Putsham has incurred your displeasure by letting Allfoxen House to Mr. Wordsworth. As it was through
me that Mr. Wordsworth was introduced to Mr. Bartholomew as a tenant, I take the liberty of addressing to you
this letter, simply to state the circumstances attending
the business, and to say a few words for Mr. Wordsworth
and his connections. . . . As for Mr. Wordsworth, I
believe him to be in every respect a gentleman. I have
not known him personally long, but I had heard of his
family before I knew him. Dr. Fisher, our late Vicar,
and one of the Canons of Windsor, had often mentioned
to me, as his particular and respected friend, Mr. Cookson, Mr. Wordsworth's uncle, and also one of the Canons
of Windsor. This circumstance was sufficient to con-
vince me of the respectability of Mr. Wordsworth's
family. You may, upon my honour, rest assured that
no tenant could have been found for Allfoxen whom, if
you knew him, you would prefer to Mr. Wordsworth.
His family is small, consisting of his sister, who has
principally lived with her uncle, Mr. Cookson, a child
of five years old, the son of a friend of his, and one excellent female servant. . . . But I am informed you
have heard that Mr. Wordsworth does keep company,
and on this head I fear the most infamous falsehoods
have reached your ears. Mr. Wordsworth is a man fond
of retirement—fond of reading and writing—and has
never had above two gentlemen at a time with him.
By accident Mr. Thelwall, as he was travelling through
the neighbourhood, called at Stowey. The person he
called on at Stowey took him to Allfoxen. No person
at Stowey nor Mr. Wordsworth knew of his coming.
Mr. Wordsworth had never spoken to him before, nor,
indeed, had anyone of Stowey. Surely the common
duties of hospitality were not to be refused to any man:
and who would not be interested in seeing such a man
as Thelwall, however they may disapprove of his sentiments or conduct ? God knows we are all liable to err,

and should bear with patience the difference in one another's opinions. Be assured, and I speak it from my own knowledge, that Mr. Wordsworth, of all men alive, is the last who will give anyone cause to complain of his opinions, his conduct, or his disturbing the peace of anyone. Let me beg you, madam, to hearken to no calumnies, no party spirit, nor to join with any in disturbing one who only wishes to live in tranquillity. I will pledge myself in every respect that you will have no cause to complain of Mr. Wordsworth. You have known me from my youth, and know my family—I should not risk my credit with you in saying what I could not answer for.—Believe me, with sincere respect, your very obedient and obliged—THOMAS POOLE.

" *September* 16, 1797."*

Mrs. Sandford tells a curious anecdote about Poole's cousins at Upper Stowey:

" Once Tom Poole, being there with his friends, begged Penelope to sing ' Come, ever-smiling Liberty !' (' Judas Maccabæus ') for Coleridge and Wordsworth. Many years afterwards she related the circumstance to her daughter, and told how she persistently selected another song. ' I could not sing it,' she said; ' I knew what they meant by *their* liberty.' "

A spy could hardly have come into this extremely patriotic neighbourhood without his business being discovered, and there can be no doubt that a spy came to observe the friends. Probably much wise advice was offered in this case by ignorant villagers puzzled by the unconventional dress and manner of the strangers, and by officious persons who felt that they owed it to the country to see that no Jacobins were tolerated in Somerset. These petty persecutions, and especially the descent and discomfiture of the spy, must have amused the two poets, and added a delightful spice of romance to their daily walks. We must remember how young they were. Coleridge could not refrain from telling the story with

* The rough draft of this letter is in the British Museum, and shows by its many erasures and corrections that Poole felt he was undertaking a very delicate mission.

mock-solemn detail, in the midst of a very serious part
of " Biographia Literaria."

Wordsworth, in the Fenwick note to " Anecdote for
Fathers," after referring rather apologetically to his acquaintance with Thelwall, says: " The visit of this man
to Coleridge was, as I believe Coleridge has related, the
occasion of a spy being sent by Government to watch
our proceedings, which were, I can say with truth, such
as the world at large would have thought ludicrously
harmless." He gave to the composition of this poem
the date 1798, and told Miss Fenwick,

" the name of Liswyn Farm was taken from a beautiful spot on the Wye,* where Mr. Coleridge, my sister,
and I, had been visiting the famous John Thelwall, who
had taken refuge from politics, after a trial for high
treason, with a view to bring up his family by the
profits of agriculture, which proved as unfortunate a
speculation as that he had fled from. Coleridge and
he had both been public lecturers; Coleridge mingling
with his politics Theology, from which the other elocu-
tionist abstained, unless it was for the sake of a sneer.
This quondam community of public employment in-
duced Thelwall to visit Coleridge at Nether Stowey,
where he fell in my way. He really was a man of
extraordinary talent, an affectionate husband, and a
good father. Though brought up in the city, on a
tailor's board, he was truly sensible of the beauty of
natural objects."

It is likely that Wordsworth's attitude toward Thelwall
in 1797 was by no means so detached and superior as
he wished to make it appear when he dictated this sadly
inaccurate and condescending note. Coleridge, writing
to a friend, says: " John Thelwall is a very warm-
hearted, honest man; and disagreeing as we do, on almost
every point of religion, of morals, of politics, and
philosophy, we like each other uncommonly well. He
is a great favourite with Sara."

A letter from Coleridge to Cottle, undated, but evidently written in the spring or early summer of 1798,

* Apparently he had forgotten that Thelwall's farm was not on the
Wye, but near Brecon, in Wales, a day's walk from the Wye.

shows in the following passage that the distrust of Wordsworth continued throughout the entire time of his residence in Somersetshire, and that Mrs. St. Albyn did not relent:

" Wordsworth has been caballed against *so long and so loudly* that he has found it impossible to prevail on the tenant of the Allfoxden estate, to let him keep the house, after their first agreement is expired, so he must quit it at Midsummer; whether we shall be able to procure him a house and furniture near Stowey, we know not, and yet we must: for the hills, and the woods, and the streams, and the sea, and the shores, would break forth into reproaches against us, if we did not strain every nerve, to keep their Poet among them. Without joking, and in serious sadness, Poole and I cannot endure to think of losing him."*

Cottle treats us to an anecdote which from its flavour evidently passed through the hands of Coleridge: " The wiseacres of the village had, it seems, made Mr. W. the subject of their serious conversation. One said that ' he had seen him wander about by night, and look rather strangely at the moon ! and then he roamed over the hills, like a partridge.' Another said, ' he had heard him mutter, as he walked, in some outlandish brogue, that nobody could understand !' " But here I am afraid the amiable Cottle becomes too garrulous to be quoted further. True or not, however, his account of how he and the poets tried to unharness a horse is worth repeating for two reasons: it is no exaggeration of their ignorance of worldly ways, and it shows how

---

* Knight makes the statement (" Life of Wordsworth," I. 146) that the poet wrote on the margin of a memoir of himself, compiled by Barron Field, and never printed, opposite a statement that his removal from Alfoxden was occasioned by " caballing long and loud ": "A mistake. *Not the occasion* of my removal. Annoyances I had none. The facts mentioned by Coleridge of a spy, etc., came not to my knowledge till I had left the neighbourhood. I was not refused a continuance. I never applied for one." I have not seen the memoir to which Knight here refers. Certainly Wordsworth's recollection was at fault, as the letters and extracts given above from diaries in Mrs. Sandford's " Thomas Poole and his Friends " show, not to mention the testimony of Cottle, Coleridge, and Southey, and the manuscript of the draft of Poole's letter to Mrs. St. Albyn, which I have seen.

eager the author of " Alfred, an Epic Poem in Twenty-four Books," was to associate his name with the authors of the " Ancient Mariner " and " The Excursion ":

" I removed the harness without difficulty, but, after many strenuous attempts, I could not get off the collar. In despair, I called for assistance, when aid soon drew near.   Mr. W. first brought his ingenuity into exercise, but, after several unsuccessful efforts, he relinquished the achievement, as altogether impracticable.   Mr. Cole-ridge now tried his hand, but showed no more grooming skill than his predecessors; for after twisting the poor horse's neck, almost to strangulation, and to the great danger of his eyes, he gave up the useless task, pro-nouncing that ' the horse's head must have grown (gout or dropsy !) since the collar was put on ! for,' he said, ' it was a downright impossibility for such a huge Os Frontis to pass through so narrow a collar !'   Just at this instant the servant girl came near, and understand-ing the cause of our consternation, ' La, Master,' said she, ' you do not go about the work in the right way. You should do like this,' when, turning the collar com-pletely upside down, she slipped it off in a moment, to our great humiliation and wonderment; each satisfied, afresh, that there were heights of knowledge in the world to which he had not attained."

CHAPTER XI

THREE PERSONS AND ONE SOUL

COLERIDGE was immensely benefited in spirits by Wordsworth's companionship, though he wrote to Cottle that in spite of his friend's conversation he was depressed, for he saw no way of earning Bread and Cheese. The nectar of sympathy and the ambrosia of discourse seem to have taken the place of these humble elements, for we hear little more of them, the mundane inference being that they were unobtrusively provided by Poole. At once the brief but fervent Polar summer of Coleridge's poetic activity began. The bracing effect of Wordsworth's society is seen first in the consecutive toil which Coleridge bestowed upon his " Osorio," which probably represents more hard work than anything else he ever wrote. Sheridan had asked him to write a tragedy. The knowledge that Wordsworth was writing one encouraged him. Such progress was made that by September he had reached the middle of the fifth act, and a month later it was finished and sent to the Drury Lane Theatre. It was rejected. In 1813, in a revised form and with a new title, " Remorse," it was successfully performed, and had a long run in London, besides being acted in the provinces.

Wordsworth was not much later than Coleridge in finishing his tragedy. The latter wrote to Cottle:

" I have procured for Wordsworth's tragedy an introduction to Harris, the manager of Covent Garden, who has promised to read it attentively and to give his answer immediately; and if he accepts it, to put it in preparation without an hour's delay."

And on November 20 Dorothy Wordsworth writes:

" William's play is finished, and sent to the managers of the Covent Garden Theatre. We have not the faintest expectation that it will be accepted."

But undoubtedly they had some hopes, for they went to London, about the end of the month, and stayed three weeks. She wrote from Bristol, on the return journey, December 21:

" We have been in London: our business was the play; and the play is rejected. It was sent to one of the principal actors at Covent Garden, who expressed great approbation, and advised William strongly to go to London to make certain alterations."

The same letter expresses great sorrow and disappointment because Coleridge's play also was rejected. Wordsworth took his defeat philosophically. It stimulated him to greater exertions. He wrote in fine spirits to James Tobin, a brother of the dramatist, John Tobin: " I am perfectly easy about the theatre; if I had no other means of employing myself, Mr. Lewis's success would have thrown me into despair." This refers to M. G. Lewis's flashy tragedy, " The Castle Spectre," which was having a profitable run in London.

" There is little need," he continues, " to advise me against publishing; it is a thing which I dread as much as death itself. This may serve as an example of the figure by rhetoricians called hyperbole, but privacy and quiet are my delight. No doubt you have heard of the munificence of the Wedgwoods towards Coleridge. I hope the fruit will be good as the seed is noble. We leave Alfoxden at Midsummer. The house is let . . . so our departure is decided. What may be our destination I cannot say. . . . We have no particular reason to be attached to the neighbourhood of Stowey, but the society of Coleridge and the friendship of Poole."

He laughingly mentions having written 1,300 lines of a poem in which he has contrived to convey most of the knowledge of which he is possessed, his object being " to give pictures of Nature, Man, and Society." He says that he has carved out work for at least a year and a half, and refers to essays " which must be written with eloquence, or not at all." " My eloquence," Wordsworth says, " modestly speaking, will all be carried off, at least for some time, into my poem." He asks Tobin to collect books of travels for him, which are indispensable for his present labours, and he wishes to see " Mrs. Godwyn's Life." In Miss Wordsworth's Journal for April 14, we learn that " Mary Wollstonecraft's life, etc., came."

One essay at least he wrote, to illustrate, as he said many years afterwards, " that constitution and those tendencies of human nature which make the apparently motiveless actions of bad men intelligible to careful observers." It was published by Professor de Selincourt in *The Nineteenth Century and After* for November, 1926, having been recently found prefixed to a copy of " The Borderers " as revised for the stage in 1797, though from its tone it appears to have been composed in 1795. It is an extremely subtle but laboured study of morbid psychology, after reading which it is easy to see why the disciple of Godwin and observer of the perversions of well-meaning French extremists,

> " Sick, wearied out with contrarieties,
> Yielded up moral questions in despair."

The visit to London, after so many months of quiet country life, acted as a stimulus to Wordsworth's productive powers. He returned to Alfoxden with a quickened appreciation of nature, and realizing that not even the mighty city held a man comparable in genius, attainments, and charm, to their neighbour and friend at Nether Stowey. Coleridge's magnetism extends even to those who endeavour to fasten their attention upon Wordsworth. Whenever the two are together, it is Coleridge who catches the eye and enthrals the ear. But he comes and goes, his intellectual fire darts now here and now there, his genius varies like the colour of a star, while Wordsworth, by slow but constant motion, rises in a calculable orbit and with a steady light. When Wordsworth lived at Alfoxden, they were in each other's houses almost every day. Their communion of spirit was close, and the result was a great quickening of their poetic powers. But the new life was more immediately evident in Coleridge. During these few months he com-

posed most of his best work—not only " The Rime of
the Ancient Mariner," " Kubla Khan," and the first
part of " Christabel," but those warm outpourings of
friendly confidence, those genial conversation poems,
which are more endearing and only less wonderful:
" This Lime-Tree Bower my Prison," " Frost at Midnight," " Fears in Solitude," and " The Nightingale."

The story of how he wrote the " Ancient Mariner "
illustrates the fact that, though they could together plan
a work, it would in the end take form and spirit from
an individual mind.   On November 13, 1797, Coleridge, with Wordsworth and his sister, started from
Alfoxden about four o'clock in the afternoon, intending
to walk to Lynton and the Valley of Stones, on the
North Devon coast, about thirty-five miles distan⁺.
With their small supply of money, it seemed a rash
expenditure, but they light-heartedly put care aside by
resolving to pay the expenses of the trip from the proceeds of a poem to be written for *The Monthly Magazine*.
Thus relieved in mind, they tramped gaily over the
Quantock Hills through the dark autumn evening, and
spent the first night at the village of Watchet, on the
Bristol Channel, planning the " Ancient Mariner " as
they went.   Coleridge invented most of the story, which
he said was suggested to him by a dream of his friend
Mr. Cruikshank, a resident of the Stowey neighbourhood.   Wordsworth contributed the idea of poetic
justice for the crime of killing an albatross.   He had
just been reading Shelvocke's " Voyages," where he had
seen a description of this bird.   He also suggested the
gruesome incident of the navigation of the ship by the
dead men.   The three worked joyously together at the
poem that night, Wordsworth contributing two or three
complete lines.   But the undertaking proved more
congenial to Coleridge, and the poem is his.   The trio
completed their excursion, which took several days and
furnished many delightful and droll recollections.   Coleridge worked at the poem until it was finished, in March,
on the 23rd of which month Dorothy wrote in her
Journal: " Coleridge dined with us.   He brought his

ballad finished." But it was the night-wind off salt
water as he went, " one of three," down into Watchet
that first brought to him the Mariner's hail.

That mysterious poem, " Christabel," was begun in
1797, and contains several observations of nature of
which the originals are to be found in Dorothy's Journal
from January 21 to March 25, 1798. She was gathering
honey that spring for two " singing masons building
roofs of gold."

The two poets were associated in another literary
venture which was not so successful as the " Ancient
Mariner." It was to have been a prose rhapsody, " The
Wanderings of Cain," in three cantos, of which one, the
second, has been preserved and printed among Coleridge's poems. In the tone of reverent tenderness with
which he almost always mentions his friend, he thus,
after thirty years, tells the story of this attempt:

" The work was to have been written in concert with
another whose name is too venerable within the precincts of genius to be unnecessarily brought into connection with such a trifle, and who was then residing
at a small distance from Nether Stowey. The title and
subject were suggested by myself, who likewise drew
out the scheme and the contents for each of the three
books or cantos, of which the work was to consist, and
which, the reader is to be informed, was to have been
finished in one night ! My partner undertook the first
canto: I the second: and whichever had *done first* was
to set about the third. Almost thirty years have passed
by; yet at this moment I cannot without something more
than a smile moot the question which of the two things
was the more impracticable, for a mind so eminently
original to compose another man's thoughts and fancies,
or for a taste so austerely pure and simple to imitate the
Death of Abel ? Methinks I see his grand and noble
countenance as at the moment when, having despatched
my own portion of the task at full finger-speed, I hastened to him with my manuscript—that look of humorous
despondency fixed on his almost blank sheet of paper,
and then its silent mock-piteous admission of failure
struggling with the sense of the exceeding ridiculousness
of the whole scheme—which broke up in a laugh: and
the Ancient Mariner was written instead."

Coleridge attempted the same subject in verse, and kept the introductory stanza, " which had been committed to writing for the purpose of procuring a friend's judgment on the metre." It is interesting to observe that the rhythm and the general musical effect are similar to those of Wordsworth's ballads, " The Last of the Flock," " The Idiot Boy," and " Peter Bell," composed about the same time. The same cadences, the same loose rhyming scheme, and the same length of line, were used for a similar description of innocent boyhood in a wilderness, by the mediæval German poet Wolfram von Eschenbach, in his " Parzeval." Coleridge's stanza is as follows:

> Encinctured with a twine of leaves,
> That leafy twine his only dress !
> A lovely Boy was plucking fruits,
> By moonlight, in a wilderness.
> The moon was bright, the air was free,
> And fruits and flowers together grew
> On many a shrub and many a tree:
> And all put on a gentle hue,
> Hanging in the shadowy air
> Like a picture rich and rare.
> It was a climate where, they say
> The night is more belov'd than day.
> But who that beauteous Boy beguil'd,
> That beauteous Boy to linger here ?
> Alone, by night, a little child,
> In place so silent and so wild—
> Has he no friend, no loving mother near ?

Because of Coleridge's quicker responsiveness to intellectual impressions, we find in his poems written between November, 1797, and the summer of 1798, a more complete record of the thoughts that must have occupied Wordsworth's mind than the latter's own poems of that period reveal. Wordsworth gathered the harvest too, but not so soon. We have every reason to distrust the testimony of strangers, and even his own deprecatory remarks in old age, to the effect that he was not at that time occupied with politics. He was living in close daily intercourse with the suffering mind

from whose anxiety were struck off " France: an Ode,"
and " Fears in Solitude," in February and April, 1798.
These great poems, unsurpassed in our language as
expressions of political feeling, show that the love of
liberty still glowed as brightly as ever in Coleridge's
breast.　He still set the cause of humanity above
insular pride.　He still was tortured with a sense of the
wrongs his country had committed.　If at the same
time he realized that the Revolution in France had
deviated from its original course, if he turned heart-sick
from a race who " still promising freedom " were " themselves too sensual to be free," there was little comfort
for him in the thought either of those at home who
expected " all change from change of constituted power,"
or of those who doted on the British Constitution " with
a mad idolatry."　To his far-seeing and humane mind
it was an excruciating dilemma.　There can be no doubt
whatever that Wordsworth suffered like pangs.　The
astounding victories of Napoleon, meanwhile, were
giving to the war-fever in England the aspect of exalted
patriotism.　There was panic in the air, to which the
mutinies of the Nore and at Spithead gave a turn towards
desperation and hardness.

Lloyd having left him on account of ill-health, Coleridge was almost penniless when winter came on.
During the Wordsworths' visit to London, in December,
he received an invitation to preach to the Unitarian
congregation at Shrewsbury, and was on the point of
accepting a call to be their pastor, when Josiah and
Thomas Wedgwood, sons of the great potter, offered
him an annuity of £150 for life, without conditions, as
a mark of their appreciation of his poetic and philosophic genius.　He had scruples against preaching for
hire, and these generous and cultivated brothers hoped
to save him for the work he was best fitted to do.　Josiah
Wedgwood's letter of January 10, containing their
proposal, is as delicately worded as it is forcible:

" My brother and myself are possessed of a considerable superfluity of fortune; squandering and hoarding
are equally distant from our inclinations.　But we are

earnestly desirous to convert this superfluity into a fund of beneficence, and we have now been accustomed for some time, to regard ourselves rather as Trustees than Proprietors."

Coleridge preached on a few Sundays at Shrewsbury, but withdrew his candidature and visited the Wedgwoods. By February 3 he had returned to Nether Stowey, as we learn from an entry in Dorothy Wordsworth's Journal for that date: "Walked with Coleridge over the hills." The Journal begins January 20, 1798, and up to this point is filled almost exclusively with minute observations of nature. In the interval Nether Stowey seems to have had little attraction, and is referred to only twice. On January 25 she writes, "Went to Poole's after tea," and on January 31, "Set forward to Stowey at half-past five." After Coleridge's return there is almost daily mention of walks to and from Nether Stowey, or wanderings with him in the woods above and around Alfoxden. Twice before he came she records "an uninteresting evening," but never again. There can hardly be in all the world a story of more perfect happiness than her pages tell. The day of her felicity was still in its dewy morning hours. She had her brother with her, contented and productive. They saw and felt as one creature. When Coleridge was with them their union was not disturbed, but enlarged and rendered more complete. This happy and fruitful intimacy is disclosed in Dorothy's Alfoxden Journal. On reading those charming pages one feels that one has come upon a hidden rill of pure water, not at its very source, however, for it flows already with a full current, as if accustomed to motion. In a partnership so close, it is hard to distinguish the original contribution of each member. When, for instance, did Dorothy Wordsworth acquire her habit of exactly noting what she saw out of doors ? Surely, if she had been so interested in natural objects three years before, she would have expressed herself to Jane Pollard on this as on so many other subjects. There are preliminary touches in her letters from Racedown, and it is quite likely she began writing some sort of nature notes there, but before she began to live with her brother this strain is rarely discoverable in her writings, and then chiefly when recalling his one visit to Forncett just before his graduation, or when referring to his poetry. Her own instincts appear to have been originally domestic and social. Notwithstanding his exquisite acknowledgment in the well-known line of " The Sparrow's Nest,"

> She gave me eyes, she gave me ears,

it was he, or he and Coleridge together, who taught her to " see into the life of things." What she gave him is more fully told in the complete sentence which concludes that poem:

> She gave me eyes, she gave me ears;
> And humble cares and delicate fears;
> A heart, the fountain of sweet tears;
> And love, and thought, and joy.

After his long years of roving, unrestrained by the sweet bondage of domestic ties, her gentleness and womanly scruples, her fine discrimination and intensity of feeling, were a revelation to him. And in return he opened to her a new world, the world of natural objects. " An Evening Walk " and " Descriptive Sketches " prove that he had obtained access to this realm without her assistance, and while she was still almost a stranger to his intellectual life. We may therefore regard the wonderful pages of her Journal as a record of remarks which were at least as certainly his as her own. Their literary form, which it is impossible to praise too highly, is, however, hers. She seldom indulges in a reflection, she seldom elaborates. Facts are all that concern her; yet, though she states facts very simply, there are always a fine glow of tenderness and some heightening touch, which spiritualize the details. Take, for example, the opening sentences of the first entry:

" ALFOXDEN, *January 20th*, 1798.—The green paths down the hill-sides are channels for streams. The young wheat is streaked by silver lines of water running between the ridges, the sheep are gathered together on

the slopes.   After the wet dark days, the country seems
more populous.   It peoples itself in the sunbeams.   The
garden, mimic of spring, is gay with flowers."

Three days later she notes: " The sound of the sea distinctly heard on the tops of the hills, which we could
never hear in summer.   We attribute this partly to the
bareness of the trees, but chiefly to the absence of the
singing of birds, the hum of insects, that noiseless noise
which lives in the summer air.   The villages marked out
by beautiful beds of smoke."

Every day she and her brother walked together, sometimes in the wood that separated Alfoxden House from
the village of Holford, sometimes on the hills above,
whence they could see the turbid waters of the Bristol
Channel and the Welsh coast beyond.   They dipped
into the coombes, or little valleys sloping to the sea,
where autumn lingered long and spring came early.   A
characteristic entry is that of January 26:

" Walked upon the hill-tops; followed the sheep-
tracks till we overlooked the larger coombe.   Sat in the
sunshine.   The distant sheep-bells, the sound of the
stream; the woodman winding along the half-marked
road with his laden pony; locks of wool still spangled
with the dewdrops; the blue-grey sea, shaded with
immense masses of cloud, not streaked: the sheep
glittering in the sunshine.   Returned through the wood.
The trees skirting the wood, being exposed more directly
to the action of the sea-breeze, stripped of the network
of their upper boughs, which are stiff and erect, like
black skeletons; the ground strewed with the red berries
of the holly.   Set forward before two o'clock.   Returned
a little after four."

She notes " the ivy twisting round the oaks like
bristled serpents," and how at night " the shadows of
the oaks blackened, and their lines became more strongly
marked " when " the moon burst through the invisible
veil which enveloped her."

There are but few touches due to sentiment or fancy.
The actual is sufficiently wonderful.   It is as if she were
seeing this infinite world for the first time.   She was
very happy, in high health and spirits.   The ordinary

sights and sounds of country life were so exhilarating that to record them was a joyous solemnity, and she did not care to speculate upon their significance. To treat them as symbols would have seemed a strangely perverse and impertinent course. Sometimes, with a faculty rarely found except in children and painters, she sees things as they appear to be, and not as she knows they really are. For example, one evening she notes that the sea was " big and white, swelled to the very shores, but round and high in the middle." Could words possibly produce a more detailed and yet unified picture than this on February 24 ?—

" Went to the hill-top. Sat a considerable time over-looking the country towards the sea. The air blew pleasantly round us. The landscape mildly interesting. The Welsh hills capped by a huge range of tumultuous white clouds. The sea, spotted with white, of a bluish-grey in general, and streaked with darker lines. The near shores clear; scattered farm-houses, half concealed by green mossy orchards, fresh straw lying at the doors; hay-stacks in the fields. Brown fallows, the springing wheat, like a shade of green over the brown earth, and the choice meadow plots, full of sheep and lambs, of a soft and vivid green; a few wreaths of blue smoke, spreading along the ground; the oaks and beeches in the hedges retaining their yellow leaves; the distant prospect on the land side, islanded with sunshine; the sea, like a basin full to the margin; the dark fresh-ploughed fields; the turnips of a lively rough green. Returned through the wood."

One scarcely knows whether to admire more such a distinct stroke as that " lively rough green " of the turnips, or the general composition of the picture, which is so plainly a day in late February or early March. Again, she mentions a prospect " *curiously* spread out for even minute inspection, though so extensive that the mind is afraid to calculate its bounds."

Their walks were usually in the afternoon and even-ing, and they brought home bundles of sticks which they gathered along the way. Sometimes Basil was with them, sometimes Tom Poole, and very often Coleridge. The latter was at Shrewsbury preaching in December, and till January 29, when he visited the Wedgwoods. He probably returned to Nether Stowey on February 3, and came at once to Alfoxden. On that date he is mentioned for the first time in the Journal. " A mild morning," Dorothy writes, " the windows open at breakfast, the redbreasts singing in the garden. Walked with Coleridge over the hills." Less methodical than even the Wordsworths, he appears to have had no scruple about breaking in upon their work at any time of day or night. So we find, under date of February 4: " Walked a great part of the way to Stowey with Coleridge." February 6: " Walked to Stowey over the hills." And so throughout this month and the next, and till April 9, few were the days on which the three did not meet somewhere. From about April 9 to 18 Coleridge was in Devonshire, visiting his relatives at Ottery St. Mary, and on his return the pleasant intercourse began again.

Most of the entries are very brief. When Coleridge had talked to his heart's content, there was probably no time left except for the daily tasks, such as " hanging out linen." They did not keep country hours— never, at least, when he was of the party. Three successive entries show how the time flew—March 25: " Walked to Coleridge's after tea. Arrived at home at one o'clock. The night cloudy but not dark." 26th: " Went to meet Wedgwood at Coleridge's after dinner. Reached home at half-past twelve, a fine moonlight night; half-moon." 27th: " Dined at Poole's. Arrived at home a little after twelve, a partially cloudy, but light night, very cold." On a day of very high wind " Coleridge came to avoid the smoke; stayed all night," and they walked in the wood. Next day she " walked to Crookham [Crewcombe she means] with Coleridge and Wm. to make the appeal. Left Wm. there, and parted with Coleridge at the top of the hill." This perhaps refers to the difficulty with Mrs. St. Albyn about staying at Alfoxden. She frequently refers to her brother's being tired or ill. Apparently the Coleridges stayed with them for some days in March, and shortly afterwards she mentions poems which her brother was composing, among them " The Thorn," " A Whirl-blast from Behind the Hill," and " Peter Bell." A striking example of how she and her brother thought the same thoughts and used the same words is to be found by comparing his poem, " A Night-Piece," with the entries in her Journal for January 25 and 31. She writes:

" The sky spread over with one continuous cloud, whitened by the light of the moon, which, though her dim shape was seen, did not throw forth so strong a light as to checquer the earth with shadows. At once the clouds seemed to cleave asunder, and left her in the centre of a black-blue vault. She sailed along, followed by multitudes of stars, small, and bright, and sharp. Their brightness seemed concentrated (half-moon)." And again: " Set forward to Stowey at half-past five. A violent storm in the wood; sheltered under the hollies. When we left home the moon immensely large, the skies scattered over with clouds. These soon closed in, contracting the dimensions of the moon without concealing her."

The poem is as follows:

The sky is overcast
With a continuous cloud of texture close,
Heavy and wan, all whitened by the Moon,
Which through that vale is indistinctly seen,
A dull, contracted circle, yielding light
So feebly spread, that not a shadow falls,
Chequering the ground—from rock, plant, tree, or tower
At length a pleasant instantaneous gleam
Startles the pensive traveller while he treads
His lonesome path, with unobserving eye
Bent earthwards; he looks up—the clouds are split
Asunder,—and above his head he sees
The clear Moon, and the glory of the heavens.
There in a blue-black vault she sails along,
Followed by multitudes of stars, that, small
And sharp, and bright, along the dark abyss
Drive as she drives; how fast they wheel away,
Yet vanish not !—the wind is in the tree,
But they are silent;—still they roll along
Immeasurably distant; and the vault,

Built round by those white clouds, enormous clouds,
Still deepens its unfathomable depth.
At length the Vision closes; and the mind,
Not undisturbed by the delight it feels,
Which slowly settles into peaceful calm,
Is left to muse upon the solemn scene.

Nearly fifty years later the poet said of these lines:
" Composed on the road between Nether Stowey and
Alfoxden extempore. I distinctly recollect the very
moment when I was struck, as described, ' He looks up
—the clouds are split, etc.' "

It is in the Alfoxden Journal that we read the first of
Dorothy Wordsworth's many remarks on the exhaustion
which it cost her brother to compose poetry. On
April 20 she writes: " Walked in the evening up the
hill dividing the Coombes. Came home the Crookham
way, by the thorn and the ' little muddy pond.' Nine
o'clock at our return. William all the morning engaged
in wearisome composition. The moon crescent. *Peter
Bell* begun."

On Wednesday, May 16, she writes: " Coleridge,
William, and myself, set forward to the Chedder rocks;
slept at Bridgwater;" and under date of Tuesday the
22nd she writes: " Walked to Chedder. Slept at Cross."
Here these precious jottings come to an end.

It seems likely that after visiting the wonderful limestone gorge at Cheddar, they proceeded, perhaps by
way of Wells and Bristol, to the valley of the Wye,
and made the visit to Thelwall's farm which is mentioned in the Fenwick note to an " Anecdote for Fathers."
It was about forty miles west of the Wye, and beyond
a mountain range.

In May also probably occurred the visit of William
Hazlitt to Nether Stowey, to which we owe a marvel-
lously vivid description of Wordsworth as he then appeared. We may depend upon Hazlitt to have set down
aught in malice that occurred to him. He would not be
inclined to change a single feature by way of flattery.
We have, indeed, to be on our guard with him, against
the venom of his rancour, as when he declares that

Wordsworth had the free use of Alfoxden, and consequently grew soft-hearted towards Toryism. Anyone
who is at all well acquainted with Hazlitt's method of
suggesting falsehood will know how to value this insinuation.   Of the close accuracy of his portraiture
there is, however, no reason to doubt.   He was an
almost unrivalled master of personal description, and
his account of Wordsworth corresponds trait for trait,
down to the twitching lines of the mouth, with a drawing made by W. Shuter in April, to which Dorothy
referred in her Journal of April 26.*

When Coleridge preached at Shrewsbury in January,
Hazlitt, who was a lad of nineteen, walked ten miles to
hear him. The poet-philosopher-preacher completed his
conquest during a subsequent visit at Hazlitt's home,
and dazzled the boy by inviting him to visit Nether
Stowey in the spring. Hazlitt's reminiscences, which
he called " My First Acquaintance with Poets," were
published, in substance, in 1817, and afterwards ampli-
fied and reprinted. I quote from the " Memoirs of
William Hazlitt," 1867:

" I arrived," says Hazlitt, " and was well received.
. . . In the afternoon Coleridge took me over to All-
Foxden, a romantic old family mansion of the St.
Aubins, where Wordsworth lived. It was then in the
possession of a friend of the poet, who gave him the free
use of it. Somehow that period (the time just after the
French Revolution) was not a time when *nothing was
given for nothing.* The mind opened, and a softness
might be perceived coming over the heart of individuals,
beneath ' the scales that fence ' our self-interest. Wordsworth himself was from home, but his sister kept house,
and set before us a frugal repast ; and we had free access
to her brother's poems, the ' Lyrical Ballads,' which
were still in manuscript or in the form of ' Sibylline
Leaves.'   I dipped into a few of these with great satisfaction, and with the faith of a novice. I slept that
night in an old room with blue hangings, and covered
with the round-faced family-portraits of the age of
George I. and II., and from the wooded declivity of the

* See the frontispiece.

adjoining park that overlooked my window, at the dawn of day, could

> . . . hear the loud stag speak.

" That morning, as soon as breakfast was over, we strolled out into the park, and seating ourselves on the trunk of an old ash-tree that stretched along the ground, Coleridge read aloud, with a sonorous and musical voice, the ballad of ' Betty Foy.' I was not critically or skeptically inclined. I saw touches of truth and nature, and took the rest for granted. But in the ' Thorn,' the ' Mad Mother,'* and the ' Complaint of a Poor Indian Woman,' I felt that deeper power and pathos which have been since acknowledged,

> In spite of pride, in erring reason's spite,

as the characteristics of this author; and the sense of a new style and a new spirit in poetry came over me. It had to me something of the effect that arises from the turning up of the fresh soil, or the first welcome breath of Spring,

> While yet the trembling year is unconfirmed.

Coleridge and myself walked back to Stowey that evening, and his voice sounded high

> Of Providence, foreknowledge, will, and faith,
> Fix'd fate, free-will, foreknowledge absolute,

as we passed through echoing grove, by fairy stream or waterfall, gleaming in the summer moonlight! He lamented that Wordsworth was not prone enough to believe in the traditional superstitions of the place, and that there was a something corporeal, a *matter-of-fact-ness*, a clinging to the palpable, or often to the petty, in his poetry, in consequence. His genius was not a spirit that descended to him through the air; it sprung out of the ground like a flower, or unfolded itself from a green spray, on which the goldfinch sang. He said, however (if I remember right), that this objection must be confined to his descriptive pieces; that his philosophic poetry had a grand and comprehensive spirit in it, so that his soul seemed to inhabit the universe like a palace, and to discover truth by intuition, rather than by deduction. The next day Wordsworth arrived from Bristol at Coleridge's cottage. I think I see him now. He answered in some degree to his friend's description of

---

* " Her eyes are wild."

him, but was more gaunt and Don Quixote-like. He
was quaintly dressed (according to the *costume* of that
unconstrained period) in a brown fustian jacket and
striped pantaloons. There was something of a roll, a
lounge in his gait, not unlike his own ' Peter Bell.'
There was a severe, worn pressure of thought about his
temples, a fire in his eye (as if he saw something in
objects more than the outward appearance), an intense,
high, narrow forehead, a Roman nose, cheeks furrowed
by strong purpose and feeling, and a convulsive inclination to laughter about the mouth, a good deal at variance
with the solemn, stately expression of the rest of his
face. Chantrey's bust wants the marking traits, but he
was teased into making it regular and heavy. Haydon's
head of him, introduced into the *Entrance of Christ into
Jerusalem*, is the most like his drooping weight of
thought and expression. He sat down and talked very
naturally and freely, with a mixture of clear gushing
accents in his voice, a deep guttural intonation, and a
strong tincture of the northern *burr* like the crust on
wine. He instantly began to make havoc of the half
of a Cheshire cheese on the table, and said triumphantly
that ' his marriage with experience had not been so productive as Mr. Southey's in teaching him a knowledge
of the good things of this life.' He had been to see the
' Castle Spectre,' by Monk Lewis, while at Bristol, and
described it very well. He said ' it fitted the taste of
the audience like a glove.' This *ad captandum* merit
was, however, by no means a recommendation of it,
according to the severe principles of the new school,
which reject rather than court popular effect. . . . We
went over to All-Foxden again the day following, and
Wordsworth read us the story of ' Peter Bell ' in the
open air; and the comments made upon it by his face
and voice was very different from that of some later
critics ! Whatever might be thought of the poem, ' his
face was a book where men might read strange matters,'
and he announced the fate of his hero in prophetic tones.
There is a *chaunt* in the recitation both of Coleridge and
Wordsworth, which acts as a spell upon the hearer, and
disarms the judgment. Perhaps they have deceived
themselves by making habitual use of this ambiguous
accomplishment. Coleridge's manner is more full, ani-
mating, and varied; Wordsworth's more equable, sustained, and internal. The one might be termed more
dramatic, the other more *lyrical*."

The reader must disentangle for himself what is original in this passage from what was woven into it upon reflection and after the lapse of years. There may well be some inaccuracies, but on the whole this is much the most complete and interesting portrayal of Wordsworth in youth or early manhood that we possess. The precise date, and even the month, of Hazlitt's visit is uncertain. He says:

" Thus I passed three weeks at Nether Stowey and in the neighbourhood, generally devoting the afternoons to a delightful chat in an arbour made of bark by the poet's friend Tom Poole, sitting under two fine elm trees, and listening to the bees humming round us, while we quaffed our *flip*."

He describes a jaunt along the coast from Dunster to Lynton, with Coleridge and a young man from Stowey. Coleridge told him that he and Wordsworth had once intended making the Valley of Rocks, near Lynton, the scene of a prose tale, and that the " Lyrical Ballads "

" were an experiment to be tried by him and Wordsworth to see how far the public taste would endure poetry written in a more natural and simple style than had hitherto been attempted; totally disregarding the artifices of poetical diction, and making use only of such words as had probably been common in the most ordinary language since the days of Henry II "

A picture of the sordid side of rural life, composed by Wordsworth about this time, and known in his family as the " Somersetshire Tragedy," was not deemed fit for publication, and was destroyed by Professor Knight !

The lease of Alfoxden expired June 24, and two days later the Wordsworths were homeless wanderers again. The poet gave the following account of their first movements :

" We left Alfoxden on Monday morning, the 26th of June, stayed with Coleridge till the Monday following, then set forth on foot towards Bristol. We were at Cottle's for a week, and thence we went toward the banks of the Wye. We crossed the Severn Ferry, and walked ten miles further to Tintern Abbey, a very beautiful ruin on the Wye. The next morning we walked along the river through Monmouth to Goderich Castle, there slept, and returned the next day to Tintern, thence to Chepstow, and from Chepstow back again in a boat to Tintern, where we slept, and thence back in a small vessel to Bristol."

The most precious result of this journey was the poem entitled " Lines written a few miles above Tintern Abbey," of which Wordsworth says, in the Fenwick note: " No poem of mine was composed under circumstances more pleasant for me to remember than this. I began it upon leaving Tintern, after crossing the Wye, and concluded it just as I was entering Bristol in the evening, after a ramble of four or five days with my sister. Not a line of it was altered, and not any part of it written down until I reached Bristol. It was published almost immediately after in the little volume of which so much has been said in these notes "—*i.e.*, " Lyrical Ballads."

ALFOXDEN.

CHAPTER XII

"LYRICAL BALLADS"

WE are now approaching the most momentous event in Wordsworth's life, so far as his connection with the public is concerned. For many months he and Coleridge had been preparing to make what proved to be one of the most gallant adventures in literary history. They had exerted themselves to produce enough poetry to fill a volume, and were already planning with Cottle for its publication. The two poets had been in communication with Cottle on the subject of printing their tragedies. In a letter to Cottle dated merely 1798, Coleridge says: "I am requested by Wordsworth to put to you the following questions: What could you, conveniently and prudently, and what would you give for—first, our two Tragedies, with small prefaces, containing an analysis of our principal characters? . . . Second, Wordsworth's Salisbury Plain and Tale of a Woman; which poems, with a few others which he will add, and notes, will make a volume." To this Cottle appends the statement: "I offered Mr. Coleridge and Mr. Wordsworth thirty guineas each, as proposed, for their two tragedies; but which, after some hesitation, was declined, from the hope of introducing one or both on the stage. The volume of Poems was left for some future arrangement."

According to Cottle, he met Wordsworth for the first time at Stowey, though, as we have seen, there is reason to think their acquaintance began at Bristol long before the poet settled in Somersetshire. The passage in Cottle's "Reminiscences" is very interesting:

"A visit to Mr. Coleridge at Stowey had been the means of my introduction to Mr. Wordsworth, who read me many of his Lyrical Pieces, when I immediately perceived in them extraordinary merit, and advised him to publish them, expressing a belief that they would be well received. I further said he should be at no risk; that I would give him the same sum which I had given to Mr. Coleridge and to Mr. Southey, and that it would be a gratifying circumstance to me, to have been the publisher of the first volumes of three such poets, as Southey, Coleridge, and Wordsworth; such a distinction might never again occur to a provincial bookseller. To the idea of publishing he expressed a strong objection, and after several interviews I left him, with an earnest wish that he would reconsider his determination. Soon after Mr. Wordsworth sent me the following letter:

> " ' Allfoxden,
> " ' 12th April, 1798.
> " ' My dear Cottle,
> " ' . . . You will be pleased to hear that I have gone on very rapidly adding to my stock of poetry. Do come and let me read it to you under the old trees in the park. We have a little more than two months to stay in this place. Within these four days the season has advanced with greater rapidity than I ever remember, and the country becomes almost every hour more lovely. God bless you.
> " ' Your affectionate friend,
> " ' W. Wordsworth.' "

The invitation was repeated by Coleridge and again, in the following note, by Wordsworth:

> " Dear Cottle,
> " We look for you with great impatience. We will never forgive you if you do not come. I say nothing of the ' Salisbury Plain ' till I see you. I am determined to finish it, and equally so that you shall publish.
> " I have lately been busy about another plan, which I do not wish to mention till I see you; let this be very, very soon, and stay a week if possible; as much longer as you can. God bless you, dear Cottle,
> " Yours sincerely,
> " Allfoxden,　　　　　　　　" W. Wordsworth.
> " 9th May, 1798."

Cottle prints in the same connection, but without date, a long letter from Coleridge, which shows that he and the Wordsworths were trying to raise money for some unusual expense, undoubtedly their trip to Germany. It was perhaps written at about the same time as Wordsworth's of May 9. There is no mention of Cottle's visit in Dorothy's Journal, but it might have occurred between May 9 and 16, when she made no entries. Omitting several sentences already quoted, the letter is as follows:

" My dear Cottle,

" Neither Wordsworth or myself could have been otherwise than uncomfortable, if anybody but yourself had received from us the first offer of our Tragedies, and of the volume of Wordsworth's Poems. At the same time, we did not expect that you could, with prudence and propriety, advance such a sum as we should want at the time we specified. In short, we both regard the publication of our Tragedies as an evil. It is not impossible but that in happier times, they may be brought on the stage: and to throw away this chance for a mere trifle, would be to make the present moment act fraudulently and usuriously towards the future time. . . . We consider the publication of them an evil on any terms; but our thoughts were bent on a plan for the accomplishment of which a certain sum of money was necessary, (the whole,) at that particular time, and in order to this we resolved, although reluctantly, to part with our Tragedies: that is, if we could obtain thirty guineas for each, and at less than thirty guineas Wordsworth will not part with the copy-right of his volume of Poems. We shall offer the Tragedies to no one, for we have determined to procure the money some other way. If you choose the volume of Poems, at the price mentioned, to be paid at the time specified, i.e. thirty guineas, to be paid sometime in the last fortnight of July, you may have them; but remember, my dear fellow ! I write to you now merely as a bookseller, and entreat you, in your answer, to consider yourself only; as to us, although money is necessary to our plan, yet the plan is not necessary to our happiness; and if it were, W. could sell his Poems for that sum to someone else, or we could procure the money without selling the Poems. So I entreat you again and again, in your answer, which must be immediate, consider yourself only. . . .

" At all events, come down, Cottle, as soon as you can, but before Midsummer, and we will procure a horse

easy as thine own soul, and we will go on a roam to
Linton and Linmouth, which, if thou comest in May, will
be in all their pride of woods and waterfalls, not to
speak of its august cliffs, and the green ocean, and the
vast Valley of Stones, all which live disdainful of the
seasons, or accept new honours only from the winter's
snow. At all events come down, and cease not to
believe me much and affectionately your friend,

"S. T. COLERIDGE."

Cottle says that he accepted these invitations, and
spent a week with Coleridge and Wordsworth at Alfoxden
House, during which time, besides the reading of manuscript poems, they took him on the proposed " roam."

" At this interview," he says, " it was determined
that the volume should be published under the title of
' Lyrical Ballads,' on the terms stipulated in a former
letter : that this volume should not contain the poem
of ' Salisbury Plain,' but only an extract from it ; that
it should not contain the poem of ' Peter Bell,' but consist rather of sundry shorter pieces more recently written.
I had recommended two volumes, but one was fixed on,
and that to be published anonymously. It was to be
begun immediately, and with the ' Ancient Mariner ' ;
which poem I brought with me to Bristol."

Cottle had good reason to expect great things of
Wordsworth. In " Early Recollections," I. 251, and
" Reminiscences," p. 143, he writes :

" Mr. Coleridge says, in a letter received from him
March 8th, 1798, ' The giant Wordsworth—God love
him ! When I speak in the terms of admiration due to
his intellect, I fear lest these terms should keep out of
sight the amiableness of his manners. He has written
near twelve hundred lines of blank verse, superior, I
hesitate not to aver, to anything in our language which
any way resembles it.' "

It is a pleasure to know that nine years afterwards the
flame of Coleridge's admiration burned just as brightly,
for Cottle says that in 1807 he received a letter from
him, saying of Wordsworth : " He is one whom God
knows I love and honour as far beyond myself as both
morally and intellectually he is above me."

The poets objected to some of the details proposed by Cottle, and there was more correspondence on the subject. In the course of the summer, the Alfoxden idyll being at an end, Coleridge removed to Westbury, two miles from Bristol. After the Wye excursion, as we have seen, the Wordsworths returned to Bristol, about July 9, and appear to have remained there six weeks. The Bishop of Lincoln, quoting either from letters of Miss Wordsworth or from some journal of hers now lost, reports that on July 18, 1798, she wrote: " William's poems are now in the press; they will be out in six weeks "; and on September 13: " They are printed, but not published . . . in one small volume, without the name of the author; their title is ' Lyrical Ballads, with other poems.' Cottle has given thirty guineas for William's share of the volume."

It was printed at Bristol on or about September 1. The impression consisted of five hundred copies. As originally printed, the title-page was:

" Lyrical Ballads/with/A few other Poems./Bristol:/Printed by Biggs & Cottle,/For T.N.Longman, Pater-Noster Row, London./1798."

It was an octavo in paper boards. Other copies have the following title-page:

" Lyrical Ballads,/with/A few other Poems./London:/Printed for J. & A. Arch, Gracechurch-street./1798."

Only one criticism of the book appeared, so far as I know, before December, and that was Southey's very unfavourable and condescending article in *The Critical Review* for October.

On August 27 Wordsworth and his sister arrived in London, having seen the University of Oxford on the way. Where they stayed or how they occupied themselves in London is not known. We do not touch solid ground again until Dorothy begins her Journal of their travels, without which their residence in Germany would be almost a blank to us. We know that the tour had been long in contemplation, and was carefully planned. As early as March 11, 1798, Wordsworth had written to James Losh, a friend at Carlisle, urging him to join the travelling party, which was to include both Mr. and Mrs. Coleridge. It was their plan, he said, to pass two years in Germany. They hoped to settle near a university, and, if possible, in a mountainous district. On account of the expense of travelling, they wished to find this place not far from Hamburg. All these requirements point to Göttingen. Wordsworth also confides to Losh that he has written 706 lines of a poem, which he hopes to make of considerable utility. " Its title," he says, " will be The Recluse; or, Views of Nature, Man, and Society." We are not at all bound to suppose that these lines were ever included among the 1,200 or 1,300 previously mentioned.

They purposed in those two years " to acquire the German language," and to furnish themselves " with a tolerable stock of information in natural science." This is what he tells Losh, in behalf not only of himself, but of his sister and the Coleridges. M. Legouis in his admirable chapter on Wordsworth's Relation to Science, has shown that these were not words written at random, but that many of the subjects already chosen by the poets and many peculiarities in the work they had already accomplished were determined by a wish to study " facts of the soul " in a scientific manner. Their purpose was to observe actual cases, unhampered by the factitious distinctions between the normal and the abnormal set up by psychologists, and to enrich the science of mind, at that time so meagrely furnished with examples.

There is even a hint of these scientific pretensions in a letter from Charles Lamb to Southey, dated July 28, 1798:

" Samuel Taylor Coleridge, to the eternal regret of his native Devonshire, emigrates to Westphalia—' Poor Lamb ' (these were his last words) ' if he wants any *knowledge* he may apply to me '—in ordinary cases, I thanked him, I have an ' Encyclopædia ' at hand, but on such an occasion as going over to a German university, I could not refrain from sending him the following propositions, to be by him defended or oppugned (or both) at Leipsic or Gottingen."

Then follows a list of propositions, similar to a list which Lamb had sent to Coleridge himself, and all implying that the latter was a liar, a sophist, and a sentimentalist. Charles Lloyd had poisoned Lamb's mind with false reports about their friend. Lamb had for once allowed his playfulness to turn into something like mischief. Coleridge had taken offence. Their old comradeship had been rudely broken. Dorothy Wordsworth had been brought into the quarrel by the meddlesome Lloyd. Coleridge wrote a generous letter, full of patience and true humility, to his mistaken friend, beginning, " Lloyd has informed me through Miss Wordsworth that you intend no longer to correspond with me."* The summer of 1798 was thus rendered a time of much unhappiness for Coleridge. His former pupil, Charles Lloyd, had slandered him. He may have suspected his wife's brother-in-law and his former associate, Southey, of trying to undermine his literary reputation, and at least he felt hurt by Southey's self-righteous aloofness. He thought he had lost the love of his oldest friend, Charles Lamb, and the dream of having the Wordsworths always near him at Alfoxden was shattered. Nether Stowey was no longer Arcady, but a stupid out-of-the-way village. His cottage was no longer the delightful trysting-place of gods and muses, but the mean, cramped, and almost squalid house which Poole long before warned him it was. Moreover, for a man who naturally disliked public controversy, and desired to cultivate his mind in tranquillity, he was achieving entirely too much notoriety. He said very truly that his name " stank." A group of clever young Tory writers, in *The Anti-Jacobin*, were assailing, amid general applause, the reputation of poets, orators, and pamphleteers, who had been so imprudent as to favour the Revolution. They drove this routed and discouraged band before them in a savage pursuit. To be overtaken by the light cavalry

---

* Mr. E. V. Lucas expresses his opinion (" Works of Charles and Mary Lamb," VI. 116) that about this time Lamb wrote his pathetic lines, " The Old Familiar Faces," and that the friend mentioned in the next to the last stanza was Coleridge.

of *The Anti-Jacobin* was not only unpleasant, but dangerous. In the issue for July 9, 1798, Coleridge was distinctly mentioned, and Wordsworth probably alluded to, in the scurrilous verses entitled " New Morality." Priestley, Wakefield, Thelwall, Paine, Williams, Godwin, and Holcroft, are pilloried as admirers of Lepaux, a member of the French Directory, and leader of the Theophilanthropists; and in the same passage occur these lines:

> *Couriers* and *Stars*, Sedition's evening host,
> Thou *Morning Chronicle* and *Morning Post*,
> Whether ye make the Rights of Man your theme,
> Your country libel, and your God blaspheme,
> Or dirt on private worth and virtue throw,
> Still, blasphemous or blackguard, praise Lepaux !

> And ye five other wandering bards, that move
> In sweet accord of harmony and love,
> Coleridge and Southey, Lloyd, and Lamb and Co.,
> Tune all your mystic harps to praise Lepaux !

The newspapers mentioned were Whig journals. Many of Coleridge's poems were first printed in *The Morning Post*. *The Anti-Jacobin* was succeeded in July by another publication of the same character and tendency, *The Anti-Jacobin Review and Magazine*, which contained caricatures by Gillray, in which Coleridge and Southey are represented with asses' heads, and Lloyd and Lamb as toad and frog. In a set of verses, " The Anarchists," Coleridge, Southey, Lamb, and Lloyd, are held up to ridicule, but there is no allusion to a fifth member of the company. Paine, Priestley, Thelwall, Godwin, Wakefield, and Holcroft, figure also in this libel.

The plan of taking Mrs. Coleridge to Germany was given up. She and the two children, Hartley and Berkeley, were left at Nether Stowey, and about September 10, Coleridge joined the Wordsworths in London. The anonymous volume of joint authorship, " Lyrical Ballads, with a Few Other Poems," was published, probably just after his arrival, and Coleridge arranged with Johnson, the bookseller, to publish his " Fears in Solitude, written in 1798, during the alarm of an invasion; to which are added France, an Ode; and Frost at Midnight."

" Lyrical Ballads " contained the following poems: "The Rime of the Ancyent Marinere "; " The Foster-Mother's Tale "; " Lines left upon a Seat in a Yew-tree which stands near the Lake of Esthwaite "; "The Nightingale: a Conversational Poem "; " The Female Vagrant "; " Goody Blake and Harry Gill "; " Lines written at a small distance from my House, and sent by my little Boy to the Person to whom they are addressed "; " Simon Lee, the old Huntsman "; " Anecdote for Fathers "; " We are Seven "; " Lines written in early Spring "; " The Thorn "; " The last of the Flock "; "The Dungeon "; " The Mad Mother "; " The Idiot Boy "; " Lines written near Richmond, upon the Thames, at Evening "; " Expostulation and Reply "; " The Tables turned—an Evening Scene, on the same subject "; " Old Man travelling "; " The Complaint of a forsaken Indian Woman "; " The Convict "; " Lines written a few miles above Tintern Abbey." Of these twenty-three pieces, four were written by Coleridge— " The Rime of the Ancyent Marinere," " The Foster-Mother's Tale," " The Nightingale," and " The Dungeon." The ineffective titles of Wordsworth's contributions show how incapable he was of perceiving small occasions of ridicule. It is a pity that many of his best poems are marred with ill-sounding labels instead of having real names appropriate to their contents. He erred in this way not through indifference to popularity, but through a sort of pedantry, a habit of paying too close attention to his own mental history.

On Friday, September 14, William and Dorothy Wordsworth, Coleridge, and a young man from Stowey named John Chester, left London by stage-coach. They reached Yarmouth at noon next day, and sailed for Hamburg in a packet-boat on Sunday morning. Of their voyage, and the first few weeks of their sojourn in Germany, we have detailed but not very systematic accounts in a Journal kept by Miss Wordsworth and some letters of Coleridge printed in *The Friend* for

November 23, December 7, and December 21, 1809, and reprinted in " Biographia Literaria " under the title of " Satyrane's Letters." The travellers appear to have been in very gay spirits. Coleridge's description of the passage sounds like the aimless rattle of a clever boy. He exhibits the prejudices of a person who has never been outside of his native land. He objects to the speech, the manners, and the complexions, of the foreigners on board, except a French *émigré*, with whom he and his friends continued to associate for some time after landing.

On arriving at Hamburg, Wordsworth went to seek lodgings, while the others, immobile through ignorance of foreign ways and languages, guarded the luggage. His knowledge of French served them in good stead. After breakfasting with their French friend, they passed the day in sight-seeing, and went to the French Theatre. They visited the English bookseller, Remnant, where they bought Bürger's poems and Percy's " Reliques." Their characteristic interest in country life led them to various small towns in the neighbourhood—Blankenese, Harburg, and Altona. They made the acquaintance of one of the numerous brothers of the poet Klopstock, perhaps Victor, the newspaper editor, who introduced them to Christoph Daniel Ebeling, professor of history and Greek at the Hamburg academic gymnasium, and afterwards the well-known librarian of the city.

At Herr Klopstock's house they met at dinner his brother, Friedrich Gottlieb, the poet, who, Dorothy tells us, " maintained an animated conversation with William during the whole afternoon." On another occasion Coleridge and Wordsworth called on the aged German poet, and had a long conversation in French, Wordsworth acting as interpreter. Coleridge now and then interposed a question in Latin. Klopstock confessed that he knew very little concerning the history of German poetry and the elder German poets; " the subject had not particularly excited his curiosity." But he talked of Milton and Glover, and " thought Glover's blank verse superior to Milton's," but, after all, he appeared not to know much about Milton, whom he had read in a prose translation when he was fourteen. Wordsworth proceeded to set him straight, giving " his definition and notion of harmonious verse, that it consisted (the English iambic blank verse above all) in the apt arrangement of pauses and cadences, and the sweep of whole paragraphs." The talk covered a wide range; the venerable author, in his feeble state of health, aroused the sympathy of his young English admirers; and when they left him they walked on the ramparts, " discoursing together on the poet and his conversation," till their attention was diverted to the beauty and singularity of the sunset and the effects on the objects round them. Wordsworth returned more than once to talk with Klopstock, and they discoursed not only on poetry, but on the Kantian philosophy, on Wolf, Nicolai, and Engel, on Rousseau, on the drama. Wordsworth expressed his preference for Dryden over Pope. Klopstock spoke favourably of Goethe, and especially of Wieland, but said that Schiller could not live. Wordsworth took copious notes of these conversations, and it is evident that he was well versed in contemporary German literature. Klopstock, they found, had once been an enthusiast for the French Revolution, but was now quite turned against it.

The friends must have realized that they could never learn German if they kept together, and on Sunday, October 1, Coleridge and Chester set out for Ratzeburg, a small town about thirty-five miles to the north-east. Two days later the Wordsworths took the diligence to Brunswick. " Dorothy and I," he wrote to Poole, " are going to speculate further up in the country." In the same letter which contains this announcement he remarks: " I have one word to say about Alfoxden: pray, keep your eye upon it. If any series of accidents should bring it again into the market, we should be glad to have it, if we could manage it." Over wretched roads they travelled by diligence across the Luneburg Heath, and into the Harz Mountains. It took them nearly two days to reach Brunswick, and one day more

to get to Goslar, which was their destination. In this
ancient and beautiful little city they appear to have
remained at least till January. In summer it would
have been a delightful residence, owing to its situation
among the hills; but they soon exhausted its winter
attractions, and, failing to make many acquaintances,
were forced to lead a very secluded life. Miss Wordsworth described it as a lifeless town, and complained
that if a man wished to go into society, and had his
wife or sister with him, he would be obliged to give
entertainments. So they tried to learn German from
the family with whom they lived, and by reading.
" William," wrote she to Mrs. Marshall, " is very industrious. His mind is always active; indeed, too much so.
He over-wearies himself, and suffers from pain and
weakness in the side."

The Wordsworths, while at Goslar, lived in a house
which is still standing—No. 86, Breite-strasse. It was
built after the great fire of 1728, was formerly No. 107,
belonged to St. Stephen's parish, and was occupied
in 1799 by the widow of Georg Christian Ernst
Deppermann.

Coleridge, meanwhile, was meeting many people and
enjoying many advantages at Ratzeburg, for which he
said he had to pay dear. " Including *all* expenses," he
wrote to Poole, " I have not lived at less than two
pounds a week. Wordsworth (from whom I receive
long and affectionate letters) has enjoyed scarcely one
advantage, but his expenses have been considerably less
than they were in England." Coleridge was amassing
material for a Life of Lessing, a work suited to his
genius, and called for by the needs of his time, but
which he never wrote. Wordsworth's surroundings at
Goslar are thus described in the Fenwick note to the
poem beginning " A plague on your languages, German
and Norse ":

" A bitter winter it was when these verses were composed by the side of my Sister, in our lodgings at a
draper's house in the romantic imperial town of Goslar,
on the edge of the Hartz Forest. In this town the

German emperors of the Franconian line were accustomed to keep their court, and it retains vestiges of
ancient splendour.   So severe was the cold of this
winter, that, when we passed out of the parlour warmed
by the stove, our cheeks were struck by the air as by
cold iron.   I slept in a room over a passage which was
not ceiled.   The people of the house used to say, rather
unfeelingly, that they expected I should be frozen to
death some night."

On January 4, 1799, Coleridge wrote to Poole:
" Wordsworth has left Goslar, and is on his road into
higher Saxony to cruise for a pleasanter place; he has
made but little progress in the language."   Ten days
later, in a letter to his wife, he says: " I hear as often
from Wordsworth as letters can go backward and forward in a country where fifty miles a day and night is
expeditious travelling !   He seems to have employed
more time in writing English than in studying German.
No wonder ! for he might as well have been in England
as at Goslar, in the situation which he chose and with
his unseeking manners.   He has now left it, and is on
his journey to Nordhausen."   He thinks Wordsworth is
hampered by having his sister with him, because the
Germans cannot understand a young woman's being
given so much freedom, and will not admit the pair
to their homes.   " Still," he goes on, " male acquaintance he might have had, and had I been at Goslar
I would have had them; but W., God love him,
seems to have lost his spirits and almost his inclination for it."
Coleridge left Ratzeburg on February 6, and arrived
at Göttingen on the 12th, by way of Hanover.   Had
the Wordsworths been still at Goslar, he would hardly
have passed so near without visiting them.   On the
other hand, Mr. Gordon Wordsworth informs me that
there exists a letter from Dorothy dated " Nordhausen,
Feb. 27, '99," from which it is clear that she and her
brother had left Goslar on February 23, a Saturday,
and, travelling either on foot or in a post-waggon, and
sleeping every night in a fresh place, had got as far as

Nordhausen, and their evident plan was to continue the
process. She says the morning of the 23rd was " a
delightful morning," and speaks of the fir-woods. The
tone of her letter seems to imply that she, at least,
was making this journey for the first time. Had it not
been for this letter, I should have had no hesitation
in saying that they left Goslar early in January. There
is nothing more till April 23.

Coleridge came to Göttingen provided with letters of
introduction to the university librarian and one of the
professors, matriculated at once, and plunged into
study. It was here that he received, a few weeks
later, the news of his little son Berkeley's death, and
in writing to Poole about that sad event, and how it
shook his sense of security, he says, April 6: " Some
months ago Wordsworth transmitted me a most sublime
epitaph. Whether it had any reality I cannot say.
Most probably, in some gloomier moment, he had fancied
the moment in which his sister would die :

EPITAPH.

A slumber did my spirit seal,
I had no human fears;
She seemed a thing that could not feel
The touch of earthly years.
No motion has she now, no force,
She neither hears nor sees:
Mov'd round in Earth's diurnal course
With rocks, and stones, and trees !

Two or three unpublished letters of Coleridge to
Wordsworth, written while they were both in Germany,
express his longing to be with his friends: " I am sure,"
he writes, " I need not say how you are incorporated
into the better part of my being; how, whenever I spring
forward into the future with noble affections, I always
alight by your side." He sends them some experiments
he has made in hexameter verse, which were long afterwards included among his printed works. Even through
his technicalities there pierces a note of pathos. He is
lonely and ill and weak :

William, my teacher, my friend ! dear William and dear Dorothea !
    *   *   *   *   *

William, my head and my heart, dear Poet that feelest and thinkest !
Dorothy, eager of soul, my most affectionate sister !
Many a mile, O ! many a wearisome mile are ye distant,
Long, long, comfortless roads, with no one eye that doth know us.
O ! it is all too far to send to you mockeries idle :
Yea, and I feel it not right !   But O ! my friends, my beloved !
Feverish and wakeful I lie,—I am weary of feeling and thinking;
Every thought is worn *down*,—I am weary, yet cannot be vacant.
Five long hours have I tossed, rheumatic heats, dry and flushing,
Gnawing behind in my head, and wandering and throbbing about me,
Busy and tiresome, my friends, as the beat of the boding night-
    spider.
    *   *   *   *   *

" The last line which I wrote I remember, and write it for the truth of the sentiment, scarcely less true in company than in pain and solitude :

William, my head and my heart ! dear William and dear Dorothea !
You have all in each other; but I am lonely, and want you !' "

The Wordsworths were far less constant' this winter than Coleridge in their attachment to a place of abode. The Bishop of Lincoln, who was favoured with information which is now lost, is explicit in his statement that they left Goslar on February 10.   He implies that they went pretty far south, " *to a more genial climate* "; for he writes of the poet : " He felt inspired by the change of place.   When he set forth from this imperial city [Goslar], so dull and dreary as it had been to him, and when the prospect of a transition from its frost and snow to a more genial climate opened upon him, he seemed to be like one emancipated from the thraldom of a prison : it gave life and alacrity to his soul."   Clement Carlyon,* an English medical student, arrived at Göttingen on March 22, 1799.   Coleridge had arrived on February 12.   In the interval the Wordsworths appear to have visited Coleridge.   " Soon after Coleridge's arrival at Göttingen," writes Carlyon,† " Mr. Wordsworth and his sister came from Goslar to pay him a

---

* Clement Carlyon: " Early Years and Late Reflections," I. 16.
† *Ibid.*, 196.

visit, and I have been informed, by one well acquainted with the fact, that the two philosophers rambled away together for a day or two (leaving Miss Wordsworth at Göttingen), for the better enjoyment of an entire inter-communion of thought, thereby becoming the whole world to each other, and not this world only, which in their metaphysical excursions was probably but a secondary consideration." Carlyon testifies to Cole-ridge's admiration for Wordsworth, saying: " When we have sometimes spoken complimentarily to Coleridge of himself, he has said that he was nothing in comparison with him." The visit to which Carlyon refers must have been very brief, and after it the Wordsworths disappear for about eight weeks.

Considering how many a time in their lives they were seized with a sudden and irresistible impulse to wander, and with almost no baggage, it would not be surprising if they made a long journey; and unless we are to suppose that a date in the Fenwick note to the poem entitled " Stray Pleasures " is incorrect, they ventured into France. In that note the poet is repre-sented to have said to Miss Fenwick, speaking of certain floating mills: " I noticed several upon the river Saône in the year 1799, particularly near the town of Chalons, where my friend Jones and I halted a day when we crossed France."

Coleridge found at Göttingen an agreeable circle of English students, several of whom were Cambridge men. He was known even then as a " noticeable " man, the very adjective that Wordsworth applied to him years afterwards in the stanzas beginning " Within our happy Castle there dwelt One." And even his English companions, Chester, two brothers named Parry, Green, and Clement Carlyon, the last of whom wrote a prolix account of their adventures together, have received from association with him a certain interest for posterity. He was admitted to the society of his professors, and became intimate with at least one German student, a son of Professor Blumenbach. With this young man he made many excursions far and near,

and engaged in endless debates, which usually turned
into monologues.   As is frequently the case with
travellers in their first year abroad, the contrast between
foreign ways and the customs of his own country
brought out his latent chauvinism.   He declaimed
against French politics and German religion, even
arguing with the celebrated theologian Eichhorn.* Yet
though shocked at the neglect of religious worship
which prevailed among the students, both English and
German, he never went to church, as one of the Cambridge men reports.   Walking with his comrades on
the well-shaded city wall or tramping through the
neighbouring forests, he edified them with long discourses on ecclesiastical history," gravelled the pastors
of the German Church," recited and expounded his own
poems, read and showed them his tragedy " Osorio,"
and in every way, through jest and earnest, played
like a magician upon their simpler natures.   Coleridge
could not be suppressed, but Wordsworth, with those
" unseeking manners " of his and that love of quiet,
left scarcely a trace of his presence in Goslar.   On
April 23, 1799, Coleridge wrote to his wife:

" Surely it is unnecessary for me to say how infinitely
I languish to be in my native country, and with how
many struggles I have remained even so long in Germany ! I received your affecting letter, dated Easter
Sunday; and had I followed my impulses, I should have
packed up and gone with Wordsworth and his sister,
who passed through (and only passed through) this
place two or three days ago. If they burn with such
impatience to return to their native country, *they* who
are all to each other, what must I feel with everything
pleasant and everything valuable and everything dear
to me at a distance—here, where I may truly say my
only amusement is—to labour !"

In a letter to Poole, dated May 5, he writes:

" Wordsworth and his sister passed through here, as
I have informed you. I walked on with them five
English miles, and spent a day with them. They were

* See a letter from one of the Parrys in Carlyon's " Early Years and
Late Reflections," I. 100.

melancholy and hypp'd. W. was affected to tears at the thought of not being near me—wished me, of course, to live in the North of England near Sir Frederic Vane's great library. . . . W. was affected to tears, very much affected. But he deemed the vicinity of a library absolutely necessary to his health, nay, to his existence. It is painful to me, too, to think of not living near him: for he is a *good* and *kind* man, and the only one whom in *all* things I feel my superior. . . . I still think Wordsworth will be disappointed in his expectations of relief from reading, without society; and I think it highly probable that where I live there he will live, unless he should find in the North any person, or persons, who can feel with and understand him, can reciprocate and react upon him. My many weaknesses are of some advantage to me; they unite me more with the great mass of my fellow-beings—but dear Wordsworth appears to me to have hurtfully segregated and isolated his being. Doubtless his delights are more deep and sublime, but he has likewise more hours that prey on his flesh and blood."

We have seen that Wordsworth and his sister passed through Göttingen on their way home, about April 20. Where they resided or travelled in the meanwhile, I do not know. In a letter to Thomas Poole, dated July 4, Miss Wordsworth writes:

" We found living in Germany, with the enjoyment of any tolerable advantages, much more expensive than we expected, which determined us to come home with the first tolerable weather of the spring. We left Coleridge and Mr. Chester at Göttingen ten weeks ago, as you probably have heard, and proceeded with as little delay as possible, travelling in a German diligence to Hamburg, whence we went down the Elbe in a boat to Cuxhaven, where we were not detained longer than we wished for our necessary refreshment, and we had an excellent passage to England of two days and nights: We proceeded immediately from Yarmouth into the North, where we are now staying with some of our early friends at a pleasant farm on the banks of the Tees. We are very anxious to hear from Coleridge,—he promised to write us from Göttingen, and though we have written twice we have heard nothing of him."

Clement Carlyon records Coleridge's comings and goings, his excursion to the Brocken in May, his trip to Cassel, his departure for home on June 24, his affectionate references to his wife and children, his expressions of attachment to his country. Coleridge carried out his intention of studying natural history and heard the lectures of Professor Blumenbach on that subject. He also made considerable additions to his knowledge of German literature and German philosophy. But his poetical activities slackened.

Wordsworth, on the contrary, was more productive during the early months of 1799 than at any previous period of equal length. His mind was thrown back upon his own past. He composed several long pieces of blank verse, which he said in after years were intended as part of " The Prelude." It seems more likely that " The Prelude " was not really planned until a year later. These passages of reminiscence sprang spontaneously from his power of living in the past. His gift of observation, which had been cultivated to an almost dangerous point at Alfoxden, was now half dormant. He gave up, for a time, his researches in psychology. The strain of political excitement was relaxed. Coleridge was not with him to stimulate speculation. He was therefore driven to live upon his memories. He wrote that winter the description of skating on Esthwaite, of the boy hooting to the owls across Windermere, of nutting near Hawkshead. Passing over the varied experiences of the past twelve years, he thought of his old schoolmaster and composed the lines beginning " I come, ye little noisy Crew," and " Matthew " and " The Two April Mornings " and " The Fountain." In two instances he followed methods which he had begun to cultivate at Alfoxden: he composed " The Danish Boy," he tells us, " as a prelude to a ballad-poem never written," and a subtle, deeply reflective poem, " Ruth," likewise in ballad form. The latter is a study of moral evil, prompted and mitigated by the influences of natural beauty. The subject is the abandonment of an innocent woman by her husband, a man of genius and charm. Wild nature, amid whose glories he had roved, made this man indifferent to human feeling and to moral obligation. But to the heart-broken Ruth, nature, with grand impartiality, gave solace in her years of sorrow.

It is a curious theme, and as Wordsworthian as any detail of its treatment. Both Wordsworth and Coleridge applied themselves more than once to the study of seduction. The latter had already written his three poems to Unfortunate Women—" Pale roamer through the night ! thou poor Forlorn !" " Maiden, that with sullen brow," and " Myrtle-leaf that, ill besped." There are many points of similarity between Wordsworth's two poems, " The Thorn " and " The Mad Mother," written in 1798, and " Ruth," written early in 1799, the most obvious being that in all of them the poet shows profound sympathy with minds disordered by betrayal, and profound knowledge, too, of the workings of such minds. In the ruin of the faculties which once adapted these poor women to social life, they have preserved, he shows us, a healthful relation to nature. Upon nature they fall back for consolation when hopes of human love have failed. Not quite the same subject, but one very much like it, had engaged his attention in " The Ruined Cottage." This is also true of " The Borderers." The material for " Vaudracour and Julia," although it may not have received substantial form until 1805, was supplied to him in 1792. It, again, is a tale of thwarted love, ending in separation and madness. Wordsworth rarely trusted himself to describe the effects of the passion of love. He knew too well the intensity of his own nature, and feared the result of any slackening of self-control; and of minds abnormal or perverted, or threatened at least with insanity, he had known only too many among his nearest associates.

At Goslar he wrote also that unique ballad, " Lucy Gray." It was founded, he informs us, on a circumstance told him by his sister. Nothing could surpass the simplicity and naturalness of this poem before the next to the last stanza is reached. At that point the suggestion of something preternatural is made, yet without disturbing the sense of reality. This touch is added with marvellous delicacy. The poet was prepared to make it by those studies of the weird which he and Coleridge had pursued at Alfoxden. " Lucy Gray " is a more perfect example of its kind than any other of Wordsworth's contributions to " Lyrical Ballads." His creative energy here, for the first time perhaps, worked through a medium of pure imagination, and on an impulse purely artistic.

" A Poet's Epitaph," dated 1799, is another instance of Wordsworth's rapidly unfolding versatility. The first half of this piece is in a vein of high moral satire—a vein not previously revealed in him; a reader who came upon it unawares might say, " This is by Burns or else by some poet born two or three generations after Burns." On the other hand, the five stanzas beginning

> But who is He, with modest looks,

which describe the true poet's gifts and limitations, though transcending in boldness and precision any lines previously written by Wordsworth, possess qualities which are immediately recognized as peculiar to him.

The five so-called " Lucy poems," which Wordsworth stated were written in Germany, fill one of the most entrancing pages in our literature. Lovely in themselves, they gain an added interest from the questionings they raise in the mind of every thoughtful reader. Have the poems all one subject ? Was Lucy a real person or a creature of imagination ? Who was she ? What passion and what pain do these lines half confess and half conceal ? To say much about them would be to desecrate their tender and exquisite beauty. No lover of poetry would wish to resolve all their mystery. Yet one is obliged to take account of several views which have been held in regard to their meaning. The traditional opinion is that they were inspired by the poet's love for his sister. When we recall the ecstatic language in which she more than once voiced her yearn-

ing for him in absence, and how her solicitude hovered
over him and lapped him in tenderness when she had
regained him, we must admit that if his nature was like
hers, this view is not untenable. As we have seen, it
is the only guess that Coleridge could make when he
read the " sublime epitaph," " A slumber did my spirit
seal." Another view is that this Lucy is as purely an
ideal creation as the child in his ballad. In that case,
we must believe these poems little less than miracles.
Taken together, they are unsurpassed for poignancy of
passion. The love of woman never inspired utterance
more tenderly reverent. If they had no origin in personal experience, we must reckon Wordsworth among
the greatest objective or dramatic artists. A third view
is the only one which an unprejudiced reading of the
poems alone would be likely to suggest: that the poet
had loved and lost. From every indication, of feeling,
of musical tone, and even of metrical detail, the five
pieces, " Strange fits of passion have I known," " She
dwelt among the untrodden ways," " I travelled among
unknown men," " A slumber did my spirit seal," and
" Three years she grew in sun and shower," appear to
have one and the same subject. And, in spite of Fenwick notes and all other external testimony, I am half
convinced that the two pieces, " I met Louisa in the
shade," and " Dear Child of Nature, let them rail,'
were conceived at the same time and from the same
impulse as " Three years she grew in sun and shower."
All attempts to look more closely into the secret have
thus far been made in vain. Lucy turned her wheel
" beside an English fire "; the " springs of Dove " are
in England: yet when could the poet, without the
knowledge of his friends, have met and so deeply loved
a young English girl ? Brief must the vision have been,
brief and eternal as the moment in Dante's life where
incipit Vita Nova. My own opinion is that an actual
experience of love and sorrow, quite definite and personal,
was the origin of these poems, and that the traits of
a real woman, her loveliness, her innocent wildness,
were fondly recalled under the name of " Lucy."

But the name, I believe, and the several touches of local detail, have slight significance, if any.

When Wordsworth and his sister passed through Göttingen in April, 1799, they had been more than seven months abroad. Their experiences had not been altogether satisfactory. Accustomed to the soft winters of England, they had suffered much from cold, and, unfortunately, did not wait to see a German May steal through the sweet valleys of the Harz. There is no evidence that they acquired any sympathetic knowledge of German life or an intimate acquaintance with the language. They lived very economically, spending far less than Coleridge. For more than six months after returning to England they were without a home or any distinct prospects for the future.

Wordsworth returned to England with no abatement of his democratic principles, and both he and Dorothy avoided the older generation of their family. She wrote to Poole on July 4, giving their address as " Mr. Hutchinson's, Sockburn, near Northallerton, Yorkshire." They are undetermined, she says, where to reside, and have no house in view. William wishes to be near a good library, and, if possible, in a pleasant country. She asks Poole to let them know if he hears of a suitable place in his neighbourhood.

Wordsworth wrote anxiously to Cottle about the sale of " Lyrical Ballads." His first letter, undated, was probably written late in May, for he says, " We left Coleridge well at Göttingen a month ago." He does not know that Cottle has transferred the book to Arch. " We have spent our time pleasantly enough in Germany," he declares, " but we are right glad to find ourselves in England, for we have learned to know its value."

By June 2 he had heard from Cottle, and expressed his regret at having lost a good opportunity of connecting himself with the publisher Johnson, in whose hands the poems were likely to have had a quicker sale. Cottle was going out of business, and the author desired to know who was to own the copyright. He was in

need of money, and asked for the balance due to him.
In a letter of June 24, he makes the astounding statement:

> " From what I can gather it seems that The Ancyent
> Marinere has, on the whole, been an injury to the volume;
> I mean that the old words and the strangeness of it
> have deterred readers from going on. If the volume
> should come to a second edition, I would put in its place
> some little things which would be more likely to suit the
> common taste."

Nothing is said about how Coleridge might feel if this
were done. One cannot imagine the author of the
" Ancient Mariner " making such a proposal with reference to the " Lines Written a Few Miles above Tintern
Abbey " or " The Idiot Boy." No doubt it was based
upon an agreement between the two poets; yet one
could wish for a more generous way of putting things.

" Lyrical Ballads " had not been badly received. The
challenge of its Advertisement had fallen almost un-
heard in a noisy world. There were few to remark the
truth and the audacity of the now famous declaration:

> " The majority of the following poems are to be con-
> sidered as experiments. They were written chiefly with
> a view to ascertain how far the language of conversation
> in the middle and lower classes of society is adapted to
> the purposes of poetic pleasure. Readers accustomed
> to the gaudiness and inane phraseology of many modern
> writers, if they persist in reading this book to its con-
> clusion, will perhaps frequently have to struggle with
> feelings of strangeness and awkwardness: they will look
> round for poetry, and will be induced to inquire by what
> species of courtesy these attempts can be permitted to
> assume that title."

But there had been one article, which, though not likely
to harm the fortunes of the book, was manifestly intended to rebuke the authors. It appeared in *The
Critical Review* for October, 1798, and was written by
Southey. Its appearance so soon after the publication
of the book has given very plausible ground to the
opinion that he planned his attack before he saw it,

and he has even been charged with persuading Cottle
to transfer it to Arch, in order not to include the former
in the ruin he intended to make.   It has also been suggested that he thought Coleridge was the author of all
the poems.   His review was certainly neither kind nor
fair.   He had had many an opportunity of realizing the
inferiority of his own genius to that or either one of
the joint authors.   Only the shallowest self-conceit
could have enabled him to brush aside lightly any
poetic theory that they might propound.   " Of these
experimental poems, the most important," he says, " is
the Idiot Boy, the story of which is simply this "—and
he goes on to anatomize it.   It is easy enough to raise
a laugh over the " story " of this poem, and over some
of the phrases in it, that are so simple as to appear
grotesque.   But he might have found so much to praise !
Instead of this, after quoting some of the most " childish " stanzas, he magisterially pronounces his verdict :

" No tale less deserved the labour that appears to
have been bestowed upon this.   It resembles a Flemish
picture in the worthlessness of its design and the excellence of its execution.   From Flemish artists we are
satisfied with such pieces : who would not have lamented,
if Corregio or Rafaelle had wasted their talents in painting Dutch boors or the humours of a Flemish wake ?"

He is altogether displeased with " The Thorn."   Of
the " Ancient Mariner " he complains that, though
many of the stanzas are laboriously beautiful, they are
in connection absurd or unintelligible.   " We do not,"
he says, " sufficiently understand the story to analyze
it."   It is strange that a man with any claim to be a
poet should entertain the distressing thought of analyzing the " Ancient Mariner "; and there could be nothing
more inept than to describe it as " a Dutch attempt at
German sublimity."   Finally, he condescends to admit
that " genius has here been employed in producing a
poem of little merit."   Curiously enough, he approves
of " The Female Vagrant," and he gives high praise to
the " Lines Written above Tintern Abbey."   He laments
that the author stooped to write such pieces as "The

Last of the Flock," " The Convict," and most of the ballads. There is an intolerable air of superiority in his concluding paragraph: " The ' experiment,' we think, has failed, not because the language of conversation is little adapted to ' the purposes of poetic pleasure,' but because it has been tried upon uninteresting subjects. Yet every piece discovers genius, and ill as the author has frequently employed his talents, they certainly rank him with the best of living poets."

Charles Lamb, though he had too readily sided with Lloyd in his quarrel with Coleridge, was disappointed with Southey's article. He thought it unappreciative, and told him so: " If you wrote that review in ' Crit. Rev.,' I am sorry you are so sparing of praise to the ' Ancient Marinere.' "   He also declares " Tintern Abbey " one of the finest poems ever written.

Wordsworth felt the blow more deeply than he would admit. He pretended to care only because the criticism must affect the sale of the book. He exclaims, in a letter to Cottle: " He knew that I published those poems for money, and money alone. He knew that money was of importance to me. If he could not conscientiously have spoken differently of the volume, he ought to have declined the task of reviewing it."

According to Cottle's account, Wordsworth ascribed the bad sale of " Lyrical Ballads " to two causes— " first the ' Ancient Mariner,' which, he said, no one seemed to understand; and, secondly, the unfavourable notice of most of the reviews." Considering that the authors had disposed of their copyright, we might wonder why Wordsworth should be so anxious about the money loss, did we not also learn from Cottle that the latter had obtained ownership once more of what was regarded as a worthless property, and then given it to Wordsworth, " so that whatever advantage has arisen, subsequently, from the sale of this volume of the ' Lyrical Ballads ' . . . has pertained exclusively to Mr. W."

Mrs. Coleridge, reflecting, no doubt, her brother-in-law's opinion, wrote to Poole from Bristol, in March,

1799: " The Lyrical Ballads are laughed at and disliked by all with very few exceptions "; and again, on April 2: " The Lyrical Ballads are not liked at all by any." She also added, in a queer little postscript: " It is very unpleasant to me to be often asked if Coleridge has changed his political sentiments, for I know not properly how to reply.   Pray furnish me."

The little book was noticed at some length in *The Monthly Review* for June, 1799, and on the whole unfavourably.   Wordsworth did not see this article until several weeks later, but he heard of it.   The anonymous writer divided his blame and his even more offensive condescension equally between the poems by Wordsworth and those by Coleridge.   He supposed, of course, that they were all written by the same author.   He sees in their natural diction only an imitation of an ancient and rude style of ballad verse.   In their spirit he detects a dangerous radicalism, the teaching of Rousseau.   The " Rime of the Ancient Mariner " is " the strangest story of a cock and a bull that we ever saw on paper."   " The Yew-tree " seems a seat for Jean-Jacques.   " The Female Vagrant " " seems to stamp a general stigma on all military transactions," and the perception of this truth sets the reviewer off on a defence of the supposed necessity of militarism.   " In ' The Dungeon,' candour and tenderness for criminals seem pushed to excess," and with a Tory's traditional solicitude for low " rates," the reviewer inquires: " Have not jails been built on the humane Mr. Howard's plan, which have almost ruined some counties, and which look more like palaces than habitations for the perpetrators of crimes ?"   " The Convict " shows " misplaced commiseration, on one condemned by the laws of his country."   This article, like almost everything else published in *The Monthly Review* in the last decade of the eighteenth century, indicates the general alertness to detect and crush all manifestations of the " levelling " spirit.   One cannot say that its author was blind to the merits of the book, nor indeed that he was mistaken in thinking he had discovered one of the chief motives of its composition.

Why did not Wordsworth boldly accept the challenge ? Apart from the supposition—for which we have up to this point seen no evidence—that his political philosophy had already begun to change to a more conservative type, there were reasons inherent in his character. Wordsworth was not one of those men who enjoy combat. Only a self-distrusting or excessively prudent young man could have suppressed, as he did, the Letter to the Bishop of Llandaff. The manifold impressions made upon him by his close view of the French Revolution he kept to himself for many years, and the reception of " Lyrical Ballads," which was, after all, only what might have been expected, made him write timorously to Cottle : " My aversion from publication increases every day, so much so, that no motives whatever, nothing but pecuniary necessity, will, I think, ever prevail upon me to commit myself to the press again.'